A CENTURY OF TRACTION ENGINES

FRONTISPIECE

A Century of TRACTION ENGINES

Being an historical account of the rise and decline of an industry whose benefits to mankind were and are incalculable

By W. J. HUGHES

Past President of the Road Locomotive Society; Member of the Newcomen Society and of the National Traction Engine Club

DAVID & CHARLES: NEWTON ABBOT

7153 4230 4

For my second Grandson
TIMOTHY EDWIN CLARKE
who found the fascination of
steam and the steam engine at
the early age of four years

First published by Percival Marshall & Company Limited 1959
New impression by the present publishers 1968
Third impression 1970

Printed in Great Britain by
Latimer Trend & Company Limited Whitstable
for David & Charles (Publishers) Limited
South Devon House Newton Abbot Devon

CONTENTS

ILLUSTRATIONS

Foreword

A steam of rich distilled perfumes. . . . MILTON
Manholin', on my back, the cranks three inches off my nose. KIPLING

FOR MANY YEARS NOW, large numbers of the British public have been seen wending their way to a completely new form of entertainment – traction engine rallies. Held in different parts of the country, these meetings are frequently attended by thousands of people; on occasion, when the television cameras have been present, the audience has probably been in the millions.

Such is the fascination of steam, that people will travel a couple of hundred miles or more to see in action machines which not so long ago were commonplace.

Such is its fascination, that men will buy a veritable wreck of an engine to save it from the scrap yard, and will then spend two or three years in dismantling it, and removing the rust, and renewing the worn or broken parts, and painting and polishing and refurbishing, until one day she stands there in her glory, ready to live again.

Then the trapped finger ends and the skinned knuckles are ignored, the toil and sweat and dirt forgotten, as the safety valves sizzle, and the hollow 'tum-tum-tum' is heard in the chimney, whilst the flywheel slowly turns over. The eccentrics gently tumble, the rods flash in the sun, and over all hangs that indefinite, indefinable, indescribable aroma of coal smoke, and hot oil, and steam! Such is the fascination of it all.

And yet, even among its most ardent devotees, how many are aware of the equally fascinating history of the traction engine during its century of development? The trials, the errors, the successes, the freaks – all play their part in the story, which it is the purpose of this book to try to tell.

It is a story worth the telling, too, for let there be no doubt about it: the traction engine and its brethren – the ploughing engine, the road roller, the road locomotive, the tractor – have been of inestimable service to mankind. In agriculture, in road making, in road haulage and in opening up and developing virgin lands abroad, steam power played a part without which the world would be very much different today.

No history of the traction engine could be a complete one. Many well-known firms have disappeared, and their records with them. In the 'salvage' drives of two world wars, much material has been destroyed. Yet a great deal *does* remain, if one takes the trouble to look for it, and later in the book I shall list possible sources for the earnest student who wishes to carry his researches further. Incidentally, I hope he enjoys the task as much as I have done!

This book is partly founded on a lecture which I have delivered to numerous learned societies over very many years. During that period, however, my knowledge has increased greatly, and so has my collection of material. The latter includes numerous albums full of photographs, many books and catalogues, and a large number of portfolios of blue-prints, photostats, newspaper and magazine cuttings, letters, and other trophies of the chase.

So that, even allowing for the expansion of a two-hour lecture into a full-length book, and the consequent inclusion of more facts and pictures, my chief dilemma has not been what to include in the book, but what must be left out! It has not been easy to put aside some of my cherished illustrations, but to have included them all would have made a volume so big and expensive that few could have afforded to buy it.

In the circumstances, then, I have tried to tell the story of the traction engine and road locomotive from first to last, within a reasonable compass. I have endeavoured to avoid too much technicality for the lay mind to comprehend, yet to include sufficient to keep the interest of the more technically-minded reader. And above all, I have omitted those irritating footnotes giving references and 'sources', which keep the eye jumping from the reading matter to the foot of the page and back again. The average reader will not be bothered to confirm the references anyway, and the earnest researcher will find confirmation in the Bibliography.

I am grateful indeed to many kind individuals and firms for assistance in the compiling of my collection, and thus in the writing of this book. Wherever copyright has been involved I have sought permission to use the material, which has always been given gladly. Only in one or two cases am I unaware of the source, and if in publication I have infringed any rights – though I think not – I apologise profoundly. I also apologise for any unintended omissions from the following lists.

The individuals to whom my thanks are due include Messrs. T. H. Allen, John M. Ball, Norman E. Box, P. W. Bradley, S. Breedon, Thomas Bridson, E. S. Brook, Ashley Butterwick (Canada), Kevan J. Coulton, C. H. Cutts, A. R. Dibben, Alan Duke, Ian N. Fraser, John L. French, W. Falder, F. J. Finn, T. Glover, F. Hal Higgins (U.S.A.), E. G. Hobson (South Africa), T. Ison, Stuart P. Johnstone, A. C. Lawrence, H. W.

Matthews, B. H. Maycock, E. Morgan, J. P. Mullett, Stephen Mustill, C. D. Nicholl, Alf Pepper, D. Phipps, R. G. Pratt, C. E. Shackle, Ian Sinclair (Australia), B. D. Stoyel, P. J. Tambling, John H. Trounson, T. D. Walshaw, D. N. Wright, F. D. Woodall, D. H. Yarnell.

For permission to reproduce engravings and other figures, and in some cases to quote extracts from their pages, I am indebted to the Editors of *The Engineer*, *Engineering*, *The Folkestone Herald*, *The Illustrated London News*, and *Model Engineer*. The extracts from Air Marshal Sir Hugh Lloyd's book *Briefed to Attack* are quoted by kind permission of Hodder and Stoughton, Ltd., and David Higham Associates, Ltd.

My thanks are due also to the Director of the Science Museum, to the staffs of the Derbyshire County Library and the Sheffield City Public Libraries, to the Borough Librarian of Folkestone, R. Howarth, Esq., A.L.A., and to the following firms: Allens of Oxford Ltd., Aveling-Barford Ltd., The Brightside Foundry and Engineering Co. Ltd., Davey Paxman and Co. Ltd., John Freeman and McLeod Ltd. (Penryn, Cornwall), John Fowler and Co. (Leeds) Ltd., Wm. Foster and Co. Ltd., Richard Garrett Engineering Co. Ltd., Longmans, Green and Co. Ltd., Marshall, Sons and Co. Ltd., J. and H. McLaren Ltd., Ruston and Hornsby Ltd., The Technical Press Ltd., and The Wantage Engineering Co. Ltd.

To my late wife Dorothy must go much credit for her encouragement in my work, and to my daughter Mrs Glenys M. Clarke I am very grateful for having deciphered and typed out my manuscript, all in her spare time.

To conclude this foreword, perhaps I may mention the existence of the Road Locomotive Society and the National Traction Engine Club, which both serve the cause of steam road traction, though perhaps in rather divergent ways. There is also the British Fairground Society which is interested in showmen's engines as well as other fairground aspects. Should any reader be interested in membership of any or all of them, I shall be happy to supply details of the secretaries' addresses, on receipt of a stamp.

I

INTRODUCTION

. . . and, last of all, with inimitable power, and 'with whirlwind sound' comes the potent agency of steam. In comparison with the past, what centuries of improvement has this single agent comprised in the short compass of fifty years! DANIEL WEBSTER

THE TECHNOLOGICAL HISTORY OF the world includes very many triumphant discoveries inaugurated and developed by Great Britain. One of the greatest of these was the steam engine, whose invention ushered in the Industrial Revolution from which so many more epoch-making discoveries – even nuclear power – were to spring. In fact at its present stage of development at least, nuclear power depends itself on the power of steam for its practical application to peaceful purposes.

It was natural that in the country of its birth, agile minds should soon be seeking fresh ways in which to press the steam engine to the service of mankind. The problem of mechanical transport had long occupied the thoughts of dreamers, but the practical solution of the problem had to await the arrival of steam and, in turn, the development of the direct-acting high-pressure engine, for land transport at least.

Freed from the incubus of the great beam and the heavy condenser, together with the tremendous cylinder and piston which was demanded by Watt's low-pressure type of engine and boiler, the high-pressure engine could be made of much smaller dimensions for an equal power. It was just what the road and rail transport people had been awaiting. Steam was in the haulage business at last.

Early designs of road engines were frequently developed by trial and error, rather than by inspiration. Others were promoted by people of little or no mechanical knowledge, who produced abortions which sometimes, however, received extremely kind notices in the press, and were then no more heard about.

In the first instance, the application of steam on the roads was to carriages, and there is a great temptation to discuss the trials and tribulations, the successes and failures, of such men as Gurney, Hancock, Russell, Hill, Maceroni, and Dance. But to do this would not lie in the orbit of this book, whose aim is rather to trace the development of the British traction engine and road locomotive from the first to the last.

None the less, there is one steam-carriage builder who should be mentioned – the father of them all, Richard Trevithick. It was he who first developed the high-pressure steam engine, and who was the first engineer to convey passengers by steam on an English road.

Murdock's little model of 1781 is often cited as the first successful road engine, but it never achieved the dignity of growing up. The same must be said of Symington's model coach of 1786, highly successful as it was in

Fig. 1. Trevithick's steam carriage of 1801.
Merveilles de la Science.

miniature. Any further development of Murdock's ideas was discouraged by his employer James Watt, who was so bigotted against steam road locomotion that he actually put a covenant in the lease of his residence that 'no steam carriage should on any pretence be allowed to approach the house'. In Symington's case, it was the designer himself who refused to build a full-sized machine, in fairness to those who would have backed him financially, because he thought the state of the roads, and the difficulty of providing fuel and water thereon, would prevent its success.

Trevithick, however, built a full-sized road engine which was first tried out on Christmas Eve, 1801. It carried seven or eight people 'like a bird' up Camborne Beacon, and was highly successful in other trials. Granted

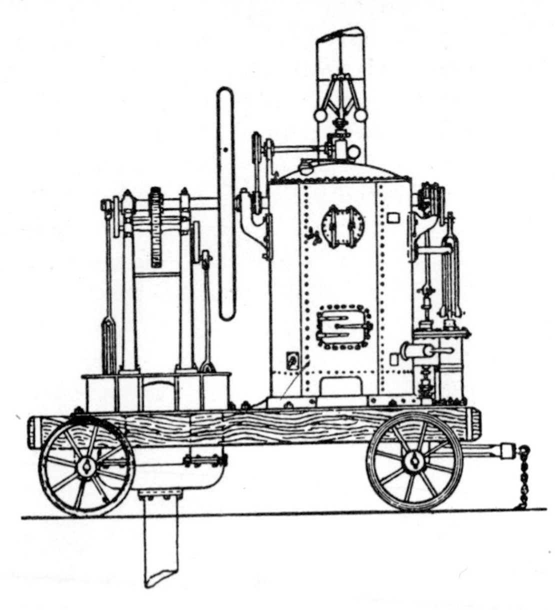

Fig. 2. Nathan Gough's portable engine of 1830.
Feilden's Magazine.

a patent in 1802, Trevithick and his partner Vivian next built a carriage in London (Fig. 1). This had a wrought iron boiler, with the horizontal cylinder enclosed within it. The forked piston rod drove forward to a crosshead working in slides, from which a return connecting rod drove the crankshaft behind.

Final drive to the ten-foot diameter hind wheels was by gearing, with a clutch each side in lieu of differential gear. The framing was wrought iron, and the coach body, set high, was suspended on springs. It could carry ten persons.

Despite the machine's success, further financial backing was not forthcoming, and the partners' capital became exhausted. The coach was removed, and the engine sold to drive a mill, which it did for many years. And Trevithick was thus led to devote most of his energies to the railway, to the benefit of the latter but the detriment of road locomotion.

Meantime, however, he had laid down the principles on which the portable steam engine was founded: and it was the portable which became the basis of the traction engine. In fact, the first traction engine on record was a portable engine with chain drive added, as we shall see in the next chapter.

In 1802, when, as Wansbrough says, steam engines of even small power were 'about as portable as a parish church', Matthew Murray was granted a patent for an engine which was 'transferable without being taken to pieces', which could be used for 'any process or manufacture requiring circular motion, or for irrigating land, or for the various purposes of agriculture'. This was a step in the right direction, but only a small one, and little came of it.

However, by this time Trevithick was building high-pressure stationary engines which had the exhaust turned up the chimney – a requisite for the portable and later the traction engine. By 1812, he was producing true portable engines for agricultural purposes, mounted on wheels, and weighing only 15 cwt., at a price of 60 guineas.

Trevithick himself described the engine, in a letter to Sir John Sinclair, 'Respecting the engine for threshing, chaff-cutting, or sawing, I am now making one about two-thirds the size of that made for Sir Charles Hawkins, which will be portable on wheels, and may be removed from place to place as easily as a one-horse cart . . . The steam can be raised, and the engine moved a distance of two miles, and the threshing machine at work within an hour'.

But during the next twenty years or so, there was little or no progress, due largely to the disturbed state of the country, the high price of corn, and the rioting and machine wrecking, all of which would do little to encourage the farmer who wished to employ machinery himself.

In 1830, Nathan Gough of Salford commenced the manufacture of 'portable and self-moving engines', but although an illustration of his portable has survived (Fig. 2), I have not been able to trace any actual

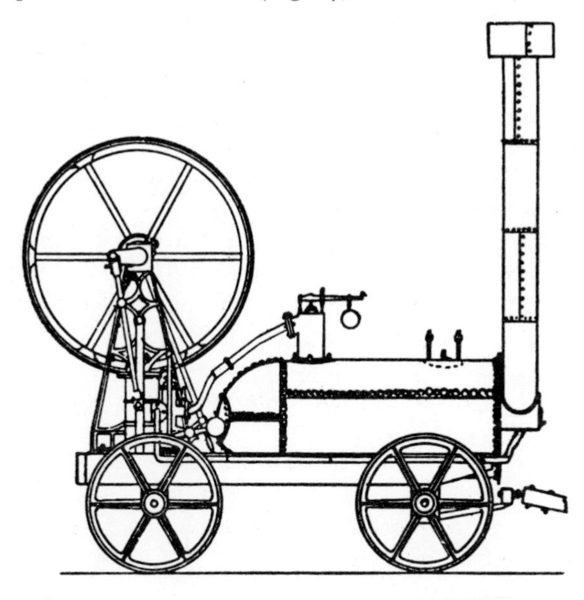

Fig. 3. Howden's 6 n.h.p. portable engine of 1839.
Feilden's Magazine.

record of a self-moving engine. If he did in fact build one at all what a pity that nothing regarding it has survived, so that it could take its rightful place! But Fletcher doubts that he did.

As will be seen, Gough's portable was mounted on a timber frame, and had a vertical boiler and cylinder. A forked connecting rod drove upwards and obliquely backwards to the overhung crank, the shaft being carried in cast brackets bolted to the boiler. In the particular case illustrated the shaft was extended to drive dual water pumps mounted on the same undercarriage; presumably the latter was shorter in length for the portable on its own.

Other portable engines were built by various small country engineers and foundries, but the next I have been able actually to trace is Howden's 6 h.p. of 1839 (Fig. 3), which was exhibited at the Wrangle show of the Lincolnshire Agricultural Society. Here we have a horizontal boiler with a return flue, mounted on a timber frame. The piston rod drives up to a crosshead, from which a rod drives downward to a further crosshead guided by slides on the cylinder front, and then back by return connecting rod to the overhung crank. The exhaust pipe runs forward to turn the blast up the chimney.

This singularly misguided gentleman, by the way, only built twelve portable engines altogether, and then gave up their manufacture because he was afraid the country would become over-stocked! How wrong he was – by the end of the nineteenth century one firm alone had built more than 33,000 portables!

But now we are rapidly approaching the first of a long and honourable line of self-moving road engines, produced by a firm whose name is happily still well known in the world, Ransomes, Sims and Jefferies of Ipswich. Robert Ransome was born in 1753, the son of a Norfolk schoolmaster. After apprenticeship to a Norwich ironmonger, he started in the same trade, and soon opened a small iron foundry.

In 1785, he obtained a patent for tempering cast-iron plough shares, and four years after started the business in Ipswich that was later to become so famous. Though principally concerned in the production of agricultural implements, the firm's interests grew wider, and in 1817 we find them installing a gasometer and supplying gas to the town. The following year saw J. and R. Ransome build the second Stoke Bridge of cast iron.

In 1830, Robert Ransome died, and the title became J. R. and A. Ransome. The first steam engine used in Ipswich was installed at their foundry in 1831. Next year the manufacture of lawn mowers commenced. A new riverside foundry was built in 1837, and so began the Orwell Works.

The English Agricultural Society held its first Royal Show at Oxford in 1839, to which Ransomes sent six tons of exhibits, over 100 miles, by wagons and horses. The firm was awarded the Society's gold medal. It was, of course, the Royal Shows, sponsored by the Royal Agricultural Society of England, as the organisation became in 1840, which were to have such a profound effect on the perfecting of the portable and traction engine, as well as steam cultivation, in after years.

Ransomes' first portable steam engine appeared at the Liverpool Royal Show in 1841, and it was this engine which was destined to become self moving, in the following year.

2

THE PERIOD OF EXPERIMENT

Steam, the enemy of space and time, with its enormous strength and delicate adaptability . . . EMERSON

THE MACHINE WHICH RANSOMES' exhibited in 1841 had a vertical boiler with rounded top, mounted on a wooden platform. The engine itself was of the so-called disc type, built under Davies' patent. For the non-technical, it should be noted that long before Parsons invented his steam turbine, there were many efforts to supersede by pure rotary motion the relatively inefficient reciprocating engine, which, however, still remained paramount. Davies' patent was just one such abortive effort to do away with piston, cylinder, connecting rod and crank, though space does not permit a description.

The Royal Show of 1842 was held at Bristol, and Ransomes sent the portable in a modified form (Fig. 4). It was on a platform which had been

Fig. 4. Ransomes' self-propelled portable engine of 1842.
Feilden's Magazine.

extended to carry a small threshing machine and, more important, a sprocket was mounted on the engine-shaft, with a larger one bolted to one hind wheel.

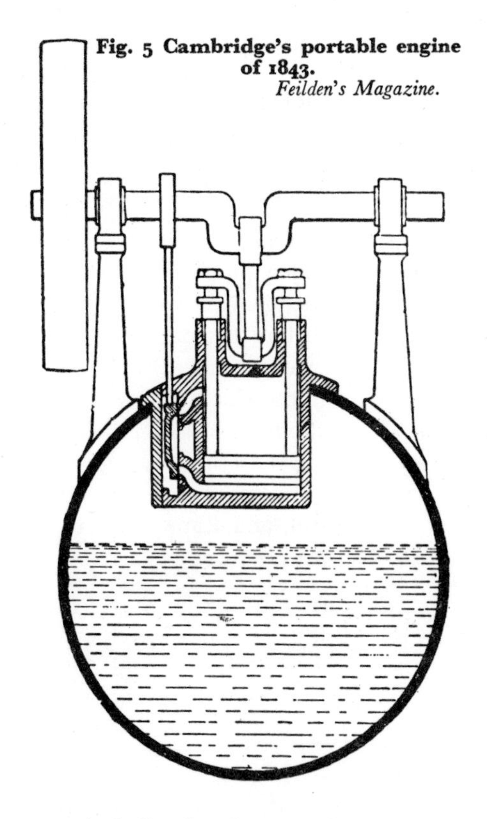

Fig. 5 Cambridge's portable engine of 1843.
Feilden's Magazine.

When the engine was required to drive the threshing machine, this was dismounted from the platform, and placed on the ground, in the second position shown in the illustration, to be driven by belt from the flywheel. Threshing complete, and the machine back on the platform, a pitch chain was applied to the sprockets, and horse-shafts fastened to the fore-carriage.

Here the reader may well enquire why the horse, when the machine was self propelling? The simple answer is that the horse was required to *steer* the engine, and it was a function he was called upon to do with many future designs too! But the fact that the engine propelled itself often used to spoil the horse, who would subsequently balk when harnessed to a load he had to *pull*.

Returning to the Ransomes engine, the work done on test at the show was estimated at 5 h.p., the quantity of water evaporated per hour at 36 galls., and the consumption of coke as 56 lb. This gives the steam used as 72 lb. per h.p. hour, and the evaporative efficiency of the boiler as 6.4 lb. of water per lb. of coke, showing that the boiler was of much greater efficiency than the engine.

The judges remarked that 'the engine travelled along at the rate of four to six miles an hour, and was guided and manœuvred so as to fix it in any particular spot with ease. It turned also in small compass'. On one occasion it is reported to have run away, and gone through a hedge, but despite these reckless propensities, the engine was awarded a prize of £30.

After this optimistic note, it is depressing to have to say that farmers still remained prejudiced against a steam engine in the stackyard. The machine had to be brought back to the works, and eventually the thresher went to one purchaser, and the engine to another.

Man's instinct, however, is to persevere, and portable engines continued to appear at the Royal Shows during the 1840's. Design was very free and varied, but there was a great prejudice against using horizontal cylinders, which was not only confined to the portable engine. As a result we find vertical cylinders used even with horizontal boilers, Cambridge's design for 1843 being shown in Fig. 5. To reduce overall height, he has used the marine-engine idea of twin piston rods, with a bent crosshead which dips downwards into the deeply-recessed top cylinder cover.

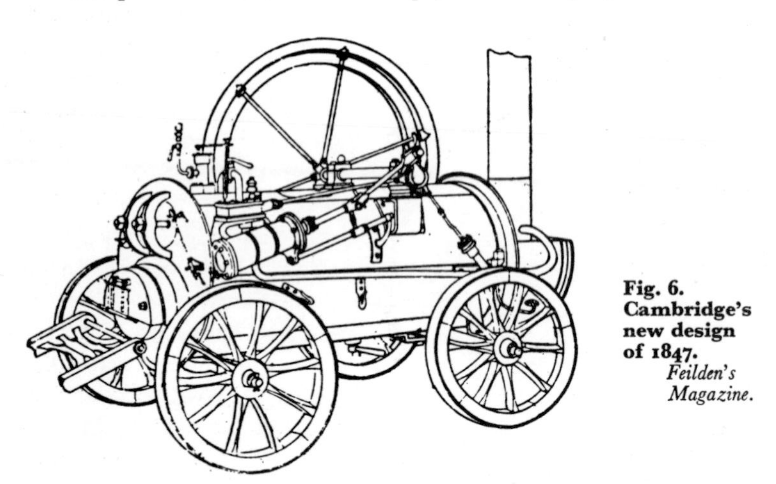

Fig. 6. Cambridge's new design of 1847. *Feilden's Magazine.*

In 1846, Cambridge exhibited an engine which, says Wansbrough, seems to have been made from the following recipe: 'Take a small pillar letter-box, bore out the lower part to fit a piston, and apply a slide valve and bottom cover; put a crankshaft through near the closed top with the crank inside: couple to the piston by a connecting rod. Fill the space above the piston, which is single acting, with exhaust steam, and immerse the whole in the boiler as far as it will go. Boil till further notice'.

Following this *tour-de-force*, it is pleasing to relate that at Northampton in 1847, Cambridge was awarded the prize of £50 for a portable of much more orthodox design (Fig. 6). True, the cylinder is not yet quite horizontal, but the engine possesses many features which were to become standard practice. The crankshaft is carried in bearings mounted on top of the boiler, and there is an eccentrically-driven feed pump. A vase-like dome is fitted for the Salter safety valve, and additionally carries a whistle, whilst a large manhole and a glass water gauge are features of the boiler too.

An engine of this type, still working, was exhibited at the Kilburn show in 1879 (as also was a Trevithick engine of 1811), and at least two are known to have worked until after the turn of the century, so they must have been well built, and satisfactory runners.

During the 1847 trials, the Cambridge engine was worked at 68 lb. pressure, and at 250 r.p.m., both figures well in advance of the time.

At the 1848 meeting at York, Hornsby of Grantham won the first prize of £50 with the portable shown in Fig. 7 (which also appeared at Kilburn in 1879, by the way). This had the unusual but sound feature of a round

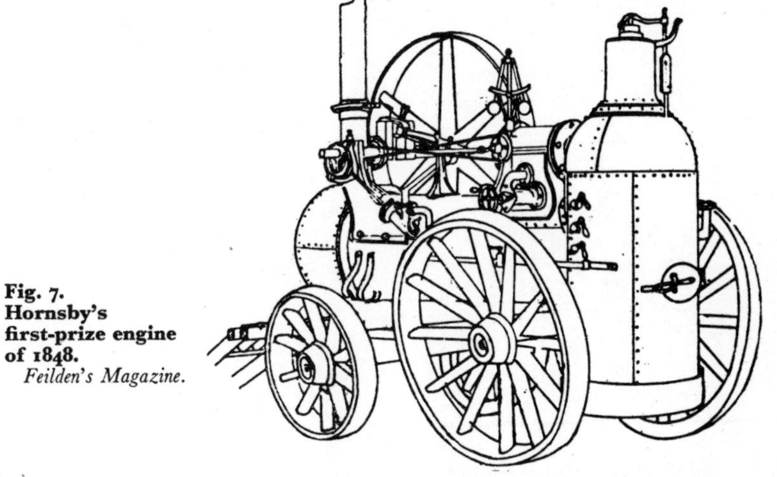

Fig. 7. Hornsby's first-prize engine of 1848.
Feilden's Magazine.

firebox, which thus needed no stays, and which was used seventy-odd years later by Robeys in their steam wagons, tractors and light rollers. (See Figs. 164–5.)

The Hornsby portable also had the cylinder steam jacketed by being enclosed in a casing built on to the boiler top, and this was of course a very important feature. Most steam engines of the day, and especially portables, had cylinders which were not even lagged, so that the steam jacket made the cylinder much more efficient.

The cylinder was 10 in. in diameter by 14 in. stroke, with the steam ports very close to the ends of the cylinder – another feature for reducing steam consumption, since less steam was wasted in filling the passages. It was an idea which Fodens used many years later which contributed to the great success of their traction engines.

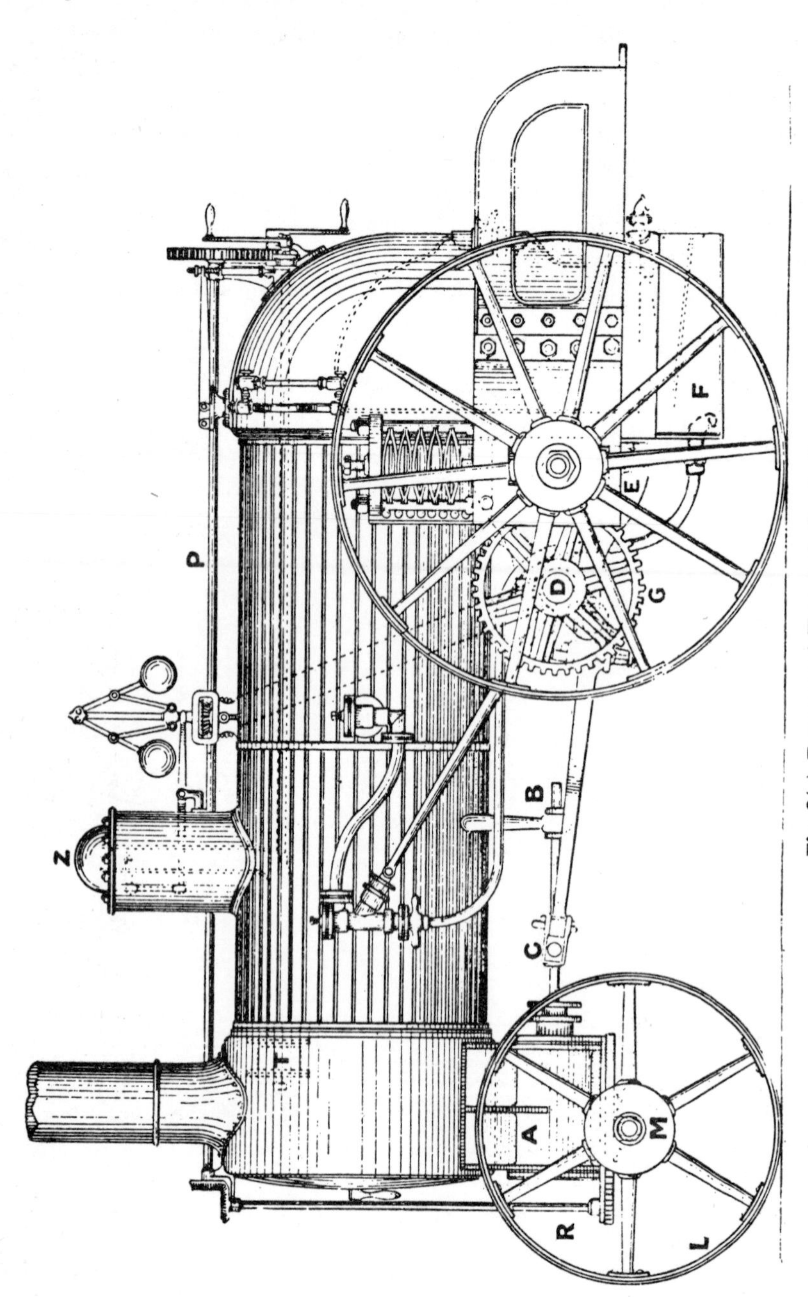

Fig. 8(a) Ransomes' 'Farmer's Engine'.
English and American Traction Engines and Steam Cars.

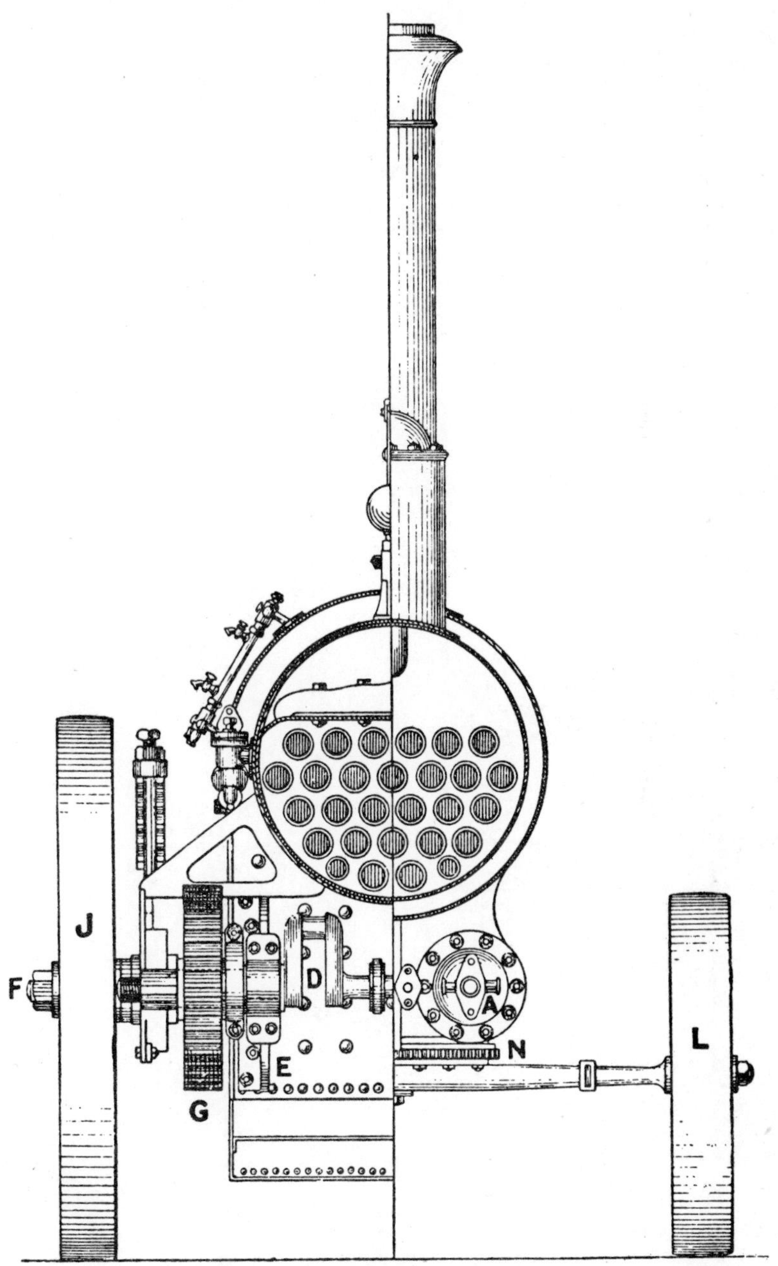

Fig. 8(b) Front view of the 'Farmer's Engine'.
English and American Traction Engines and Steam Cars.

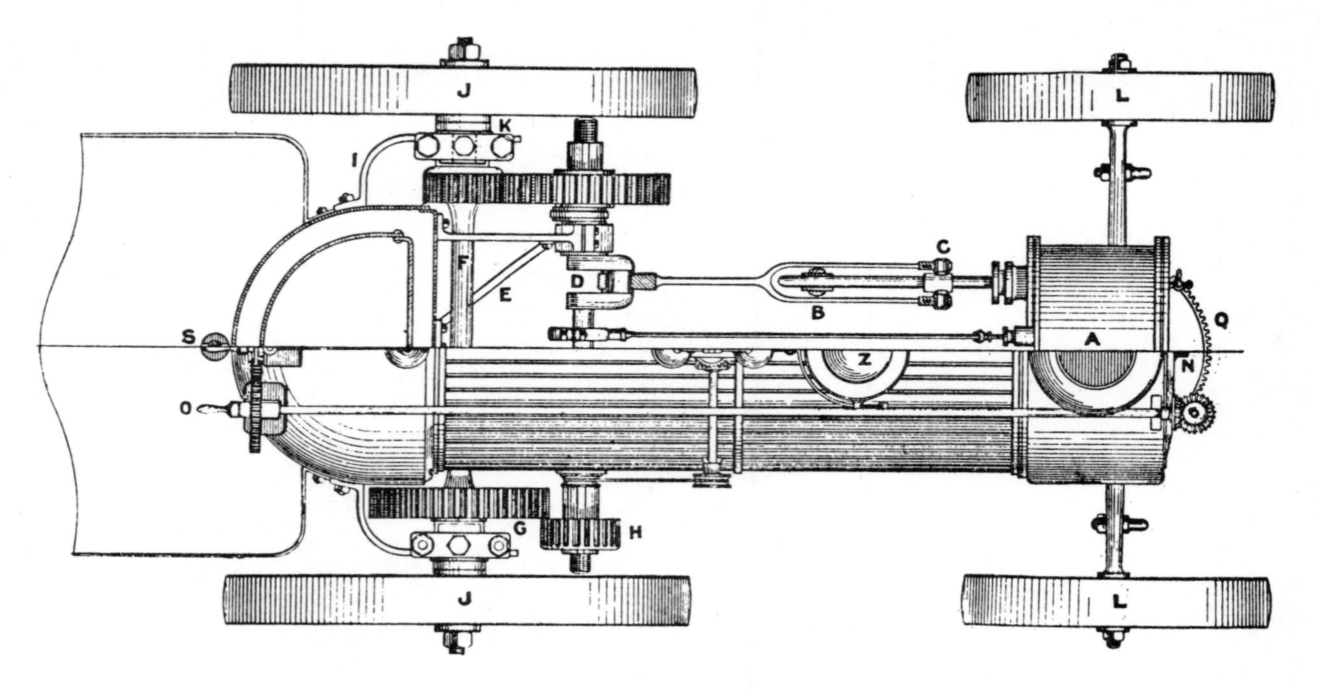

Fig. 8(c) Plan of the 'Farmer's Engine'.
English and American Traction Engines and Steam Cars.

Meantime Clayton and Shuttleworth were the first firm to build a portable of more or less 'modern' appearance, in 1848, with the horizontal cylinder (unjacketed but wood lagged) on the firebox top, driving forward to a bent crankshaft carried in cast brackets on the boiler top. This design was built in three sizes, of 4, 5 and 6 h.p., with 6¼-in., 7-in. and 7¾-in. bore cylinders respectively. In each case the stroke was 12 in. and the working pressure 45 p.s.i.

In all this period there seems to have been no further attempt to build a self-propelling engine, but in 1849 Ransomes exhibited another, this time at the Leeds Royal. The engine had actually been built in Leeds, at the Railway Foundry of E. B. Wilson and Co., to the designs of Robert Willis, and it somewhat resembled an inside cylindered railway locomotive in its layout, though with ingenious arrangements to fit it for road and stationary work. (Figs. 8 (a), (b) and (c).)

There were two cylinders A 6¼ in. by 10 in., the extended piston rods sliding in brackets B. From the crossheads C, forked connecting rods took the drive back to the crankshaft D, running in wrought-iron brackets bolted to the front of the firebox. Each end of the crankshaft was splined, bearing in one case a pinion and in the other a spur wheel. On the hind axle, on the corresponding sides, were a spur wheel and a pinion respectively. By this means, two gear ratios were available, of 1 to 2¼, and 2¼ to 1; alternatively, with both gears slid out of engagement, the crankshaft could run free.

The hind axle was supported in the curved wrought-iron brackets I, bolted to the firebox sides, with leaf springs above. Also bolted to the firebox sides were brackets carrying the wrought-iron footplate behind.

Considerable comment was caused by the boiler, of which the whole longitudinal seam was *welded* – not, of course, with the methods applicable today, but by bringing to welding heat in the hearth and then by skilled forgemen applying their hammers. This on a barrel 5 ft. 6 in. long, was no mean feat! Another unusual (for that period) point was that the joints between barrel and smokebox, and barrel and firebox, were made by flanging the parts themselves, and not by using angles rivetted on.

The hind wheels, 4 ft. in diameter, and front wheels, 2 ft. 8 in., were built up in wrought iron, with round spokes rivetted to a welded rim. In the former, the naves were bushed with brass, bored out to a force fit on the axle, and secured by nut and washer. The front wheels of course ran free on their axle.

Also before its time was the footplate steerage, in which a small pinion, attached to the handle on its stub-shaft, meshed with a larger one on a shaft P running along the boiler top. From here bevel wheels worked a vertical shaft R, on the bottom of which a pinion meshed with a toothed rack bolted to the front axle.

From the regulator handle S, a shaft passed through the boiler to a regulator in the smokebox, shown sectionally in Fig. 9. The cast-iron valve face, W, was held into its tapered socket by the set screw, and the brass valve itself, U, was keyed to the shaft, with a helical spring to keep it on the seat when there was not enough steam pressure. There were two steam apertures VV, which corresponded to similar ones in the valve face W. From the valve chest, the steam passed out through orifice X into a pipe connected to the cylinder valve chest.

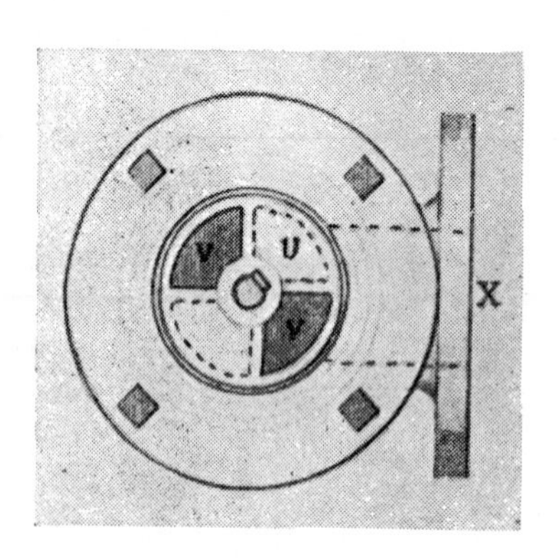

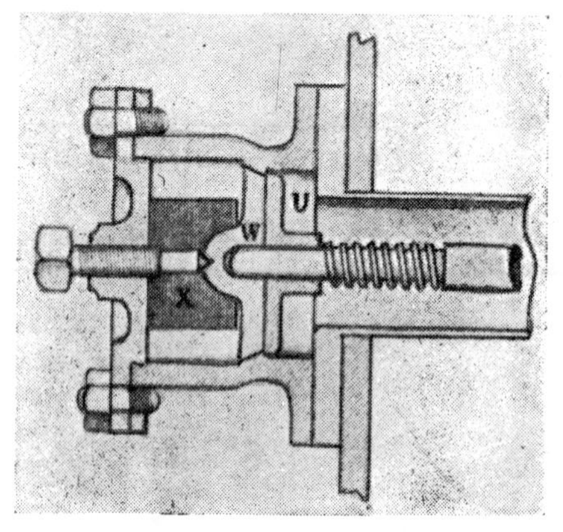

Fig. 9. Regulator valve of the 'Farmer's Engine'.

The Artizan.

The regulator steam pipe was bent up at right angles to collect the steam from the dome Z, and was capped, so to speak, by a butterfly valve worked from the Watt-type governor. This was driven by a cord from a pulley on the crankshaft. At the opposite side of the crankshaft was the eccentric from which the feed pump, on the boiler side, was driven. The pump obtained its supply from the tank F underneath the ashpan, so that the feed water was heated to some extent.

When it was required to use the engine stationary, the drive could be taken in three ways: firstly directly from the crankshaft, with a universal joint and coupling rod screwed on at either end, secondly via the gearing with the same arrangement screwed on the hind axle, and thirdly using the hind wheel or wheels to take a driving belt or belts. In both the latter cases, the firebox had to be jacked up.

The performance was quite useful, and after carrying off the first prize at the 'Royal', it was well tested by Ransomes and May (for another partner had come into the firm), driven by J. C. Wilson from the builders. It threshed two days at Mr. Mumford's farm at Bramford, and another at nearby Mr. Wood's. From there it went to Mr. Frost's, near Freston, ascending 1-in-11 Freston Hill 'at a brisk walking pace' *en route*. This was in slow gear: on the level, 'it performed twelve miles within the hour easily'.

On test, it could raise steam to the working pressure of 45 p.s.i. in 45 minutes, using 41 lb. of coal. When threshing, it used from 50 to 55 lb. of coke per hour, evaporating in the same time 41 gallons of water, driving two four-horse threshing machines, and threshing 260 coombs of grain in a working day of 10 hours. The total weight of the engine in full working order was 2½ tons, but it also hauled a small four-wheeled tender with additional coal and water.

The Practical Mechanic's Journal says: 'Such is the general detail of this "farmer's engine", which, we are sure, only requires to be known to be pretty universally introduced . . . For large farms, we conceive that this engine will be a most effective assistant: and even on those of limited extent, if at all conveniently located, its powers of locomotion on a common road will render it quite available, as it can be quickly taken from one farm to another'.

And yet, despite this optimistic report, which today does not seem unjustified, it is sad to relate that, like the previous 'self propeller', this engine too failed to achieve success. The farmers were prejudiced still against self-moving engines, and it is reported that after about two years' use, the 'farmer's engine' was on its last legs, chiefly because it was too lightly built to stand up to the terrible road conditions of that era. It was well designed and well built – but it *was* before its time! So Ransomes, discouraged, dropped the idea of a self-moving engine, and it was several years before it came up again.

3

FEATURES OF A MODERN ENGINE

A machine, receiving at distant times and from many hands new combinations and improvements, and becoming at last of signal benefit to mankind, may be compared to a rivulet swelled in its course by tributory streams, until it rolls along a majestic river, enriching, in its progress, provinces and kingdoms. STUART

BEFORE WE PROCEED ANY further in seeing how *our* rivulet swelled in its course, let us have a look at our majestic river, so that we may know just which tributory streams to look for. In other words, let's inspect features of a modern type of engine, and briefly discuss its construction. We shall then know, as we study the older designs, which features of these have stood the test of time, and which have been discarded.

Now of course, although to a layman all traction engines look more or less alike, this is only an outward similarity. Some makers actually vary considerably in *details* of design from others: thus it is with traction engines as with motor cars or vacuum cleaners or air liners. (And, let it be said, each maker swears, and has his partisans who also swear, that his machine is much better than any of the others!)

A handy traction engine to discuss will be the Clayton and Shuttleworth of 1898, chiefly because I have four nice clear engravings of it which show all the points I want to talk about.

In passing, engravings are frequently better than photographs for the study of detail, if only because the artist usually puts in *all* the detail, which sometimes is blurred on a photo. Moreover, a photograph reproduced in, say, a catalogue, has invariably been 'retouched'. This is all very well if the retouching artist knows what he's doing, but sometimes he doesn't, and uses his imagination. There is, for instance, one classic example in a Burrell catalogue (and on a coloured plate in my possession) where a chain descends mysteriously from the belly tank, makes half a turn round the steerage worm-wheel, and ascends again into the belly tank, equally as mysteriously. Some imagination that retoucher had!

Nathaniel Clayton and Joseph Shuttleworth joined forces in 1842 to found this famous firm, which built many thousands of steam engines of many kinds, until in 1929 it failed, with Burrell and others of the Agricultural and General Engineers group, and was absorbed by Marshalls. The engine we are about to study was from the drawing board of William Fletcher, doyen of all designers, and author of dozens of articles and at least two magnificent books (see Bibliography).

Early in his career he was leading draughtsman and assistant manager at a Southern manufacturers', and then manager at a Norfolk establishment. There followed eight years as chief draughtsman at Marshalls, from where he went to Ransomes, then to Claytons, and finally to Davey, Paxman's.

For all these firms he designed traction engines, road locomotives and portables, and it is probable that he thus exerted a greater influence on general appearance as well as excellence of design than any other man except, perhaps, Thomas Aveling. All his designs bear the hall-mark of classic simplicity, elegant proportions, and fitness for purpose which characterise this present example, the 6 n.h.p. Clayton and Shuttleworth.

The term nominal horse power (n.h.p.) is really a hangover from early days, probably deriving from the 'horse power' machines or horse works devised to use horses for driving threshing machines and other barn machinery. One type of horse works was a kind of treadmill, where one, two, or three horses, side-by-side, walked on inclined endless belts which moved beneath them, the power thus generated being taken off through a shaft, gearing and universal joints. Another kind was a sort of windlass, the horses being harnessed to the arms, and walking round in a circle. This type was in use until the 1890's or later: a 'one-horse' machine (Fig. 10) was awarded a silver medal at the 'Royal' at Carlisle as late as 1880.

Thus the manufacturer of a 4 h.p. portable would intend to purvey to non-technically minded farmers that his engine developed the same power as a 'horse power' in which four horses were used. In actual practice, the term was quite wrongly used, one nominal horse power being deemed to be equal to '10 circular inches of piston area'. To work out what this

Fig. 10. A horse-power machine.
A Text-Book of Farm Machinery.

Fig. 11. Clayton and Shuttleworth's traction engine of 1898, seen from the off-side.
A Chapter in the History of the Traction Engine.

Fig. 12. Nearside view of the 1898 Clayton and Shuttleworth.
A Chapter in the History of the Traction Engine.

meant, or was supposed to mean, take the square of the cylinder bore and divide by ten to obtain the n.h.p. Example: a cylinder of 9-in. bore: $9 \times 9 = 81$: 8 n.h.p. engine! Or cylinder $6\frac{1}{4}$-in. bore: $6\frac{1}{4} \times 6\frac{1}{4} = 40$ nearly: 4 n.h.p. engine.

This system, of course, took no account of the boiler pressure or even of the stroke, but it did serve as a rough and ready measurement, in early days when the usual pressure was about 45 lb.

Looking at our Clayton engine, we see the locomotive-type boiler which is the chassis, so to speak. The barrel is relatively short, so that on a down incline the firebox crown would not be uncovered, nor on a reverse slope would the front end of the fire-tubes.

The sides of the outer firebox are extended upwards and backwards, to carry the bearings for the shafts; they have a curved plate – the 'arch plate' – riveted between them to form the top of the firebox wrapper. The extended plates are called the hornplates, and were invented by Thomas Aveling in 1870.

Riveted to the boiler is the smokebox, and riveted under that is the perch bracket, carrying the bearing in which the fore-carriage fork rotates. The latter is a fork fitting over the front axle, with a pin passing through both to allow the axle to tilt on uneven ground.

Mounted on the front axle is the round spudpan, to carry the spuds or paddles – the angle, or T-irons which can be attached to the hind wheels to give extra grip on soft ground. The steerage chains are attached to the spudpan, and from beneath the front fork a stay or strut is carried back to the firebox throatplate to give additional support to the fore-carriage.

Looking now specifically at the off-side (Fig. 11) we see the cylinder near the smokebox. It is steam jacketed (another Aveling patent) and acts as a steam dome also. Twin safety valves are mounted on top of it. The crosshead is guided by a bored-out trunk, though some makers used bars instead.

Four shafts (crankshaft, two countershafts, and hind axle) are used, being carried in brass bearings mounted in steel brackets accurately fitted to holes bored in the hornplates. Many makers use 'bent-from-the-round-bar' crankshafts, but after forging our Clayton has had the cheeks machined. An eccentric on the crankshaft drives the pump mounted on the boiler barrel: other makers had different ideas about pump positions.

The outside gearing is neatly enclosed in sheet steel casings. Two T-rings form the rim of the hind wheel, with cross strakes riveted on at an angle, so as to preserve constant rolling contact with the ground. The inner ends of the spokes are cast into the hub, the outer ends being palmed out and rivetted to the T-rings.

Bolted on to the back of the hornplates is the tender, with the water tank underneath and coal bunker behind the footplate. Also bolted to the hornplate, and often directly to the bolts securing the hind axle bearing, is the draw strap, which passes back along the tank side to the channel-section drawbar. The strap and bar are both riveted to the tender, but it is they which take the strain of haulage, and *not* the tender.

Beneath the draw strap is a manhole giving access to the tank, and above it a cast pocket with a hinged lid (which also forms a footstep) to allow the tank to be filled. Forward of the pump, on the boiler side, is a tool box forming a footboard too, with a neat little access ladder.

Now to the other side (Fig. 12), where we see a manhole in the boiler side, below the cylinder flange, giving access to the boiler interior for cleaning and washing out. On this side, too, we can see more clearly the pipe or bend which carries steam from boiler to cylinder. In many engines the steam is taken through a hole or holes in the boiler top direct into a cavity in the cylinder base and thence round the steam jacket and up to the dome.

However, that means that the whole big joint round the cylinder flange has to be made steam tight, whereas with the separate bend there are only two small joints. Moreover, with this arrangement the steam is taken more nearly from the centre of the barrel, reducing a tendency to prime when running downhill.

Above the bend is the rod which works the slide valve, which was much more used in tractions and portables than the piston valve. The valve gear is Stephenson link motion, which was the gear almost, but not quite, exclusively used by British makers.

A high-speed cross-armed governor, spring loaded, is used, connected to a large-area equilibrium valve, when working stationary. The heavy flywheel assists in smooth running. Behind it may be seen the regulator lever, sticking up, and the gear-change lever, cranked.

The steerage chains wrap round a drum carried in brackets fastened to the hornplates, with a worm, worm-wheel, shaft and hand-wheel to allow control from the footplate. There is also a rod to control the opening of the ashpan damper, and a handle and screw to apply the band brake on a drum behind the winding drum.

The latter, mounted on the hind axle, carries a length of wire-rope which can be paid out and used for such purposes as hauling tree stumps out of the ground, or extracting wagons from soft ground, or even, fastened to a suitable stout tree, for hauling out the engine itself if bogged down. We shall see later how the winding drum was driven.

A fitting which many makers omit is the form-fitting seat – only an

Fig. 13. Driver's view of the Clayton and Shuttleworth.
A Chapter in the History of the Traction Engine.

idler or a namby-pamby would want to sit down during a nine- or ten-hour working day, anyway. Behind the seat is the fairlead, consisting of two vertical rollers through which the rope can be paid off at an angle, when necessary.

Then there's a small brass cap: this covers the mouth of the water lifter, on to which a hose can be attached to fill the tank from a roadside ditch, stream or pond. The lifter itself – a simple type of injector – is mounted inside the tender, though most makers do not bother to conceal it.

Looking now at the top view (Fig. 13), the change-speed arrangement may be seen behind the steering wheel. Two pinions are keyed to the crankshaft, with a spacing boss between them (which is used, incidentally, as the pulley for the governor belt). Part of the second shaft is of square section, and on this slides a boss carrying two spur wheels together. (The smaller of these is nearly hidden in Fig. 13 by the change-speed lever.)

When the lever is moved to the left, it engages the larger spur wheel with the smaller pinion, giving slow speed. Movement to the right engages the smaller spur wheel with the larger pinion, giving fast speed. In the position shown, the engine can run free. All the gearing is of best crucible cast steel, at this period.

In this view the regulator lever is nearly indistinguishable, but it is just to the right of the eccentrics, with its handle beneath the right-hand ball of the governor. The tall lever in its quadrant bolted to the right-hand hornplate is the reversing lever, of course. Below it and to the right, on the tender side, is the lever controlling the water cock to the injector, which is mounted lower down on the side.

It will be seen that the gear-change lever, regulator lever and pressure gauge are mounted on a transverse plate which is rivetted to the hornplates: this is known as the front plate. At the cylinder end of the hornplates is a similar transverse plate, cut away to clear the motion work, and known as the spectacle plate.

We will discuss the remainder of the gear drive to the hind axle in a later chapter, but the third shaft in its massive bearing brackets is prominent in this view, the twin water gauges being behind it. Some makers fit water gauges on 'stalks' so that they come outside the shaft and are more easily visible. Twin sliding doors for the firehole are visible, but most makers use the oval hinged type.

On the front view (Fig. 14), there is not a great deal to notice, but the artist has omitted the push-pole lug from its position directly under the centre of the smokebox. This was a bracket which we shall see in other engines (*vide* Fig. 128), to allow a steel pole to be attached so that the engine could push or pull a wagon or threshing machine about in shunting

Fig. 14. The C. and S. seen from the front.
A Chapter in the History of the Traction Engine.

it to an exact position. In Fig. 175 another use is seen, as a towing bracket.

Also noticeable on the front view is the fact that the Clayton engine is narrow in the width – a useful attribute when passing through farm gateways and working in crowded stackyards.

This engine, of 6 n.h.p., actually has a cylinder of 8-in. bore, and has developed over 30 horse power on the brake, the boiler making ample steam. It has hauled a load of 20 tons over a long hill near Lincoln, having an average gradient of 1 in 8½. A similar engine of 7 n.h.p. (8½-in. bore) is also reported as hauling *in fast gear* a load of 20 tons of coal on a 22-mile-long and very hilly road in Scotland, burning only 11 cwt. of coal on the journey.

In another test, an 8 n.h.p. engine (9-in. bore by 12-in. stroke) built for the Khedive of Egypt, hauled more than 26 tons up that same hill in Lincoln, 'at a good speed', says *Engineering*, 'without a stoppage, steam blowing off all the way'. In this latter engine the working pressure is 150 p.s.i., and engine revolutions 155 per min. at 2 and 4 m.p.h. on the gears. The flywheel is 4 ft. 6 in. dia. by 6½ in. face, hind wheels 6 ft. 3 in. by 16 in., and front wheels 4 ft. by 9 in.

So there we are – a handsome, well-proportioned engine typical of the traction engine at its heyday. Let us now go on to look at more of its early ancestors.

4

STILL EXPERIMENTING

One of the noblest gifts that science ever made to mankind . . .
GALLOWAY

THE EARLY HISTORY OF the traction engine is bound up inextricably with steam cultivation, as well as with the portable engine, and it is inevitable therefore that a few ploughing engines and other cultivators should creep into this book. The steam engine was bringing prosperity to Britain: the population was increasing by leaps and bounds – and the population needed feeding. In the middle of the nineteenth century emphasis was on arable farming and corn growing rather than on livestock. The age-old methods of husbandry could not prepare the ground fast enough, nor thresh the corn. Steam gave the answer to both problems.

We have already mentioned the inauguration of the Royal Agricultural Society of England, and that it was this society, with its tests, which did most to increase the efficiency, simplicity, durability and safety of the agricultural steam engine. To take efficiency alone, in 1848 the prize-winning portable engine – a Garrett – burned 11½ lb. of coal per h.p. hour; in 1850 Garrett won again with 7½ lb.; in 1851 Hornsby with 6¾ lb. came first; in 1852 the same firm achieved 4⅝ lb.; and in 1853 Claytons brought the figure down to 4⅓ lb.

In 1849, the year of Ransomes' 'farmer's engine', an Edinburgh brewer named James Usher patented a cultivating machine of which a model – which belongs to Mr. C. E. Shackle and which may well be contemporary – is shown in Fig. 15. Two cylinders at the sides of the smokebox drive a crankshaft behind the firebox, from which gearing takes the drive to the cultivator shaft and to the driving roller.

The cultivator shaft is mounted in a frame, which may be raised or lowered according to the depth of tillage required, and carries four discs or plates, on each of which are three plough shares. These are staggered, not only to vary the load, but also to make a finer tilth. Slight of Edinburgh built the first machine for Usher in 1851: it was of 10 h.p., weighed 6½ tons, and ploughed a breadth of 4 ft. 2 in., working well.

An improved model, built in 1855, had a vertical boiler, with greatly

Fig. 15. A model of Usher's rotary cultivator.
The Model Engineer.

increased heating surface, and weighed a ton less. The tillage shaft could be raised or lowered by power, cutting to a maximum depth of 9½ in. at 30 r.p.m. A harrow towing behind broke up the ground even further, and 6½ acres per 12-hour day was a normal stint.

At the Great Exhibition of 1851 there was no self-propelled engine at all, though plenty of portables. And there was also an exhibit by one John Fowler which, unlikely as it seems, was the direct ancestor of the beautiful Fowler traction, ploughing and showman's engines which still delight our eyes at today's rallies. It was his mole-draining plough.

John Fowler was born at Melksham, Wilts, in 1826, and was at first engaged in the corn trade. In 1847 he joined a Middlesbrough engineering firm, and two years later, whilst in Ireland, became impressed by the necessity of draining waste lands by mechanical power. Experiments at Bristol resulted in the mole drainer (Fig. 16) which at first was worked by horse-power machine. Having no works of his own, it was built for him by Ransomes.

In 1850 he successfully undertook to drain Hainault Forest in Essex with the device, and in 1851 he won awards both at the Exhibition and at the coincidental Royal Show. The principle is, of course, that the vertical blade or coulter carries the bullet-shaped mole, which is about 18 in. by 3 in., through the ground at a suitable depth. A 'bob', which is a little larger in diameter, trails behind to compress the soil and leave a smooth surface.

Even today this method is very popular in some areas – particularly the heavy Essex, Suffolk and Cambridgeshire clays – and the steam ploughing tackle cannot be bettered for the sheer 'guts' needed to do the job.

With the success of his mole plough (for which he was using a steam portable as early as 1852) Fowler's attention turned to the tremendous possibilities in steam cultivation. Yet whilst he was working on this, his agile mind conceived other things too – in 1852 he was granted patents for improving reaping, for sowing, for spreading manure, and for using his mole plough to lay electric telegraph cables. In 1853 he entered no fewer than 90 miscellaneous exhibits at the Royal Show!

Still working in co-operation with Ransomes, and especially their works manager, William Worby, a steam ploughing outfit was produced in 1856, and tested with success at nearby Nacton in April of that year.

I have not been able to trace a picture of the engine actually used, but there seems evidence to show that it had no drive direct to the wheels, though it could and did move itself along the headland by a small powered windlass hauling on a rope anchored ahead. To move from field to field, or on the road, the engine was hauled by horse team.

Fig. 16. Fowler's mole-drainer: the beginning of a great firm.
A Text-Book of Farm Machinery.

The implement used was the 'balance plough', which was devised by Fowler in discussion with David Greig, a farmer, and Worby (Fig. 17). It was in use with no alteration in principle for the next eighty or ninety years! The ploughman sat on the tail of the implement, steering it by altering the lock of the main wheels through a worm and wheel actuated by the steering wheel. When it reached the other side of the field, the other plough shares were put into operation, lifting the original four up in the air, and the implement was hauled back again. (See also Fig. 51.)

A prize of £500 had been offered by the R.A.S.E. 'for the steam cultivator which shall in the most efficient manner turn over the soil and be an economical substitute for the plough or the spade'. Fowler entered for

Fig. 17. Fowler's balance-plough.
Journal of the R.A.S.E.

this prize, but though the judges were satisfied with the quality of his work, they disallowed the award because they estimated the cost at 7s. 2½d. an acre, as against 7s. 0d., by horse ploughing.

In 1857, the prize was again withheld from him on the grounds that the economy was still unproved. The same judges, incidentally, remarked sadly about another competitor at these trials: 'Mr. J. A. Williams' system was anything but satisfactory in results. The judges regret to be compelled to add that the extreme discourtesy of his language and conduct towards themselves rendered their duties in the inspection of his work painful and unpleasant in a manner they never before had occasion to experience . . .'

But at Chester, in 1858, John Fowler gained the coveted award, having meantime spent ten times the amount in experimenting! The judges this time stated that his machine had a saving, as compared with horse labour, on light land of 20 to 25 per cent, on heavy land of 25 to 30 per cent, and in trenching of 80 to 85 per cent, the soil in each case being left in a far more desirable condition. The balance plough was used, of course, with different shares for the trenching. Fig. 18 shows the engine, which was adapted from an ordinary portable, with an extended frame to carry the windlass. The endless rope passed 2¾ turns round each pulley sheave to obtain a good purchase, its other end passing round a 'self-moving windlass and anchor pulley' (Fig. 19) on the opposite headland. This anchor had disc wheels, which dug in to resist the side pull of the rope and, through reduction gearing, the pulley drove a small windlass. The rope wrapped round this was attached to an anchor laid ahead, and so the anchor pulley moved ahead to match the similarly driven forward motion of the engine. The box on the anchor was filled with stones, to resist the pull of the cable tending to overturn it.

A separate tender was hauled by the engine, with a coal-bunker and a water tank the top of which formed the driver's footplate. The cost of the whole outfit was £730, and in 1858 Fowler sold twenty sets. Claytons were also building under Fowler licence, but I have no record of their production.

Meantime, returning to the Chester show, the judges were not too happy about other exhibitors, once more. The stewards reported that the visitors' way was through an avenue of steam engines, their flywheels in perpetual motion . . . 'but what would have been the effect on a visitor's

Fig. 18. Fowler's ploughing-engine of 1858.

Journal of the R.A.S.E.

Fig. 19. Fowler's self-moving anchor.
Journal of the R.A.S.E.

nerves had he known that three of these steam engines had been liable to burst at any minute? It is hardly necessary to say that the stewards . . . immediately ordered their fires to be extinguished; and the police had orders to remove any man from the show yard who should attempt to get up steam in a dangerous engine'.

And then there was the poor chap who disgraced himself at the trials of the portables. Say the stewards: 'In one instance an over-zealous engine driver was detected in the act of appropriating a handful of cinders, in order to prolong the spark of life in his expiring engine: the consequence was that the culprit was immediately tried by a sort of drumhead court-martial, and expelled the yard'.

One pictures the remaining drivers drawn up in a hollow square with the ashen-faced victim in the centre. Stern of mien, a judge advances: a sickle flashes to sever the culprit's buttons, and with sagging steps he leaves the scene of his disgrace. Poor fellow! poor fellow!

Still, there were other firms at the Chester 'Royal' whose names we have noted already, and who did not disgrace themselves. Tuxford won first prize in the 8 h.p. portables, and Hornsby was first in the 12 h.p. class. Clayton and Shuttleworth had a 7 h.p. engine fitted with reversing link motion, with 'toothed gear work for imparting motion to the main travelling wheels, which have plain tires'. (Note the spelling of that word, as common to the period.) 'The steerage was effected by a single wheel turning in a transom in front: the price was 350*l.*' Horse steerage was substituted later for the single wheel, by the way.

Recently we mentioned Garretts, and happily they are still with us. Their first steam engine was a portable exhibited in 1840 at the Norwich Show; in 1857 they produced a self-propelled engine with Boydell wheels. In 1858 at Chester, they had a double-cylindered portable of 12 h.p., which drove one wheel by pitch chain. It was horse steered, and fitted with a water tank beneath the boiler; there was a 'stage' to carry the coal and 'to serve for the driver's standing place'.

Garrett's stated that the self-propelling gear was intended to act as an auxiliary rather than to supersede horses for haulage. It had been found economical and to answer well. The charge for this addition to an engine was 5*l.* per h.p.

Another 1858 exhibitor was Frederick Savage of Lynn, who had started his business (which also still thrives) in 1850. The Savage engine was a 7 horse single-cylinder portable, mounted midway on a timber framing supported by two eight-foot diameter wheels with broad felloes, and a single wheel in front, turning in a transom, for steerage. Both the main wheels were gear driven from the crankshaft, and for turning sharp corners either wheel could be disengaged by a clutch.

This engine is stated to travel along the roads at 3 m.p.h. 'dragging a threshing machine from one farm to another, threshing the corn, and then conveying it in wagons to market, seaport or railway, and carrying back coal, oilcake, timber or manure, and this last season has prepared 120 acres of land for wheat sowing with a Coleman's cultivator'.

However, this pen of mine is rather tending to run away, and if we are not to get too much out of chronological order, we had better retrace our steps to 1854, and some Boydell engines.

5

THE BOYDELL 'ENDLESS RAILWAY'

Fulton knocked at the door of Napoleon with steam, and was rejected: and Napoleon lived long enough to know that he had excluded a greater power than his own.

HORATIO GREENOUGH, *quoted by* EMERSON

JAMES BOYDELL FIRST PATENTED his 'Endless Railway' in August 1846, and followed this with a more detailed specification in February 1854. This was for wheels to be equipped with shoes, which were stepped at the ends so that when on the ground they overlapped one another sideways and thus formed a continuous track (Fig. 20). The shoes were of wood, faced with iron, and on the back was a cycloidal guiding bracket passing through a slot in a bracket bolted to the outer face of the wheel rim. Alignment was secured by a projection on the wheel which engaged with a slot in the rear end of the shoe.

Richard Bach of Birmingham was the first to build a self-moving engine using Boydell wheels, and it must have been this machine which excited much attention at the Carlisle Show of the R.A.S.E. in 1855. Apparently he fitted the wheels and self-propelling gear to an existing portable, and Garrett's did the same in 1856. The latter was probably the engine which appeared at the Chelmsford 'Royal' in that year, when the Stewards' report said: 'Mr. Boydell again exhibited his engine, drawing with ease any implements that were attached to it: and it still remains to be proved if it will ever be found serviceable in agriculture'. Neither of these engines is preserved in picture form, it seems.

In 1856, too, Charles Burrell commenced building Boydell equipped engines, an event which has been commemorated (in July 1958) by the mounting of a bronze plaque to celebrate the birth of the first *heavy duty* steam road haulage engine at Thetford in Norfolk. The engine itself is seen in Fig. 20, ready to move out from under the shears where the wheel guards had been finally mounted.

It was driven by two cylinders of 7½ in. by 12 in., with a nominal h.p. of 12 and a weight in working order of 11½ tons. The fore-carriage had Boydell wheels too, and a horizontal hand-wheel with handles was mounted on a vertical shaft, on the lower end of which a pinion engaged

with a circular rack for steerage purposes. The overall length was 17 feet.

In April 1857, Charles Burrell patented the application of Boydell wheels to a common portable engine, the single cylinder driving one wheel or the other by a single gear. In this case, ordinary wheels were used on the front axle, which was steered by a horse in the shafts. The engine was capable of drawing a threshing machine, or a set of ploughing tackle or cultivating equipment, over rough roads, 'or indeed where no roads exist'.

It was first exhibited at the Salisbury Royal Show in 1857, and two were sold. Later it was reported that one of these machines had been in daily use for twelve months with an itinerant threshing machine, without repairs of any consequence. The additional cost of such an engine over an ordinary portable, with a water tank added beneath the boiler, was 'about 140*l*'.

Another Boydell engine which appeared at the same show was that of Collinson Hall, which worked at 'enormously high pressure' – but unfortunately we aren't told what it actually was! – and took steam from two domes, or either one at pleasure, so as always to get dry steam from the highest point. This also was employed to draw implements, and was found 'to answer every requirement as a locomotive on fields and roads'.

At Salisbury too was a Boydell engine built by Lee of Walsall, but little is known of this except that it was propelled by a pinion on the crankshaft gearing with a spur wheel on one of the propelling wheels.

Burrell's road engine and adapted portable meantime had given the demonstrations of road haulage and ploughing advertised in the poster of which Fig. 21 is a replica. This was at Croxton Park, near Thetford, and it was reported that they were highly successful.

Tuxford's of Boston were another firm building engines with Boydell wheels, and in fact the use of a watchmaker's glass on the original print of Fig. 20 appears to reveal the names Boydell-Tuxford-Boston on the nave of the hind wheel of the *Burrell* engine, so that they may well have made the wheels for that engine too. But this is admittedly arguable.

Their own engine was a three wheeler (Fig. 22), the front wheel being carried in a fork, and controlled by rack and pinion steerage, with a pointer attached at the top of the 'steering column' to indicate the lock of the wheel.

The engine framing was of sheet and angle iron, carrying a return-flue boiler, with a coal bunker and footplate behind for the stoker driver. The single-cylinder engine was of Tuxford's famous 'steeple' type in which the cylinder was inverted, driving upwards to a crosshead sliding in guide bars, from whence return connecting rods brought the drive down to the

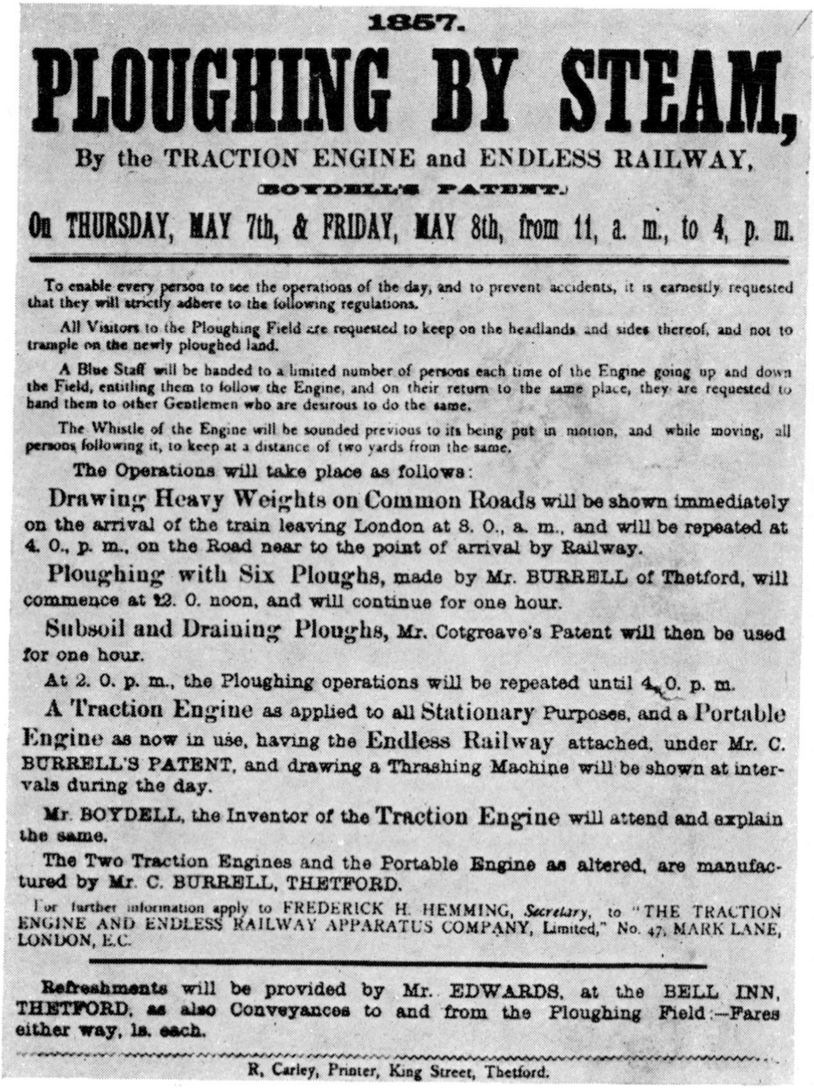

1857.

PLOUGHING BY STEAM,

By the TRACTION ENGINE and ENDLESS RAILWAY,

(BOYDELL'S PATENT.)

On THURSDAY, MAY 7th, & FRIDAY, MAY 8th, from 11, a. m., to 4, p. m.

To enable every person to see the operations of the day, and to prevent accidents, it is earnestly requested that they will strictly adhere to the following regulations.

All Visitors to the Ploughing Field are requested to keep on the headlands and sides thereof, and not to trample on the newly ploughed land.

A Blue Staff will be handed to a limited number of persons each time of the Engine going up and down the Field, entitling them to follow the Engine, and on their return to the same place, they are requested to hand them to other Gentlemen who are desirous to do the same.

The Whistle of the Engine will be sounded previous to its being put in motion, and while moving, all persons following it, to keep at a distance of two yards from the same.

The Operations will take place as follows:

Drawing Heavy Weights on Common Roads will be shown immediately on the arrival of the train leaving London at 8. 0., a. m., and will be repeated at 4. 0., p. m., on the Road near to the point of arrival by Railway.

Ploughing with Six Ploughs, made by Mr. BURRELL of Thetford, will commence at 12. 0. noon, and will continue for one hour.

Subsoil and Draining Ploughs, Mr. Cotgreave's Patent will then be used for one hour.

At 2. 0. p. m., the Ploughing operations will be repeated until 4. 0. p. m.

A Traction Engine as applied to all **Stationary** Purposes, and a **Portable Engine** as now in use, having the **Endless Railway** attached, under Mr. C. BURRELL'S PATENT, and drawing a Thrashing Machine will be shown at intervals during the day.

Mr. BOYDELL, the Inventor of the **Traction Engine** will attend and explain the same.

The Two Traction Engines and the Portable Engine as altered, are manufactured by Mr. C. BURRELL, THETFORD.

For further information apply to FREDERICK H. HEMMING, *Secretary*, to "THE TRACTION ENGINE AND ENDLESS RAILWAY APPARATUS COMPANY, Limited," No. 47, MARK LANE, LONDON, E.C.

Refreshments will be provided by Mr. EDWARDS, at the BELL INN, THETFORD, as also Conveyances to and from the Ploughing Field:—Fares either way, 1s. each.

R, Carley, Printer, King Street, Thetford.

Fig. 21. Replica of a Burrell poster of 1857. *The Engineer.*

crankshaft. As will be seen, the motion was all enclosed, as it was in their portables too, which had the same engine design.

The Tuxford engine shown weighed about 12 tons, yet could turn in a 30-foot diameter circle. There was a 'remarkably neat friction box' by which either side-wheel could be thrown into or out of gear, when turning. Various sizes were built, the prices ranging from 550*l.* for an engine of up to 20 h.p., driven on one wheel only, up to 1,020*l.* for an engine up to 32 h.p., driven on both wheels and fitted with the disconnecting apparatus. The Burrell engines cost from 750*l.* to 800*l.*, by the way.

Many Tuxford locomotives went to Cuba; the *Illustrated London News* reports one being shipped from Liverpool, 'with a series of cars, drays and ploughs for attaching to it. This engine forms the third shipped within the last four months for the same gentleman, Senor Glacide Gener of Matanzas. They are all intended for sugar plantations, and are to plough, to draw cane from the fields to the mill, and to carry manufactured sugar from the mill to a railway station a few miles distant'.

Clayton and Shuttleworth also built three-wheeled Boydell engines at Lincoln, but beyond the fact that one of these was exported to Odessa in May 1858, I can trace no further information.

Many Burrell-Boydell engines were also exported, to Cuba, Spain and South America, and they were extensively tested and used in Her Majesty's dockyard and arsenal at Woolwich, too. A typical example was of a heavy siege gun with a carriage and tender with 16 men, totalling about 18 tons, being hauled by a 9-ton engine from Woolwich Arsenal up Burrage Road to Plumstead Common, and down a steep incline to Waterman's Field in return. The steepest ascent was 1 in 10, and descent 1 in 8, but the engine managed easily. On another trial a larger engine successfully took 43 tons over the same route.

Nevertheless, most makers by 1860 had realised the defects of the system, and did not continue with the Boydell patent wheels. What were the defects? *The Engineer* sums them up neatly. 'Boydell's engine . . . failed in a detail only, but that was enough to condemn it. In going to its work on hard roads, the shoes were quickly knocked to pieces by direct impact; and as there was no device to provide for lateral tipping when one edge or the other of a shoe got on a stone or other obstruction, the cycloidal guides were frequently broken.'

The *Journal* of the R.A.S.E. complained of heavy wear and tear, and the very great consumption of oil and grease. *Mechanic's Magazine* said: 'A couple of Boydell's engines found their way to Woolwich amid a flourish of trumpets. But later on the Government offered these road locomotives to the highest bidder, with the highly suggestive recommendation that

Fig. 12 Tuxford's Boydell engine of 1858

Photo: Science Museum

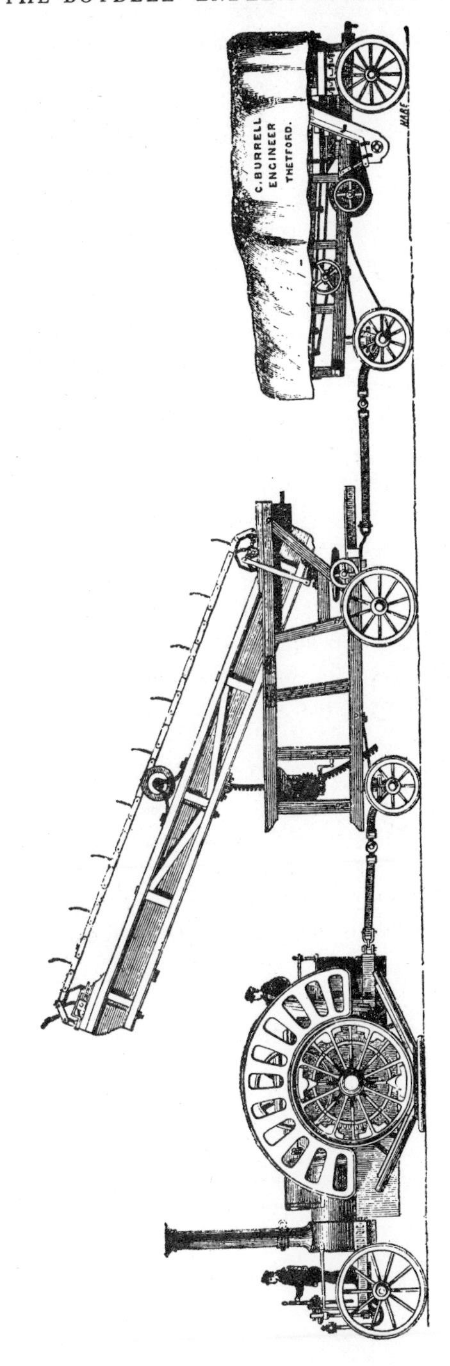

Fig. 23. The Burrell-Boydell of 1862 drawing a threshing-machine.
Catalogue of the 1862 Exhibition.

they could easily be converted into stationary engines – a fact apparently deemed necessary to secure a purchaser.'

Still, Burrell doggedly kept on, reluctant to drop the idea; he patented an improvement whereby the cycloidal guide passed through a slot in the wheel rim itself, instead of a bracket on the outside; he made the guide and other wearing parts of steel. But the swan-song of the Burrell-Boydell was at the International Exhibition of 1862, from the catalogue of which Fig. 23 is extracted showing the engine hauling a train of threshing machinery.

The 1862 engine was of 10 b.h.p., with two cylinders of 6½-in. diameter by 12-in. stroke. The gearing of case-hardened wrought iron gave a single ratio of 1 to 8, and a normal travelling speed of 4 m.p.h., at which the engine could take 20 tons on the level, or 10 tons up 1 in 20. The steering wheel was now vertical, with a worm and worm-wheel to turn the vertical shaft with its pinion meshing with a rack on the front axle. The engine had been lightened considerably, now weighing only 7 tons against its predecessor's 9 to 10 tons.

It was stated in *The Engineer* that 'the workmanship is apparently of a very superior quality', and indeed one would expect this from Burrell. But at last even he had to acknowledge himself beaten, and it appears that the costly and disappointing experiment ended with the 1862 Exhibition. James Boydell had died in June, and so did not share the final frustration.

True, there were many magnificent individual exploits carried out by these engines, as may be found reported in various journals of the period, but we have to be objective about the performance as a whole. And the plain fact is that the Boydell endless railway had too many breakages to be a success. Some engines were scrapped outright; others had plain wheels substituted for the Boydell ones: others again *were* converted into stationary engines, as suggested by the Government.

Meanwhile, Charles Burrell addressed himself in other directions, and we shall see with what results in later chapters.

6

BRAY'S TRACTION ENGINE

Look abroad, and contemplate the infinite achievements of the steam power.
KENNEDY

AT ABOUT THE TIME that Charles Burrell was trying out his first Boydell engine, a Folkestone marine engineer named William Bray was designing a traction engine to be fitted with wheels of his own devising, for which he took out a patent in 1856, when he was forty-four years of age. An improved specification was patented in 1859.

Bray was the chief engineer of the steamer *Lord Warden*, owned by the South Eastern Railway Company, and the design of his patent wheels was plainly inspired by the feathering floats of the paddle wheels with which he was so familiar.

Fletcher says that the engine itself was introduced in 1856, but the earliest printed reference I have is from the *Folkestone Chronicle* of July 18th, 1857, which, after some rather lyrical preamble, says 'this invention . . . consists of an ingeniously constructed locomotive traction engine, which is capable of being used with the greatest ease, on common roads or arable land; the steering apparatus, which guides a single wheel in front, is so complete that it admits of the machine being turned short at a right angle, or entirely round in its own length'.

The description of the driving wheels which is given next may be followed on Fig. 24, though this picture is actually of a later engine. The article goes on: 'By a peculiar application of the eccentric motion attached to the ends of the shaft, which also forms the axle of the two main wheels, a series of cogs or teeth are projected through the surface of the wheels, from a quarter of an inch to three inches, and which are made to move in or out as the wheels revolve, causing them to bite or grip the ground – and acting also as brakes, so that the engine can be brought to a dead stop even in descending a steep incline. The wheels are made to move free on the shaft, while the eccentric is fixed to rotate with it, and each wheel is capable of being thrown out of gear'.

What is not mentioned is that the rotary position of the axle, and so of the eccentrics, is altered by a worm and worm-wheel, controlled by the

Fig. 24. William Bray drives his engine of 1858. *The Illustrated London News.*

handle grasped in Fig. 24 by the driver. Rods may be seen joining the teeth to the eccentric strap, with a 'master' rod just to the right of centre near the bottom. Now if the eccentric throw is at the top, the teeth will project fully at the top, but not at the bottom. But if the driver rotates the eccentrics so that the throw is at the bottom, the teeth will project fully at the bottom, and not at the top. In the position shown, maximum projection is towards the cylinders. The wheels run free on the axle, and are driven by pinions on the crankshaft driving intermediate two-speed gearing working directly on the large spur-wheels bolted to the inner spokes.

The *Chronicle* continues: 'It (the engine) is contrived to carry 8 cwt. of coke, sufficient for a day's consumption, and a ton of water. It is worked by means of a tubular boiler and two engines (i.e., cylinders—W. J. H.) of six horse power, the weight of the whole being less than 6 tons, while that of Boydell's Endless Railroad is 10 tons.

'This machine is intended to supply every requirement in the working of a farm, and entirely to supersede the use of horses on the land. It will require but three men to manage it, and will be capable of drawing as many as eight ploughs abreast, and doing from ten to twelve acres a day, while a single plough drawn by a team of horses can accomplish but about one acre. It can also be used for drawing loads of manure and agricultural produce – for driving threshing machines (by attaching a drum) – for rolling, harrowing, etc. – and, being fitted with two patent pumps, it will distribute liquid manure, and may also be applied as a powerful fire-engine.

'The trial of this machine was made on Wednesday last, when it proceeded up the tram-road, round by the upper station, down the Dover-road, over Radnor-bridge, up to the East-cliff, where it now stands. It was tried in the presence of several scientific gentlemen, and proved highly successful. It was originally intended to have been sent down to Salisbury for exhibition at the Agricultural show to take place there next week, but it was found advisable to make two or three trifling alterations which will delay its being brought before the notice of the public for a fortnight, when we believe it will be exhibited in different parts of the neighbourhood, for the purpose of testing its efficiency, and the most sanguine expectations as to its result are entertained by its projector, to whom too much credit cannot be given for the pains and labour he has bestowed in bringing it to perfection. We are proud to have been the first to notice this clever invention . . .'

The engine was built entirely in Folkestone, the patterns being made by a local carpenter named John Dunk, and cast by a Mr. Barrett who had a small foundry in Tontine Street.

On November 21st, in the same year, the engine is described as being used for direct traction ploughing, with 'three shares fixed in a wooden framework', whilst in February of 1858, we are told that 'a new steering apparatus' had been added to the 'otherwise improved' engine. On this occasion the engine was tested hauling two common agricultural wagons loaded with rock, up Dover Hill, and forty-four persons jumped on the wagon for good measure.

At the end of May 1858, the *Illustrated London News* published the engraving reproduced at Fig. 26, and this is undoubtedly of the engine as just described. There are two front wheels for steerage instead of the former single one, and the engine is quoted as being of 8 h.p., so that the cylinders were now of larger bore. The weight is still given as 6 tons, and it is stated that the boiler is of Baron's patent cup-surface type, working at 60 p.s.i.

Experiments at Broadmead Farm, Folkestone, are described, in which steam was raised in 40 min. and the engine was set to work with three ploughs in a frame. Over light, loamy soil, rather wet, 6 acres were ploughed in a 10-hour day at a cost of not more than 4s. per acre. Next the engine drew a load of 10 tons up Dover Hill, with a gradient varying from 1 in 7 to 1 in 11; it went both up and down with perfect ease.

The same report describes War Department experiments at the Royal Arsenal, Woolwich, when a carriage loaded with three 68-pounder guns, a total weight of 20 tons, was steamed from the Arsenal and past the Royal Artillery Barracks 'with the utmost ease', though the latter was a considerable incline. Fuel consumption was ¾ cwt. of oven coke per hour.

Returning to the illustration, which, by the way, was engraved from a photograph taken by Venables of Folkestone, the inventor is on the rear of the footplate, with one of his sons as steersman. Link motion was evidently fitted, and the regulator is just behind the chimney, with the steampipe then coming back to the cylinders. It is not clear what the lever on the smokebox is, but, being handy for the steersman, it may well be the control for throwing one hind wheel or the other out of gear for cornering. The front steerage is similar to that of the Burrell-Boydell.

On the water tank is a pump with two large barrels, with air vessel between, but unfortunately the drive linkage cannot be seen properly. A point of interest is that the boiler and cylinders are wood lagged.

The driving wheels are 8 ft. in diameter, constructed of angle and sheet iron, about 12 in. wide, the projecting teeth being 1 in. thick and 6 in. wide. The two front wheels are ordinary wagon wheels, about 4 ft. in diameter. Thursday, July 29th, 1858, saw Bray's traction engine in Westminster Road, 'and witnessed by thousands of spectators, who seemed much interested and astonished on seeing a steam engine travelling the

FOR ONE DAY ONLY!!!

JIM MYER'S

GREAT AMERICAN CIRCUS.

CONSISTING of all the Members (now in England), of the Far-famed American Company, and leading Artistes from the principal English, French, and Russian Cirques, combining an array of Equestrian, and Gymnastic Talent, unequalled in the World's History.

Will enter FOLKESTONE,

On SATURDAY, AUGUST 13th, 1859,

In Grand Procession at One o'clock.

The Magnificent Band Carriage being drawn by

BRAY'S TRACTION ENGINE

Which will also be accompanied by 50 Ladies and Gentlemen of the Establishment, on their richly-caparisoned Steeds, dressed in superb costumes, and bearing elegant banners, &c , &c.

The most beautiful Stud of Trained Horses in Europe, matchless for sagacity and high training. Also the wonderful troupe of performing Dogs and Monkeys. The greatest Clowns of the day.

Two Performances daily, Morning at 2, and Evening at 7 o'clock.

Dover, Friday, ... Aug. 12th	Hythe, Monday, . Aug. 15th
Folkestone, Saturday, ,, 13th.	Romney, Tuesday, ,, 16th

Fig. 25. The very first Showman's Engine.

The Folkestone Chronicle.

streets of London', as well they might at that period! On this occasion, it drew a truck loaded with heavy cases of several tons total weight from Maudsley's works to their wharf close to Westminster Bridge.

Maudsley, Sons and Field continued using the Bray engine, and so did Her Majesty's Government. A paragraph in *The Artizan* dated 1st November, 1858, reads as follows:

'STEAM *v.* HORSES – TRACTION ENGINES – The Lords of the Admiralty, desirous of testing the practicability and economy of employing steam power in place of horses, in the Government dockyards, have entered into an arrangement with Mr. Bray for the use of his steam traction engine. The contract is to pay at the rate of 50*l.* per month for the exclusive use of the engine in Woolwich Dockyard, for one month certain, experimentally, in the removal of timber and other heavy stores, hitherto performed by horses. On the 13th October ult., the engine steamed into the dockyard, and carried out the allotted day's work with perfect steadiness, passing the windings and acute turnings and discharging its load . . . with ease and success. The amount of fuel consumed during the day was 6 cwt., at a cost of 3s. 6d.'

That their Lordships were satisfied with the trials is evidenced by the fact that in the following February Bray's traction engines – note the plural – 'now constructing by Messrs. F. and J. Hughes, at their factory at New Cross, for service at the dockyards of Woolwich and Keyham were . . . inspected by M. Vianson, inspector of steam machinery, in the service of the King of Sardinia'.

From this paragraph, too, it seems evident that Bray's limited local facilities were not adequate for producing engines *en masse*, so to speak, and this would explain him placing the Admiralty order with Messrs. Hughes (no relative of the author!).

One of Bray's engines came to grief on April 9th, 1859, in Nelson Street, Greenwich, when it was transporting a mainshaft, weighing 22½ tons, from Penn's factory to the *Howe*, lying in Woolwich Dockyard. 'The engine was steaming up the road at about 3 m.p.h., when, in order to avoid some newly-macadamised stones, it was turned towards the kerb: but the part of the road being over some cellars, suddenly gave way, and it required the efforts of a number of labouring men, aided by powerful jacks, iron levers and plates, with enormous steam power to extricate the engine, and raise the immense weight upon the sound earth: an operation which was accomplished without further accident after little over an hour's delay, and consequent interruption of the roadway traffic.'

Another firm making the Bray engine under licence was Taylor's of Birkenhead, who at the same time were making their own 'Steam Elephant', which we shall see later. They called the Bray engine the 'Steam Horse', and in November 1859 it steamed down at 11 a.m. from London Bridge station, where it had been unloaded, arriving at Woolwich Dockyard by 12.30. An important feature was that this engine was fitted with springs: these may have been Taylor's own idea, of rubber springs, or the leaf springs to be seen on later Bray engines.

Meantime, however, Bray's traction engine had achieved the distinction of becoming the world's first showman's engine, for on August 6th and 13th, 1859, the *Folkestone Chronicle* carried the advertisement reproduced in Fig. 25, which tells its own story. Despite the crudity of the wood-cut, we can see that this American circus proprietor started the tradition of gay embellishment of the showman's engine, or rather carried it from his other vehicles to the engine – just look at the wheels and at the apron in front of the steerage platform!

It is equally obvious that the engine itself was one of the main attractions of the circus: the astute Myer realised that it would pull the crowds, especially in the area of its birth, as well as pull his vehicles!

We have not space to notice all the journalistic accounts given of Bray's engines in the next few years, but *The Engineer* in July 1861 describes a 'novel journey through the metropolis' hauling a 22-ton boiler 30 ft. long and 8 ft. in diameter, on a long truck weighing 5 tons. The engine was larger than those already described in this chapter, having a pair of cylinders 9-in. bore by 15-in. stroke. It weighed 14 tons in running order, and was working at 90 p.s.i., though designed for 120 lb. maximum.

Says the writer, 'It was, we believe, the sixteenth built on Bray's principle, and was the first with outside framing, and the second provided with springs over the driving wheels . . . The huge load was steered with, apparently, the greatest ease through a labyrinth of carts, cabs and omnibuses; and, so far as we could see, no horse abandoned himself in consequence to nervousness, much less to involuntary locomotion. The strange procession made but little noise and, for all we could see, left the paving in as good order as it found it'.

By now, Bray's Traction Engine Company had its offices in Pall Mall, and had engaged the celebrated engineer D. K. Clark as consultant. He was with the engine on the journey just described, and it is believed he was largely responsible for the design of the machine shown at the Great Exhibition of 1862 at Kensington, and depicted in Fig. 26. This was apparently like the engine of 1861, just described.

D. K. Clark himself describes this fine engine in his book *The Exhibited Machinery of* 1862, from which I have extracted Fig. 26. After a preamble about the driving wheels, he goes on: 'The engine is fitted with two

Fig. 26 The engine exhibited by Bray in 1862 *The Exhibited Machinery of 1862*

cylinders, from which the power is transmitted to the driving wheels by means of pinions on the crankshaft, working into large circular racks bolted to the inner sides of the wheels, for the quick speed: or, by means of intermediate gearing, the engine may be put on the slow speed . . . (It) is fitted with a drum, by means of which it may be employed for driving machinery: a derrick is also fitted to it, by which it may load its own wagons, and a capstan or windlass to give a purchase. The boiler is fitted into and fixed to the frame, without forming any portion of it, or being subject to any of the strain of working the engine. The driving axle has four bearings – two inside and two outside the wheels – for the purpose of steadying the engine, and the weight is placed on springs. Thus, in addition to its tractive power, the engine is qualified to act as a stationary or portable engine, a steam crane, or a steam winch, by which it has been well adapted for the service of Woolwich Dockyard, where it has been constantly and satisfactorily at work in its various capacities since it was removed from the Exhibition.

'A similar engine was employed in removing locomotive engines, marine engines and other heavy machinery, from different railway stations, manufactories and docks to the Exhibition buildings, the loads amounting in some cases, to 45 tons.'

From the *Practical Mechanics Journal* 'Record of the Great Exhibition of 1862', we learn that the cylinders were 7 in. by 10 in. and the driving wheels were forged in wrought iron, in one piece, with round felloes. The tires (original spelling – W. J. H.) were double, the outer being bolted to the inner, with a thin film of India rubber in between. Weighing 9½ tons, the engine was intended to haul 25 tons.

The catalogue of the Exhibition says that 'reference can be made to the London and North Western Railway Company, Messrs. John Penn & Son, Messrs. Maudsleys, Messrs. Humphreys and Tennant, and other engineering firms, who employed the engine, as to its power and capabilities'. The illustration in the catalogue itself is reproduced in Fig. 27, showing an engine 'of still further improved construction, being built to the designs of the Company's engineer, Mr. D. K. Clark, C.E.'. Note that this engine was *not* itself exhibited, as sometimes supposed – indeed, as I have seen stated as a fact. This machine had the cylinders and gearing ranged in a horizontal line with the axle, 'by which', says Clark, 'the details have been simplified, and the cost of the engine reduced. A traction engine of this design has been constructed for the company on this system by Messrs. Chaplin and Co., of Glasgow, fitted with their upright boiler with tapered tubes'.

Still in 1862, I have included Fig. 28 as being the first actual *illustration*

Fig. 27. The design by D. K. Clark for the Bray Traction Engine Company.
Catalogue of the 1862 *Exhibition.*

of a heavy road-haulage job I can trace. It shows a Bray engine similar to that in the Exhibition, drawing a girder 74 feet long, 5 ft. 8 in. high, and weighing 20 tons, past the Bank of England on the night of September 7th. The girder was to form part of a bridge for the London, Chatham and Dover Railway over the Manor Road, Dulwich, and by police orders the journey had to be performed between 10 p.m. and 6 a.m.

Raised first by jacks to six or seven feet off the ground, the front of the girder was supported on a four-wheeled boiler truck (with swivelling bolster) in front and on a two-wheeled trolley behind, to both of which it was securely chained. Naphtha flares were fixed all along the girder for light and warning, and it had passed from Hoxton via Moorgate Street, the Bank, London Bridge to Southwark by midnight.

Some artistic licence is evident in the picture, the engine and its load being rather larger than life in proportion to the spectators, but it does give some idea of the great interest caused by this event, even among the sophisticated crowds of the Metropolis. It makes one realise again the astuteness of Jim Myer!

My last Bray illustration (Fig. 29) is of an engine built in 1866 by Dübs and Company, now incorporated in the North British Locomotive Co. Ltd., of Glasgow. It bears the maker's number 65E, and the same company built two more traction engines, No. 594E in 1872 for Charles Randolph, and No. 1023E in 1876 for James Young. Unfortunately there is no information whatsoever about the last two.

However, I have a general arrangement drawing (dated March 7th, 1866) of No. 65E, which was built for the Ottoman Company for use in Turkey, and which, as the last figure shows, was very similar in appearance to the Clark design of 1862. There were two plate frames, as in railway loco practice, the slightly inclined cylinders being outside the frames with valve chests inside, so that the crankshaft had overhung cranks outside the bearings with the eccentrics inside.

Between the pairs of eccentrics the shaft carried two pinions of different size, one at each side, which ran loose on it. A double-ended dog clutch sliding on feathers between the pinions could engage with either, so locking it to the shaft at will.

A countershaft behind the crankshaft carried two spur wheels in permanent mesh with the pinions, and between the spur wheels was mounted the bevel-type differential or compensating gear, arranged so that whichever gear ratio was engaged the drive went through the differential. At each end of the countershaft was a pinion, engaging with an internal circular rack bolted to each wheel.

The front wheels were 3 ft. 5 in. diameter by 8 in. broad, and only

Fig. 29. A fine Bray engine built by Dübs and Co. for Turkey.
The North British Locomotive Co. Ltd.

2 ft. 8 in. apart; the hind wheels, which had the Bray feathering teeth, of course, were 5 ft. 0½ in. diameter by 12 in. broad, with 4 ft. 5 in. between. The extreme length was 18 ft. 1½ in., width 8 ft. 9 in., and height to top of chimney 9 ft. 6¼ in. The hind axle was on leaf springs, and the front one on a helical spring.

Centred 5 ft. 6¼ in. above ground, the boiler barrel was 5 ft. long by 2 ft. 6 in. diameter, and there were 64 wrought-iron tubes of 1⅞ in. o.d. The outer firebox was 3 ft. 4 in. wide and 2 ft. 9 in. long, with internal measurements 2 ft. 9½ in. by 2 ft. 2⅓ in.

Without a doubt this was one of the neatest, cleanest, and most handsome traction engines ever built. It was a credit not only to William Bray, but also to D. K. Clark and to Dübs and Company.

7

THOMAS AVELING

Strong-shouldered steam . . . EMERSON

THE STORY OF THE Bray traction engines has taken us rather far ahead, and now we must retrace our steps a little to meet another of the pioneers, Thomas Aveling, whose creations were the forerunners of a line which persists to this day in the products of Aveling-Barford Ltd.

Aveling was born in Cambridgeshire in 1824, and his father dying soon afterwards, his mother moved to Rochester, where she married a clergyman. This gentleman ruled the boy 'with a Bible in one hand and a birch in the other', and Thomas was slow and dull. Apprenticed to a farmer near Canterbury, however, and away from his stepfather, he became very bright. He married his master's niece, and commenced farming on his own account on Romney Marsh in Kent.

With his innate mechanical abilities, the young farmer soon made a name for himself in repairing the inefficient agricultural implements of the day. From this it was but a step to setting up in 1850 a small engineering shop in Rochester for this purpose. He was greatly impressed with the possibilities of applying mechanical power to agriculture, and began extensive experiments in that direction.

In 1856 he produced a steam plough, for which in 1858 the Kentish farmers presented him with three hundred guineas and a valuable piece of plate in recognition of its merit. However, the Aveling steam plough was not in evidence at the shows of the R.A.S.E. at that time, and I have not been able to trace any illustration or description of the machine.

By now, of course, the portable steam engine was becoming more popular for farm use, but Aveling realised that it would not be difficult to eliminate the team of horses needed to transport it from place to place, by making the engine self propelling. He commenced to adapt Clayton and Shuttleworth portables in 1858, as shown in Fig. 30, by driving one hind wheel by pitch chain, with an intermediate reduction gear. The pinion slid on splines on the crankshaft so that it could be engaged or disengaged at will. Steerage was by a horse in the shafts. Stephenson link motion was

Fig. 30. Aveling's conversion of a Clayton and Shuttleworth portable.
A. R. Dibben, Esq.

fitted, and the reversing lever may be seen between the cylinder and the off-side hind wheel.

Meantime Aveling pressed on with his ideas for a locomotive engine designed as such, for which he took out his first traction engine patent in 1859. Not having sufficient manufacturing resources of his own, the engine was built for him by Clayton and Shuttleworth of Lincoln. It was exhibited in 1860 at the R.A.S.E. Show at Canterbury, being listed as an '8 h.p. Patent Locomotive Engine'.

This engine (Fig. 31) had the cylinder placed over the firebox with the crankshaft at the smokebox end. The driving arrangement was similar to that on the converted portable, already described, but at the show the engine had Aveling's newly-patented 'pilot' steerage. This consisted of a single wheel in a fork, mounted in a bracket attached to the horse-shafts. From the top of the fork a lever extended backwards, with a curved T-piece at its end.

The steersman sat with legs dangling between the shafts, and guided the machine by vertical handles attached to the T-piece. It may be remarked that though Aveling patented this steerage in 1860, it had been patented previously by F. Andrews in 1826, and used by Gurney in 1828 on his steam carriage. Aveling himself used it for ten or eleven years.

In 1861, Aveling had accumulated sufficient resources to be able to build his own engines, and exhibited the engine shown in Fig. 32, at the Leeds 'Royal'. The cylinder was now steam jacketed, and mounted in the smokebox itself: this was a C. and S. patent used by Aveling, whilst Clayton's were using Aveling's pilot steerage and other points of design.

The rearward position of the crankshaft was an advantage in that a shorter driving chain could be used, giving less stretch. To allow tightening of the chain, the stub-shaft was mounted in a movable block carried in a curved slot in the crankshaft bracket, below the crankshaft itself. (See Fig. 34, which shows the device as fitted to the engine of 1862.) It will be seen that this curved slot allowed for correct mesh of the pinion and spur wheel in any position.

On the 1861 engine you will also notice the large dome, with Salter safety valve on top, and pressure-gauge behind. The steam pipe to the cylinder passes from the dome to the cylinder through the steam space of the boiler. Stephenson link motion is fitted, with reversing lever on the firebox side, and a Watt-type governor controls the engine speed when working stationary.

The driver (in this photograph Thomas Aveling himself) stands on a footplate which is the top plate of the water tank, with space for coal behind him. On the back of the tender is a toolbox, and on the side the

Fig. 31. Aveling's first engine, built by Clayton and Shuttleworth.
A Chapter in the History of the Traction Engine.

Fig. 32. The first engine built at the Aveling works. *A. R. Dibben, Esq.*

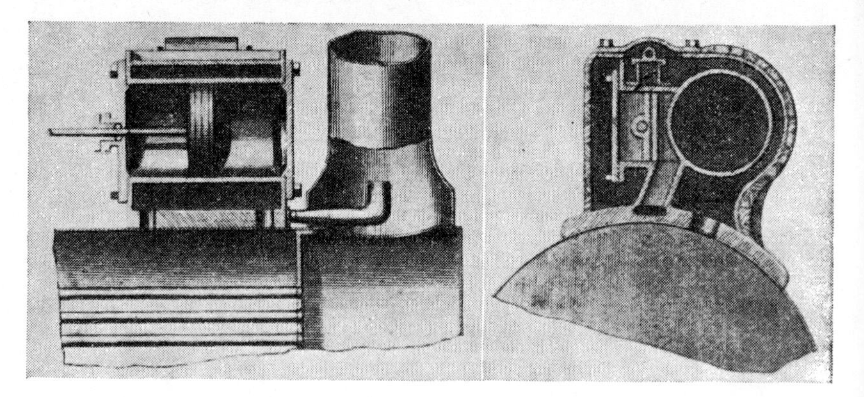

Fig. 33. Aveling's steam-jacketed cylinder.
Practical Mechanic's Journal.

water pocket, by which the tank is filled. All these are features which persisted to modern times.

Both hind wheels are driven, the large chain wheel being keyed to the hind axle; the hind wheel can run free on the axle, being driven from the boss of the chain wheel by the pin in the pear-shaped hind wheel boss passing through holes in both. On the other side, a cast boss is keyed to the hind axle, and the near-side hind wheel is driven by a pin passing into this. When turning a corner, one pin could be withdrawn to allow differential action.

The fore-carriage is carried on a vertical pin projecting downwards from the smokebox, and from the bottom of the pin a stay passes back to

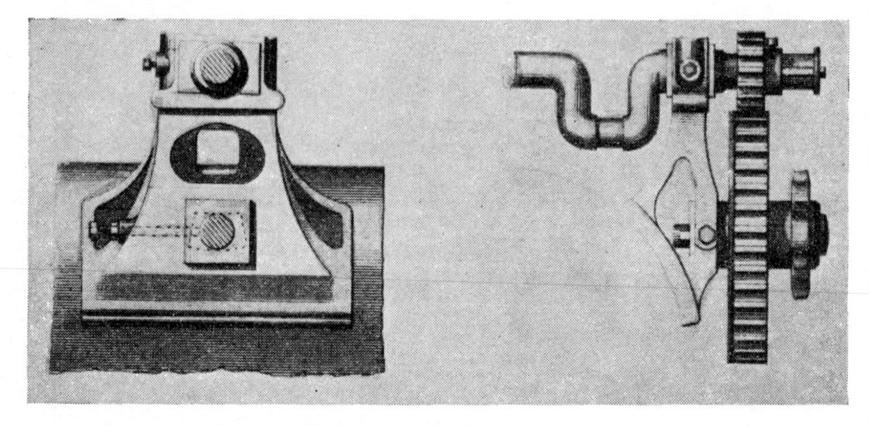

Fig. 34. Adjustment for the pitch-chain drive.
Practical Mechanic's Journal.

the firebox throatplate. The two chains dangling between front axle and firebox are to restrict the lock of the axle so that the front wheel rims do not catch on and abrade the boiler at full lock.

The hind wheels were 5 ft. 6 in. diameter by 12 in. broad, but with a central tyre 4 in. broad which bore the load on firm ground. On very soft ground, spuds or paddles of T-iron could be attached to the rims to give extra grip. Between crankshaft and hind wheel the total gear ratio was 1 to 9. The cylinder was 9 in. by 12 in., and at normal working pressure of 70 lb. the engine worked at 120 to 140 r.p.m. The chimney was a 'fine job of iron moulding, being cast in one piece, but only ¼ in. thick'.

Full to capacity with 3 cwt. of coal and 150 gallons of water, the total weight of the engine was about 7½ tons. *The Engineer* reported a trial in February 1861 when one of these engines, hauling a threshing and a cleaning machine weighing about six tons together, 'ascended and descended long inclines of 1 in 12, maintaining a uniform speed of nearly three miles

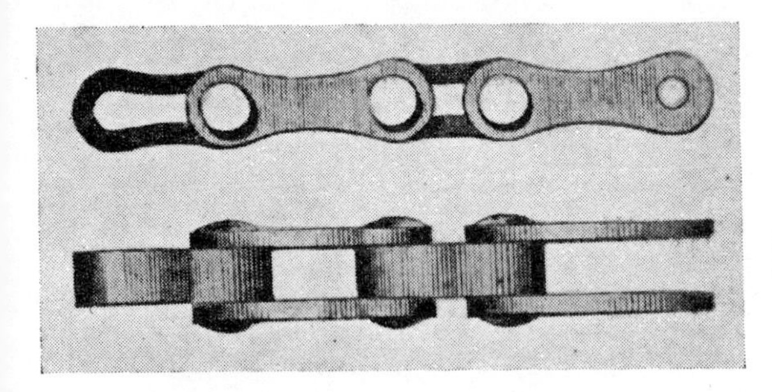

Fig. 35. Construction of Aveling's chain.
The Engineer.

an hour in both directions, generally making an abundance of steam, moving with great steadiness, and steering with the utmost ease in any direction desired'.

The engine shown in the picture is Aveling's No. 20, and it was reported in December 1861 that he had by then turned out No. 34. The price was £360.

Towards the end of the year Aveling took out his celebrated patent (No. 1295) for the separate steam-jacketed cylinder, and Fig. 33 shows the arrangement of this. The steam entered the jacket through holes in the boiler top coinciding with similar ones cast in the cylinder flange, and passed round the jacket to the steam space or dome containing the regulator valve.

The latter slid on top of a box-shaped casting containing the butterfly valve worked by the governor, from whence the steam passed into the valve chest. After passing through slide valve and cylinder, the steam was exhausted through the oval passage seen cast in the cylinder base, and so

to the blast pipe. It will be seen that the cylinder casting is completely lagged with wood and sheet iron, except for cylinder end-covers and dome.

Fig. 34 shows the arrangement of the gearing and pitch-chain adjustment already described, with an enlarged diagram of the chain itself in Fig. 35. The complete engine of 1862 is shown in Fig. 36, and it will be seen that the horse-shafts have been abandoned, the pilot steerage now being carried on angle-iron framing (Fig. 37). Other details remain very similar to the last engine described, though the reversing lever is now handier.

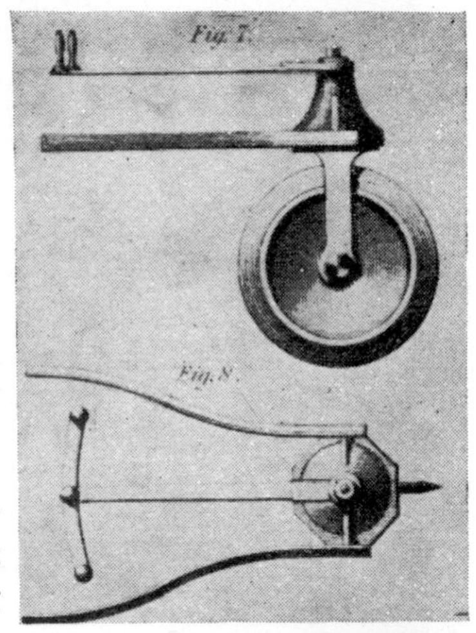

Fig. 37. Aveling's pilot steerage. *Practical Mechanic's Journal.*

A further interesting point of construction is given in Fig. 38, showing the water tank. The top, bottom, and ends were cast flanged plates, connected by wrought-iron sides which carried forward past the front plate to be riveted to the axle bearer-plates, which themselves were riveted to the firebox sides. The ends of the T-iron drawbar were forged round at right angles to bolt to the wrought-iron sides.

This engine was shown at the Great Exhibition of 1862, when *Mechanics' Magazine* said, 'one of its most important features was the excellent construction of the firebox and boiler, enabling it to raise a high pressure of steam for exerting the great power required from a traction engine'. *The Engineer* stated: 'Mr. Aveling's traction engine is the best, we think, that has yet been produced'. The firebox was of Bowling iron, with stay bolts pitched at 5-in. centres, and a pair of longitudinal stays were placed below the tubes to stay the two tube plates. Both firebox and barrel were lagged.

Weighing 8 tons empty, and about 10 tons in working order, the engine had a bore of 10 in. with a 12-in. stroke. A 'powerful friction break' was fitted on the hind axle for use on hills, and the price was now £420.

Typical of the pioneering work done by Aveling engines abroad was that of the Yudanamutana copper mines in South Australia, for whom several machines were built in 1862. The mines were 120 miles from Port Royal, over an unbeaten tract of ground, with water stations every 10 miles. By animal carriage the cost of transport was £10 a ton, but the engines reduced this to £2.

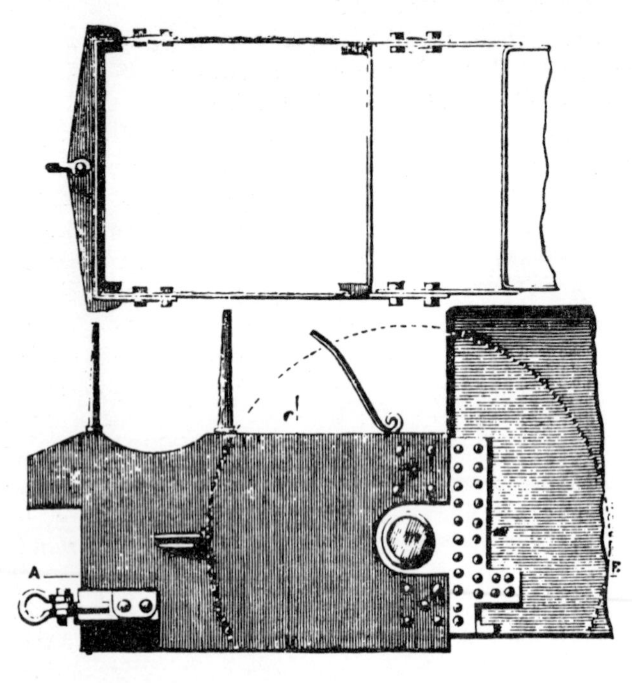

Fig. 38. Construction of the water-tank.
The Engineer.

For the very arduous duty involved, the engines were heavier and stronger than the ordinary agricultural locomotive engine, with a weight empty of 11 tons. The firebox was 40 in. long, 31 in. wide, and 20 in. deep inside, with stays at $4\frac{1}{2}$-in. centres. Fitted with 37 lap-welded tubes $2\frac{3}{4}$ in. o.d. and 5 ft. 7 in. long, the boiler barrel was 3 ft. 1 in. diameter and $\frac{3}{8}$ in. thick. The outer and inner firebox wrappers were also $\frac{3}{8}$ in. thick, with tube-plate and door-plate $\frac{1}{2}$ in. thick. Riveted inside the smokebox was the flanged tube-plate $\frac{5}{8}$ in. thick. In fact, 'the boiler construction is up to the best locomotive standard, and is thus enabled to use locomotive steam pressure of 100 to 120 pounds on the square inch'. A manhole was fitted in the smokebox tube-plate.

The cylinder and steerage were identical with the Exhibition engine: the working parts (presumably meaning the motion) were 'neatly housed in from the influx of weather', and the gearing was covered with light cast-iron splashers. But this was a two-speed design, with a sliding pinion at either end of the crankshaft, giving ratios of 1 to 20 on one side, and 1 to 14 on the other, and speeds of 2 and 4 m.p.h.

These pinions engaged with spur wheels mounted on a second shaft, behind and parallel with the crankshaft, and carried in brass bearings fitted in radial slots in the brackets. In the slot beneath each bearing was a thin cast-iron packing piece, with a thick block above the bearing, held down by a set screw. When the chain needed to be tightened, the blocks were interchanged, thus raising the shaft in the brackets.

The driving wheels were 6 ft. 6 in. diameter, with cast-iron rims 18 in. wide and cast-iron nave 15 in. diameter. Each wheel had 14 wrought-iron spokes, 2½ in. by 1 in. section, notched at the ends and cast 3½ in. into the naves, after dipping in tar. The nave was cast the day after the rim, to allow for contraction. The hind axle was 5 in. diameter, and unsprung.

The rear tank held 211 gallons, and a belly tank was fitted to hold 69 more, allowing for a journey of more than 10 miles. The first of the Yudanamutana engines was No. 53, and with the larger firebox, double gearing and extra tank, the price was increased to £530. It was designed to haul six strongly built oak wagons, each when loaded of a gross weight of 5 or 6 tons.

Another overseas company using Aveling engines was in Buenos Aires, and there is a report of one of these engines, named *El Buey*, hauling on test a load of 28 tons up a 1 in 12 hill, and crossing a ditch 4½ ft. wide and 2 ft. deep, with a load of 22 tons on soft ground.

At the Smithfield Club Show at Islington in 1863, it was stated that Aveling had completed 97 engines. The show engine was lighter than the Australian road loco, but had the same two-speed gear. The chain 'has solid block links, 2 in. wide, each finished in the shaping machine', thus giving a large bearing surface with minimum wear.

We have spent some considerable time in examining these early Aveling engines, but I feel sure that the reader will agree that it has been profitably spent. The details are most fascinating, and already many signs may be observed of the ultimate direction of traction engine design, as exemplified in Chapter Three. Aveling the pioneer was an ace designer, without a doubt, and it is good to know that his name still lives on, a century later, in the products of the well-known concern of Aveling-Barford Ltd., of Grantham.

8

MORE OF THE EARLY DESIGNS

Great inventions are never, and great discoveries are seldom, the work of any one mind. THURSTON

AT THE SAME TIME as Aveling was creating his early masterpieces, there were, of course, many other designers at work. Some were equally inspired, like Fowler and Bray: the former's name lives on in the great firm at Leeds, but the latter's star, having burned bright for a brief decade or so, faded and was no more seen.

In the early days, too, many 'mushroom' builders sprang up, anxious to cash in on the demand, and some weird and wonderful machines resulted. Many of these people were small firms with little engineering experience, less knowledge, and very primitive equipment.

The press of the day did not suffer unduly from inhibitions, and we find in the technical journals some quite outspoken comment on the output of some of these firms. As, for instance, *The Engineer*, reporting on the 1861 'Royal', says: '. . . one little engine, of two or three mule power, made by somebody in Newton-le-Willows, stood in a corner in disgrace. It had but one stay bolt in the middle of each side of the firebox, and *no* stays in the crownplate'.

Later in the year, reporting the Smithfield Club Show, the same journal remarks, with delightful irony: 'Smith Bros. of Thrapstone sent a diminutive self propeller, of about the size and cut of a parish fire engine. The boiler had flat sides, the makers having ascertained, we suppose, that square boilers are stronger than round ones. The stay bolts were put in in pairs, each pair being nearly or quite a foot from the nearest pair. A pinion on the engine shaft geared directly into an internal wheel – which might be ½ in. or possibly ⅝ in. across its face – this wheel or circular rack being part of the propelling wheel of the engine.'

This report goes on: 'It has occurred to us, when looking over a collection of 20, 50 or 100 portable engines, from almost as many makers, that . . . there must be a great deal of knowledge of locomotive construction among our village engineers . . . We would like to see some of the boiler-making investigated, also the line of truth of cylinders and guides, and of the principle bearings. We would like to see diagrams of the link motions of some of these engines and to know whether the piston takes steam before or after the end of the stroke; also whether the back pressure ever becomes so great as to reverse the engine, although we hardly suppose it does.'

Fortunately or unfortunately such examples of bucolic enterprise have not been perpetuated very often in engraving or letterpress, and we can devote our attention to more solid efforts. It must be remembered that the period of experiment in design was by no means finished, and so the mechanical details and appearance of different makes varied considerably, over a period of thirty years or more.

One of the builders who achieved success with a thoroughly sound design was James Taylor of the Britannia Works, Birkenhead, whose name we have already encountered as one of the builders of the Bray engine. Unfortunately there is little press record of the traction engine activities of this firm, but a beautiful plate does exist of the 'Steam Elephant', taken from *The Artizan* of July 1st, 1859, and reproduced as my Fig. 39.

The description accompanying the plate remarks that Boydell's and Bray's engines were 'mostly intended for hauling loaded wagons or trucks, or for hauling agricultural machines.

'Now Mr. Taylor, who is well known for the admirable steam winches, cranes, hoists, and such-like labour-saving machines invented and constructed by him, has for some time past devoted himself to designing a portable steam engine, which shall be capable of running over ground of variable degrees of hardness, drawing loaded trucks or agricultural implements, and also for performing the duties of an ordinary portable steam engine for driving or rotating machinery, for raising or lowering heavy weights and, by the application of a derrick or sheer leg, to perform the duties of a crane, besides containing within itself the means of performing various other descriptions of work, as that of a crab, winch, windlass, &c.; it may be employed for pumping water or as a fire engine.

'The engine is remarkably compact, and unlike all of the traction engines which have preceded it, is mounted upon springs, and is capable of being turned in a circle of much smaller diameter than any other portable engine designed for the same purpose heretofore constructed, and this without having to resort to any disconnecting clutch or gear for throwing the one driving wheel out, and also without any cessation of the transmission of the power of the engine through either driving wheel.'

This last paragraph makes it clear that Taylor was using differential gear in the drive; it was of the same bevel wheel and pinion type used in the majority of today's cars. Contrary to popular belief, this was invented as long ago as 1825 by Roberts (who later became a principal of the well-

Fig. 39. James Taylor's well-designed 'Steam Elephant'. *The Artizan.*

known engineering firm of Sharp, Roberts & Co. of Manchester), and was used by him in a steam carriage. On the Steam Elephant the differential gear was fitted into the two-speed spur wheel on the countershaft which may be seen below the buffer beam on the end elevation, one of the bevel wheels being plainly visible.

The boiler and machinery were carried on vertical plate frames, the former being only 4 ft. 8 in. long so that the water level was little affected on a steep ascent or descent. It was 'constructed partly with flues and partly tubular', but the exact design is not clear. It must have had return tubes, for the fire door was at the chimney end. It was 4 ft. 4 in. high and 2 ft. 9 in. wide, with 7 sq. ft. of fire-grate surface, 34 sq. ft. of 'plate-heating surface', and 24 sq. ft. of tube surface. The working pressure was 55 p.s.i., following a hydraulic test at 150 p.s.i.

The two cylinders, 6-in. diameter by 10-in. stroke, were slightly inclined from the vertical, and bolted to strong castings fastened to boiler and framing. Stephenson reversing gear was fitted, and the crankshaft carried two pinions sliding on feathers, to engage or not with the two-speed spur wheel previously mentioned. On this countershaft, with its differential gear, a chain wheel was mounted close to each end, from which the chains took the drive to a separate countershaft mounted vertically below the hind axle.

At each end of this shaft a pinion was mounted, driving an internal circular rack fastened to each hind wheel. The bearings of the shaft and the hind axle were connected by rigid links, and could slide vertically in guides fixed to the frames, the amount of movement being controlled, of course, by the leaf springs mounted above the hind axle.

In permanent mesh with a pinion on the crankshaft was a spur wheel on a shaft above and behind it, which also carried the drum for the band brake, and a large drum for a winding rope. This spur wheel in turn drove a pinion on a parallel shaft, behind and below the other, carrying a fly-wheel at one end and a crab or winch barrel at the other.

It will be seen that the steerage wheel was on a vertical shaft, at the lower end of which there was a pinion gearing with a curved rack attached to the fore-carriage, on which the front axle was mounted on leaf springs. It was claimed that 'one man may attend to the fire, the engine levers and gear, and also the steering wheel, as the whole of the levers are so arranged as to be entirely within his control'.

The hind wheels were 6 ft. diameter by 10 in. face, and leading wheels 3 ft. 6 in. by 4½ in. Water capacity was 130 gallons, 'but can easily be increased to 200 gallons if required', and the coal bunker had a capacity of 20 cubic feet. The exhaust steam was led into a chamber which collected the condensed water in the exhaust, before the latter went to the $1\frac{3}{8}$ in. diameter blast pipe. From the chamber the hot water drained into the tank, thus pre-heating it 'to a considerable degree'.

After being extensively tested at Birkenhead, the engine was employed at H.M. Dockyard at Keyham. On trial it ran at 6 m.p.h. light, and on slow speed drew a log of timber which it had previously taken twelve horses to move. It also drew easily two loaded wagons carrying 11 tons.

Concludes *The Artizan:* 'In a report made by Mr. Danvers to the Honourable the Finance, Home and Public Works Committee of the Department for India upon the traction engines of Boydell and Taylor, he speaks of Mr. Taylor's engine in high terms of commendation; and we understand that the Indian Government are likely to apply Mr. Taylor's engines very extensively.'

Whether or no this prophecy was actually fulfilled is not clear, but the Steam Elephant next appears in print (in my collection, at least!) at the Great Exhibition of 1862. This is only a small illustration which would not reproduce here, but the engine has been re-arranged somewhat, the boiler being reversed, and the steersman now having a vertical wheel at what was formerly the hind end.

D. K. Clark remarks that the springing was now on blocks of rubber, and that three speeds were fitted. A super-heater effect was obtained by passing the steam from the dome carrying the safety valve to a second dome surrounding the base of the chimney. The wheels were also of different construction, with wrought iron spokes cast into the cast-iron naves and rims. But apart from these scant details, no further particulars of Taylor's engines appear to be available.

Clayton and Shuttleworth have already been noticed as the builders of Aveling's first engines, and when the latter began to make his own, Clayton's were evidently still working to some extent in conjunction with him. We have seen how Aveling used the C. and S. cylinder arrangement in 1861 (Fig. 32) and, of course, the patentees used the same design themselves (Fig. 40). They also used Aveling's pilot steerage, thus returning the compliment.

There was, however, one big difference between the two makes: where Aveling used pitch-chain drive, with the hind axle behind the firebox, C. and S. used spur gearing, with the axle in front. An interesting but not so important feature is that Clayton's used a separate tender on two wheels. A pair of sockets was fitted to the tender at each side, into which horse-shafts could be fitted, and it could then be used as a water cart, when the engine was being employed for driving a threshing machine, or other stationary work.

Fig. 40. The 1861 design of Clayton and Shuttleworth.
A Chapter in the History of the Traction Engine.

This engine was exhibited at the Leeds Show of the R.A.S.E., together with several C. and S. portables, one of which was their engine No. 4278 – not bad for a firm which only started building portables in 1845 and did not number them until 1849! They were now turning out *fifteen engines per week* (italics by *The Engineer*), 'the Stamp End Works, at Lincoln, being the greatest manufactory in the world, and employing no less than 940 men'. The majority of these engines were going abroad, many to Russia, Austria and Hungary, the granary of Europe.

At this show, besides Aveling and C. and S., were portable and steam ploughing engines built for John Fowler by the well-known firm of Kitson and Hewitson of Leeds, for Fowler had not yet set up his own factory. Messrs. Benj. D. Taplin and Co. of Lincoln exhibited two engines with pitch chain self-propelling gear, and with horse-shafts for steerage. One of these was a 12 h.p. double-cylinder engine, and the other an 8 h.p. single.

'Another decided novelty, in connection with agricultural engines, is the application thereto of Giffard's Patent Injector,' said *The Engineer*, which then went into a panegyric on that valuable instrument. But actually there were few engines fitted with the injector – Ruston, Proctor

Fig. 41. Nathaniel Grew's first ice-locomotive.

The Engineer.

& Co. had one – for the price of £20 was certainly against it. Nevertheless, this was a pointer to its future use on traction engines.

A further feature was the improving standard of boiler making, with plates properly flanged (with a generous radius on the corners) instead of being joined by angle iron, and with stronger plates to allow of higher pressures. (Richard Bach and Co. of Birmingham had a portable designed for 100 p.s.i., which was much higher than usual at the time.)

At the Smithfield Club show in December 1861, *The Engineer* made the comments noted on pages 68-9, but then went on to say that 'the engines shown this year average remarkably well, and Kitson's, Aveling's, Ruston, Proctor & Co.'s, and Clayton, Shuttleworth & Co.'s, are certainly up to the existing standard of locomotive engine construction', meaning, of course, railway locomotive standards.

Besides Clayton's 4,541st engine, this show also saw Robey & Co.'s No. 938, Ruston, Proctor's No. 299, and Mr. William Foster's No. 64. These were all portables, except Robey's, which had steering gear as well as self-propelling motion.

Another self-propelling engine was one by Gardiner and Mackintosh of

Fig. 42. Grew's second design, shown at the 1862 Exhibition.
Catalogue of the 1862 *Exhibition.*

New Cross, a double cylinder with steering gear and pitch-chain drive, though 'the mainshaft of the engine was cut nearly through in one place, apparently to permit the clearance of the connecting rod'. Scarcely a recommendation!

Towards the end of 1860 Mr. Nathaniel Grew, A.I.C.E., designed and superintended the building of the unusual locomotive shown in Fig. 41, for Mr. Gabriel Solodornikoff of Moscow, who had the exclusive concession for the use of such machines in Russia. It was intended for use on the frozen lakes and rivers 'for the transport of tallow and other goods from the interior during the long winter season, this duty being at present performed by horses and other beasts of burden, at a very slow and expensive rate'.

The wrought-iron framing carried a loco-type boiler, with two cylinders, 6 in. diameter by 16-in. stroke. Link reversing motion was fitted inside the frames, driving the overhead valves through rocking motion. The boiler worked at 100 p.s.i., and had a large firebox to enable wood fuel to be used. The 100-gallon saddle tank was intended to be filled with snow and ice, with a steam jet for melting and for heating the feed.

Most of the weight was taken on the sprung driving axle: at the leading end the steering sledge was mounted on springs, and steered by a pinion on the lower end of the vertical shaft, which engaged with a rack on the sledge. The trailing sledge was also sprung. These sledges were made from T-iron of 2½ in. by 3 in. section riveted to wrought-iron plates, stiffened by cross-stays of angle iron. Considerable play was allowed to both sledges and axle to allow for the holes and irregularities in the ice surface.

The picture shows the machine as exported, and *The Engineer* stated that on arrival in Moscow it was intended to fix 'a house of light but warm construction' at each end of the sledge for driver and steersman, and full lagging for all steam pipes and other radiating surfaces.

In the autumn of 1861, Mr. Grew sent out a further engine, of improved construction (Fig. 42), which was successfully worked that winter on the River Neva, between Cronstadt and St. Petersburg, carrying passengers and goods. It was constructed by Neilson and Co. of Glasgow (their No. 786) and weighed about 12 tons in working order. The cylinders were 10 in. diameter by 22-in. stroke, driving to a layshaft and thence by connecting rods to the 5 ft. diameter wheels. Steerage was as before, but with a worm and worm-wheel now to turn the vertical shaft. The speed was up to 18 m.p.h. Incidentally, a 1½-in. scale model of this engine was shown at the 1862 Great Exhibition, and is now in the possession of the Science Museum, though unfortunately lack of space prevents its being on view to the public at the time of writing.

The last-named International Exhibition at Kensington had quite a

Fig. 43. Tuxford's exhibited engine of 1862.
Practical Mechanic's Journal.

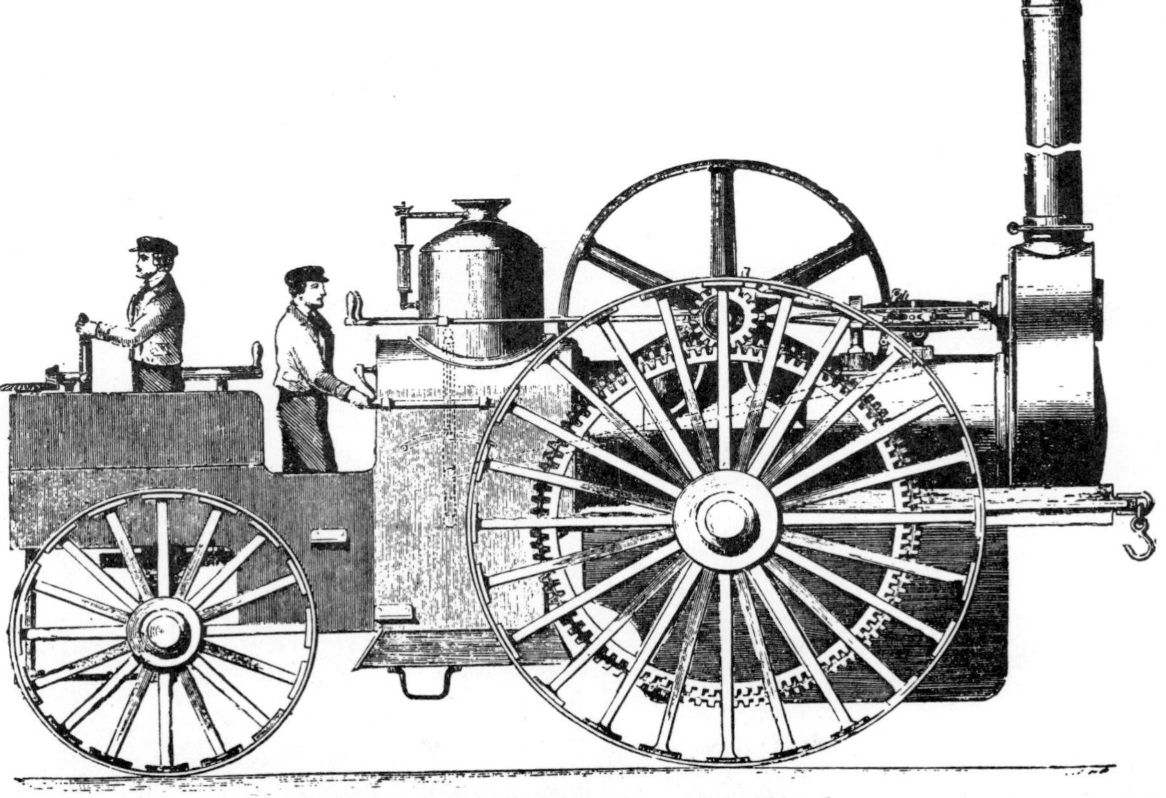

Fig. 44. The 1862 engine of Taplin and Co. of Lincoln. *Catalogue of the* 1862 *Exhibition.*

number of traction engines on view, one or two of which we have already noted. Tuxford and Sons, of Boston, had constructed a portable engine with threshing machine combined in 1842, having an oscillating cylinder mounted on top of a return-flue boiler. In 1850, they evolved a portable which had the vertical engine completely enclosed in a sheet metal housing behind the boiler, a feature which has already been described in connection with their Boydell engine of 1857.

At the Great Exhibition they showed the locomotive engine depicted in Fig. 43, which had both the steeple-type enclosed engine and the return-flue boiler. It had been shown previously at the Leeds 'Royal' in 1861. There was a single drum-like driving wheel, driven by gearing, but whether single or two speeded is not stated – probably the former.

The steerage arrangements are not clear, either, but are probably similar to the design a year or two later, which somewhat resembled that of a modern motor car – wheels mounted on stub axles swivelling on vertical pivots or kingpins, with linkage connecting the axles together and to a crank worked by the steering wheel.

Practical Mechanics' Journal states that it '. . . can be steered with great facility, will turn readily to either side, and can have its motion reversed instantaneously and be made to run backward at the desire of the driver. It is stated to be capable of ascending any moderate gradient; to draw a load equal to a ton per horse power of the engine along a fair road or over hard ground at the rate of three or four miles per hour. When no load is required to be attached, the engine travels at a proportionately higher speed – from eight to ten miles have been accomplished in the hour along the ordinary high roads.'

The same account shows a small picture of the engine hauling a threshing machine, and says that a winding drum was fitted for hauling the load up steep slopes or out of difficulties. A seat was fitted over the driving wheel 'to carry the necessary labour', though the mortar boards look rather out of place there! These locomotives were built in three sizes, 8, 10 and 12 n.h.p., the last costing £500.

The rather ungainly-looking machine seen in Fig. 44 is the 'new patent traction engine' of Taplin of Lincoln, of 16 horse power, 'fitted with extra space for water and coals sufficient for a 10-mile journey; and is built expressly for drawing heavy loads of 50 tons and upwards'. It had been re-designed with two-speed gear, with pinions sliding on the crankshaft to engage with the double spur wheel shown, and the steam-jacketed double cylinders were contained in the smokebox – perhaps under Clayton & Shuttleworth licence. This machine, too, had the 'motor car' type of steering, by the way.

Fig. 45. Robey's engine and threshing-machine.
Catalogue of the 1862 *Exhibition.*

As in some other engines of the time, the boiler could be tilted to keep it more or less horizontal when ascending or descending hills. The price was £590, with a 12 h.p. version for farm purposes at £425, whilst the firm claimed that they would quote for engines up to the unheard-of figure of 50 horse power!

Another Lincoln firm was Robey and Co., founded by Robert Robey in 1854, and now Robey and Co. Ltd., who, incidentally, are one of the few remaining firms still building steam engines at the time of writing. Fig. 45 shows the engine and threshing machine which Robey had exhibited at the Leeds 'Royal', where it won a silver medal, and at Smithfield in December 1861, and now at the Great Exhibition.

Portable engine practice is still very obvious in this design, with the wooden wheels and fore-carriage, and the hinged chimney and crutch to receive it. The steerage was via worm and wheel, with a chain pinion at the foot of the vertical shaft, and chain to the axle, and the drive was by pitch chain to one hind wheel. This was the ten-horse double-cylindered model, but though the catalogue gives no indication of what other powers were available, it is reasonable to suppose that Robey would add these details to other sizes of engine as required.

The 1862 catalogue also carried a woodcut (Fig. 46) of Robey's 'Patent Highway Locomotive', but it seems likely that this design remained on paper only, as there is no contemporary evidence of an example being built.

We have mentioned Chaplin's of Glasgow as building a Bray engine with their vertical boiler, but at Kensington (besides steam cranes, locos,

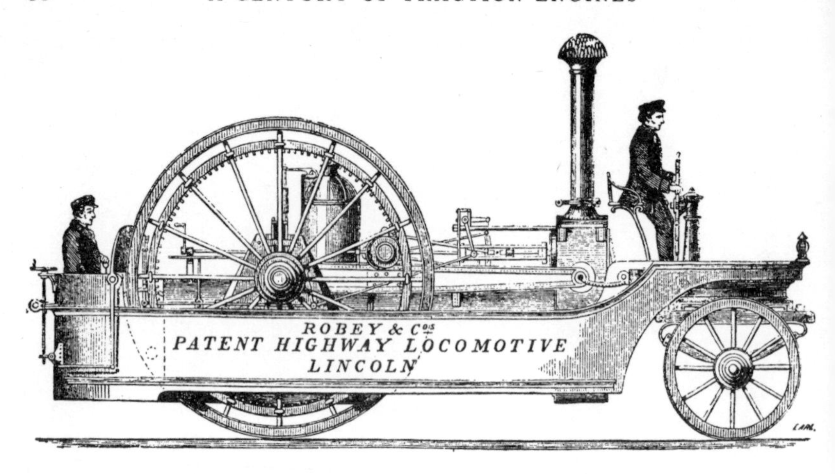

Fig. 46. Robey's 'Highway Locomotive'.
Catalogue of the 1862 *Exhibition.*

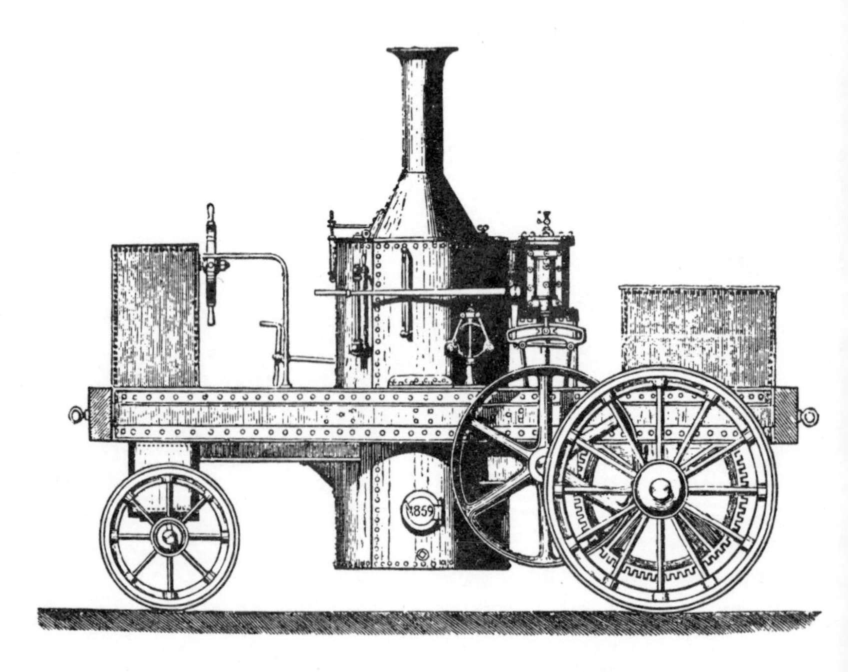

Fig. 47. Chaplin's vertical boilered engine.
Catalogue of the 1862 *Exhibition.*

and other machines) they had a 'carrying and traction engine' of their own design – though the engine illustrated in the catalogue (Fig. 47) bears the date 1859 on the fire-door! The design very much resembles their contractors' (rail) loco, but with the addition of flywheel and governor for stationary working and, of course, the necessary steerage.

No indication is given of the sizes or prices, but the railway locos were from 6 to 27 h.p., and it is stated that 'carrying' engines can be built 'adapted to carry loads up to 50 tons'. Presumably, therefore, the traction engines were built in large sizes too.

9

STEAM CULTIVATION

It has long been the hard fate of most inventors, if their inventions are of any real value, to be assailed by . . . rivals. MUIRHEAD

MEANTIME, MANY BRAINS HAD been at work on the problems of steam ploughing and cultivation, and some interesting self-moving engines were evolved. One of these was the rotary cultivator of Thomas Rickett (Fig. 48), built at the Castle Foundry in Buckingham. The double

Fig. 48. Rickett's rotary cultivator of 1858.
Journal of the R.A.S.E.

cylinders, 5½ in. by 10 in., were enclosed in the smokebox, and worked at 90 p.s.i. giving up to 180 r.p.m. when working stationary.

The return flue boiler was 5 ft. 3 in. long, and the hind wheels 4 ft. diameter by 12 in. broad, driven by the gearing shown, the final spur wheel of which engaged with a cage or lantern gear wheel on the single driving wheel. The digger-shaft, 2¼ in. square in section, was 7 ft. long, and was driven by pitch chain, with a 1 to 2 reduction, direct from the crankshaft. Different forms of cutters could be mounted on this shaft, according to the work required, and it revolved in a direction against the motion of the engine. The shaft was carried in radial arms which could be raised or lowered to vary the depth of tillage. On test at the Chester Show in 1858 the machine was found to be capable of cultivating up to 5¾ acres per day, at a cost of 9s. per acre – appreciably more than that of Fowler's steam-ploughing apparatus.

An interesting point here is the amount of wages paid per day – the engineer received 5s., with two men at 3s. each and, of course, this would be for a ten-hour day of good solid graft!

The trouble with the Rickett and other similar cultivators, however, was the weight of the engine – from 6 to 10 tons – consolidating the ground, and steam ploughing by cable was soon well to the fore. Even

Fig. 49. Fowler's clip-drum ploughing engine.
C. E. Shackle, Esq.

so there were many other attempts at direct cultivation during the century, but the same trouble still generally applied.

In cable ploughing, we have already seen the beginnings of Fowler's single-engine system in Chapter Two, but it must be remembered that there were many other systems, several using a windlass driven by portable engine, which have no further place in this book.

Fowler further developed his single-engine system by inventing the clip drum (Fig. 49) in which the rope was held fast by means of the two rows of clips or leaves D-D, as seen in Fig. 50 which shows a section of the edge of the drum. It will be seen that the rope, at E, would be gripped more tightly the heavier the pull. The clips were of chilled cast iron, which wore very well but were replaced cheaply and easily. Fig. 51 shows the system in use, with the balance plough and the self-moving anchor.

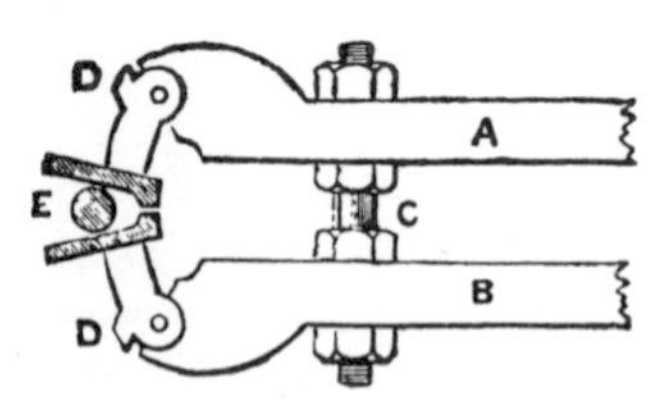

Fig. 50. Arrangement of clips.
Practical Mechanic's Journal.

The engine shown in Fig. 49 was Fowler's No. 106, and was built for him by Kitson and Hewitson of Leeds. He had laid out his own works in Leeds in 1861, but not yet achieved sufficient output to be independent. In fact, in 1862 Burrell's were also building under licence and selling Fowler engines and tackle: the illustrations of both firms in the Official Catalogue of the International Exhibition are identical, the woodcuts of the engines being copied from this very photograph.

This was a double-cylindered engine of 14 n.h.p., with bevel wheels to

Fig. 51. Arrangement of the Fowler single-engine system.
Practical Mechanic's Journal.

drive the vertical shaft, which drove the drum through the dog clutch mounted on the shaft. At the other end of the crankshaft was a small bevel pinion driving the sloping bevel wheel, the top of which may be discerned above the far connecting rod. This bevel wheel was mounted on a slanting-shaft which drove the hind axle through a further pair of bevels, with a dog clutch on the slanting-shaft too, to interrupt the drive at will.

The hind wheels were loose on the axle, but with circular bosses keyed on outside them. A friction band encircled each boss, and was secured to the broad wheel-spoke seen: thus, when the bands were tightened, the wheels were driven, but when turning a corner, one band could be slackened. To steer the engine, a vertical shaft passed through the tank, with reduction gear to a pulley, round which passed the steerage chains passing right forward to the front axle.

Note the vase-like dome, with its Salter safety valve, and direct steam pipe to the top of the valve chest, with the governor valve incorporated – typical of Fowler's thorough attention to efficiency of detail.

The experience of Mr. E. Ruck, who farmed 800 acres of arable land in the upper Thames valley, may be quoted to show how the farmer benefited from the steam plough. He had formerly used 56 oxen and some horses, with seven 4-ox teams for the morning shift and seven for the afternoon. He bought a 14 h.p. steam tackle set by Fowler (for which he paid largely by selling his oxen), and was satisfied that his tillage was better and more cheaply done by steam.

Meantime two young men of genius entered the field. Alfred Yarrow and James Hilditch had become firm friends at school, both being vastly interested in things scientific and mechanical, and with a mutually owned workshop for experiments. At the age of seventeen they made their own

Fig. 52. Arrangement of the Yarrow and Hilditch system.
Journal of the R.A.S.E.

telegraph apparatus, and erected the first over-house telegraph line in London, between their homes, half a mile apart.

Before they were twenty-one, they had taken out several patents in improvements for steam ploughing, and had lectured on the subject to the Society of Civil and Mechanical Engineers. It will be appreciated that Fowler's system involved considerable strain on the anchor pulley when the plough was travelling away from the engine and, in fact, it was not unknown for the anchor to overturn, causing considerable trouble. Fig. 52 shows how the new Y. and H. system prevented this; the single acting plough A is travelling towards the engine, working as it goes, but plough B, travelling towards the anchor pulley, is *not* working. On A reaching the engine, and B the anchor, the motion is reversed, and now B works, *travelling towards the engine*, whilst A is drawn backwards. Thus at any time the strain on the anchor is limited to the slight work of hauling back the non-working plough, with all ploughing strain taken directly by the engine. Moreover, the tail rope (round the anchor pulley) needed only to be light in section, saving cost.

The system was widely acclaimed by several leading agriculturalists, and the manufacture taken up by Coleman and Sons of Chelmsford. Among customers was the Khedive of Egypt, who purchased 24 sets for use in cultivating cotton on the Nile. This was important to Britain, to help to alleviate the distress caused in Lancashire by cessation of American supplies due to the Civil War.

In the engine itself (Fig. 53) a bevel-shaft conveyed the power to the drum-shaft, on which the drums could be thrown in or out of motion as required. The drum-shaft was continued on to the firebox, where a pinion could be meshed with a gear-wheel to drive the hind wheels at a speed up to 2½ m.p.h. Aveling's fifth-wheel steerage (not shown in the engraving) was used, and the cylinders were enclosed in the smokebox on the C. and S. principle. In 1862, *The Engineer* reported an 8 h.p. set at work cultivating seven acres a day 'which, considering the stiffness of the soil, may be looked upon as a most satisfactory result'.

Although not relevant to the present volume, we may note that coincidental with their ploughing system this lively pair of youths designed a highly successful steam carriage which had a speed of 25 m.p.h. It was built by Cowan and Co., of Greenwich, and exhibited at the 1862 Exhibition, when neither of them had yet become of age! Moreover, all this brilliant work had been done in their spare time and with no capital, for Yarrow was apprenticed at Ravenhill's, the marine engineers, and Hilditch was training as a silk mercer in the family business, which, incidentally, he carried on in due course, leaving steam engineering behind him.

Fig. 53. Ploughing engine by Yarrow and Hilditch. *The Engineer.*

Robey & Co.
Lincoln.

On conclusion of his apprenticeship, Yarrow became London representative for Coleman and Co. selling the steam ploughs, but after two years set up his own small general engineering factory. The steam carriage had had to be abandoned owing to legal obstruction, and now he let the steam ploughing go too, to devote his full energies to the new venture, which, in due course, became the world-famous marine engineering firm.

Messrs. W. Savory and Son of Gloucester had patented an interesting ploughing engine in 1861, the prototype (Fig. 54) being built for them by Robey and Co. of Lincoln. The winding drum was a 6-ft. diameter shell revolving on three pairs of wheels carried in brackets on the boiler shell. Two cylinders were placed transversely in the enclosed box over the steerage, the extended crankshaft driving the drum by pinions and internal gearing. A further extension, with a dog-clutch connection, carried a worm engaging with a worm-wheel keyed to the hind axle.

Under the drum, and parallel with it, was a screw shaft carrying a pair of guide rollers whose to-and-fro movement regulated the coiling of the rope on the drum perfectly. A separate donkey pump on the footplate replenished the boiler. Two engines were used in this system, one at each side of the field, hauling the implement (a Fowler balance plough or Howard's grubber, etc.) back and forth between them.

In 1864, at the Newcastle meeting of the R.A.S.E., Fowler himself exhibited a double-engined set with clip drums. Each engine was rated at 7 n.h.p., and the set, with a four-furrow balance plough, worked 8 acres in a 10-hour day. Working pressure was 100 lb., and coal consumption no higher than 188 lb. per acre.

This has been called Fowler's greatest achievement, but it was his last, for he died on December 4th, 1864, following an accident on the hunting field. He was only thirty-eight, but had 32 patents to his name, his own works, and a fame which was known throughout the civilised world. And he had laid the foundations of a long line of engines which themselves reached to the ends of the earth, to bring prosperity in remote places, along with the engines of other British makers, some of whose exports we have noticed already. Yet curiously enough, up to the time of Fowler's death, no pure traction engine bearing his name had appeared – his activities had been devoted almost entirely to the perfection of steam ploughing.

10

THE LATER SIXTIES

They who aim vigorously at perfection will come nearer to it than those whose laziness or despondency makes them give up its pursuit from the feeling of its being unattainable. CHESTERFIELD

THE 1860'S SAW A spate of engines of quite assorted designs. Hornsby and Sons in 1863 produced an undertype engine of the appearance shown in Fig. 55, in which the double cylinders were directly beneath the smoke-box. On the end of the crankshaft a pinion geared into a spur wheel on the countershaft, from which chains drove the hind wheels. Helical springs were used, and the engine was neat in appearance but, says Fletcher, 'we fear it was not a striking success'.

In the same year, at the Worcester Royal Show, Brown and May exhibited a spring-mounted engine, with two speeds given by separate

Fig. 55. Hornsby's undertype traction engine.
A Chapter in the History of the Traction Engine.

pitch chains at each side of the engine. Incidentally, reporting that same 'Royal', *Mechanics' Magazine* commented that Fowler's (ploughing) engine had the steerage controlled from the footplate, where it 'had no business to be'!

Clayton and Shuttleworth's engine of 1863 appeared as in Fig. 56, with the cylinder in the smokebox, having an internal pipe in the boiler to carry steam from the large dome. The drive was now by pitch chain to a countershaft passing behind the firebox, with bevel type compensating or differential gear on the shaft. A pinion on each end of the latter drove spur wheels bolted to the hind wheel hubs, rotating on the dead hind axle.

The fifth-wheel steerage had been discarded in favour of the type shown, with worm and wheel, pinion and chain to the fore axle, which, indeed, was now becoming quite popular. At the same time, Clayton's would provide 'hind steerage' if the customer desired, but of what particular type is not known.

In 1865 this firm had changed to all-gear drive (Fig. 57), and to effect this had moved the steam-jacketed cylinder (or cylinders) back, on to the first ring of the boiler barrel, so reducing the distance between the crankshaft and the countershaft. This enabled the drive to be carried through a single intermediate wheel, mounted on a stub-shaft carried on the crankshaft bracket. Apart from this, the drive was as before.

It is interesting to note that the fore-carriage was still of timber construction with only wrought or cast iron parts where absolutely necessary. In the front wheels, stronger spokes of flat section had been substituted for the round ones, and at the rear the sides of the tender had been built up to give greater coal capacity, with access now by a ladder.

Robey's engine of 1865 (Fig. 58) still had rather the look of a self-propelling portable engine, rather than a traction engine designed as such, with pitch chain to a stub countershaft beneath the footplate, and thence again to a single hind wheel. The example shown is the 10 h.p. double-cylinder model, but it would not be possible for this horse power to be effectively used in traction – that single wooden wheel would just not be strong enough to transmit the power. Hence we must acknowledge that Robey's engines were merely intended to work themselves and their tackle from farm to farm, and not to be used for serious haulage.

This book is not intended to cover the story of the steam roller (which could occupy a fair-sized volume of its own!) but as a matter of historical import we should note its introduction at least. It was in 1863 that the first British steam roller appeared, to the joint design of Mr. W. Clark, municipal engineer of Calcutta, and Mr. W. Batho of Birmingham, where the machine was built. After trials the machine was shipped to

Fig. 56. Clayton and Shuttleworth's engine of 1863.
A Chapter in the History of the Traction Engine.

Fig. 57. Clayton and Shuttleworth's engine of 1865.
A Chapter in the History of the Traction Engine.

Calcutta, and in 1864 two further machines, built in London, were sent out.

I have not traced any illustration, but it is known that these machines had two rolls at the front end, acting as drivers, and two more set side-by-side in a turntable at the rear for steerage purposes, and more than covering the gap left by the front rolls.

However, the first really successful steam roller to be worked regularly in Britain was built by Aveling and Porter. In 1866, experiments were carried out by Aveling, who replaced the hind wheels of a heavy traction engine by extra wide ones of 7 ft. diameter and 3 ft. wide, the total weight of the machine being more than 20 tons. In December of that year, *English Mechanic and Mirror of Science* reported that the machine had 'been doing good service in Hyde Park during the last two or three weeks, to the admiration of numerous spectators'.

Following the success of the experimental engine, Aveling designed his first roller as such (Fig. 59), and this was acquired by the City of Liverpool in 1867. It was an enormous machine weighing 30 tons (which proved in the event to be far heavier than really necessary), and had a single acting cylinder of 11 in. by 14-in. stroke. The two driving rolls were 7 ft. diameter by 2 ft. wide, and the steering roll was 5 ft. diameter, in two sections each 2 ft. 6 in. wide.

Over the front rolls was a 500-gallon water tank (not shown in this engraving), and the roll turntable rotated on small rollers set radially in the frame, being controlled by a ship's hand-wheel operating a chain through a worm and worm-wheel. Despite its bulk, the machine could be turned in its own length.

Before this basic design was superseded in 1871, the firm had sold a good many – two went to New York in 1869 – and one of them acquired by Hull in 1867 was still working there as late as 1926. These machines were mostly of 12 to 15 tons in weight.

Returning to traction engines, in 1866 at the Smithfield Show, Clayton and Shuttleworth showed two traction engines and Burrell one, these being the only tractions on view. *The Engineer* remarked about the former: 'We find some pleasure in stating that considerable improvements have been effected in these traction engines of late. These refer principally to apparently small matters in detail: but it is in detail that the talent of the engineer is most conspicuously displayed. The engines in question are very similar in appearance, the only marked difference being that one of 10 horse power has double cylinders, the other of 8 horse power has but one. Like ourselves, Messrs. Clayton and Shuttleworth are firm believers in double cylinders for traction engines, and the single cylinder has only

Fig. 58. Robey's engine of 1865.
Steam and the Steam Engine.

Fig. 59. Aveling's first steam-roller, 1865.
The Practical Dictionary of Mechanics.

been adopted by them in deference to the wishes of those who hold different opinions . . . the machinery may be made lighter, and the expense of repairs will be reduced by adopting the double arrangement, inasmuch as at starting the gearing is spared from jerks and the communication of power is more regular, while the weight of the flywheel may be greatly reduced as compared with the single arrangement – a matter of some importance . . . The road wheels are now made of wrought instead of cast iron; the tyres consist of a broad hoop, within which two angle irons are riveted at such a distance apart that, including the breadth of the rings, the width of the tyre is divided into four equal parts. The spokes are of wrought iron, oval in section, cast into the boss . . . and then bent so as to cross each other; the outer spokes in the boss going to the inner angle iron of the tyre, and vice versa. The spokes have T-heads, which are riveted to the angle-iron.'

This is the first description of the type of wheel which, with the substitution of T-rings for the angle-rings, was to become nearly universal for

Fig. 60. Tuxford's engine of 1867.
A Chapter in the History of the Traction Engine.

traction engines. But Clayton's had a further refinement. 'As hitherto made, the strains in such wheels have been thrown altogether on the rivets, which is highly objectionable. As constructed by Messrs. Clayton and Shuttleworth, however, the spokes when fixed into the boss are put into a kind of lathe, and their ends are submitted successively to the action of an ingeniously constructed machine by which they are all cut to the proper length and to the right curve. The hoop is then shrunk on over the spokes, and the strain is exerted not on the rivets but on the T-heads, which bear with mathematical precision on the inside of the tyre . . . We need hardly add that the workmanship of these, and that of several portable engines exhibited by this firm, is exquisite . . . the firm . . . have earned a reputation equal to that of the first locomotive shops in the kingdom.'

In the following year this firm patented and built a very unusual double-cylindered engine in which the crankshaft was, as it were, cut into two at the centre, each half revolving in its own pair of bearing brackets and with its own flywheel. Moreover, from each crankshaft a separate pitch chain drove to a chain wheel running free on a dead shaft behind the firebox, and each chain wheel carried a pinion driving spur wheels bolted to each hind wheel.

In other words, each cylinder drove its own hind wheel separately! There were two regulators and two reversing levers, and all this extra complication was to allow one wheel to be run at a slower rate than the other when turning sharp corners. In view of the fact that Clayton's had been using a very efficient form of compensating gear (which *The Engineer* called 'the excessively elegant "Jack-in-the-box" gear') for some three or four years, it is difficult to know why this very peculiar arrangement was developed. Needless to say, it was *not* perpetuated!

This engine, by the way, was Clayton's No. 7724, which gives some idea of the tremendous total quantity of portable and traction engines now being produced, even allowing for the fact that the firm was the largest manufacturer in the world. Shades of Howden, who gave up production at twelve engines because of his fear of over-stocking the country!

At the Paris Exhibition of 1867 Clayton's showed an engine almost identical with Fig. 57, but with the improved wrought-iron wheels just described which, by the way, had strakes riveted at an angle to the hind-wheel rims, similar to engines of the 'modern' period, to give a grip on soft ground. The double cylinders were 7½ in. diameter by 12-in. stroke, with valve chests between; the crankshaft was 3½ in. in diameter with a 5-ft. flywheel; and the front and hind wheels were, respectively, 3 ft. 6 in. diameter by 9 in. wide, and 5 ft. 9 in. diameter by 1 ft. 6 in. wide.

Tuxford still favoured his enclosed steeple-type engine, and Fig. 60

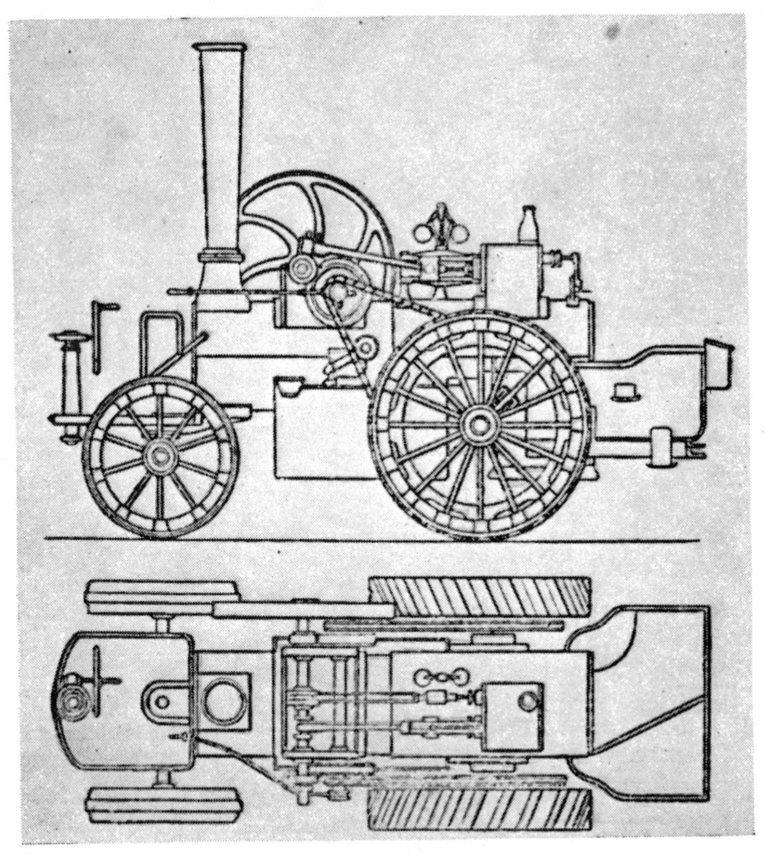

Fig. 61. Burrell's 'chain' engine.
A Chapter in the History of the Traction Engine.

shows his 1867 design, again with return-flue boiler and with front wheels on stub axles with 'motor car' type steerage, having, however, a large diameter horizontally mounted steerage wheel. Other features include the large steam dome with twin Salter safety valves, and the water supply carried in a belly tank.

Meantime, Charles Burrell, having perforce dropped his pet, the Boydell system, had gone on to develop the engine shown in Fig. 61, of which large numbers were turned out between 1866 and 1878, many of them being actually at work into the 1920's. The crankshaft carried a different sized gear pinion at either end, and there was a countershaft running across the boiler top below the motion. Near each end of this shaft was a spur wheel, to be engaged or not with the appropriate pinion, so as

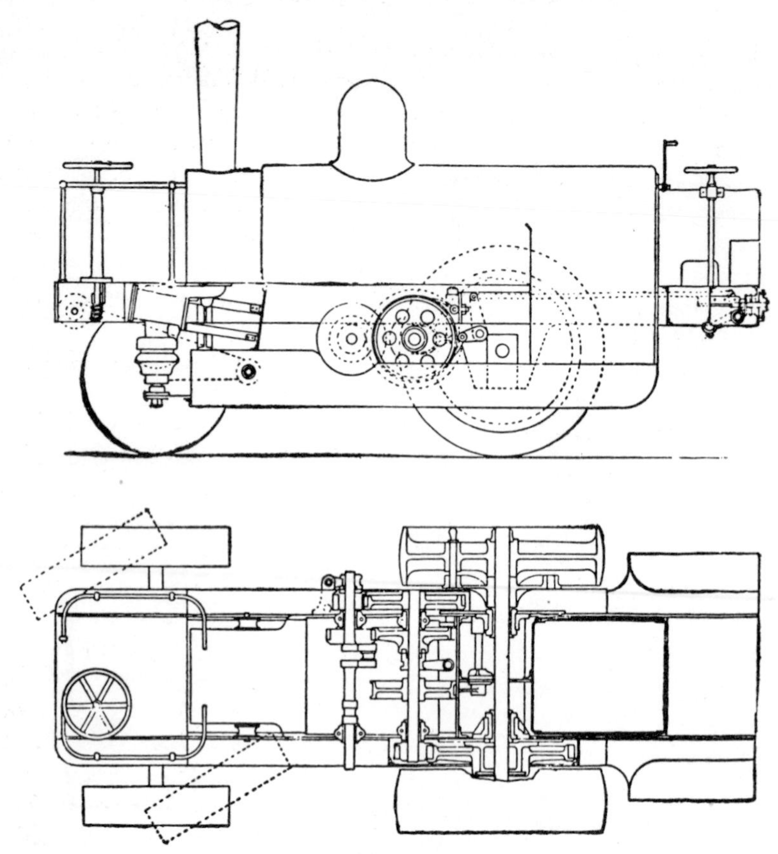

Fig. 62. Fowler undertype of 1868.
A Chapter in the History of the Traction Engine.

to give two speeds. From the countershaft a pair of chains drove the hind wheels. The engine was driven and steered from the front, with a rear platform to carry the stoker and his coal supply. Water was contained in the belly tank, and pre-heated by passing some of the exhaust steam into it.

The Fowler works had been extended during the early 'sixties to cope with the rapidly increasing business, which was still entirely devoted to ploughing tackle. However, in 1865 the firm launched out into building portable and traction engines, as well as other products, and these became an excellent selling line too.

In 1868 the firm, always ready to try new ideas, built the undertype engine shown in Fig. 63, with double cylinders over the front axle. The slow-speed gear (permanently in mesh) was outside the frame plates, with a dog-clutch sliding on the crankshaft, and the fast speed was inside, with a dog-clutch sliding on the countershaft. The latter carried a brake drum between the frames, and also drove the hind axle through gearing on the near-side, the wheel on that side being keyed to the axle. On the other side a driving boss was keyed to the axle, with holes into which a driving pin could be passed from a corresponding hole in the wheel. In turning sharp corners, the pin had to be removed to allow differential movement: a system still used at that time by many makers. The engine was very wide over its cast-iron driving wheels, and for this and other reasons did not prove a commercial success.

The *Illustrated London News* of April 10th, 1869, has an interesting (though technically not very accurate) picture of two Aveling and Porter traction engines being used in a combined land and sea assault on Dover Castle. This was during the Easter Volunteer Review, and the engines, being actually on the way to France for export, were lent to draw a battery of guns from the railway station up the Castle Hill. Incidentally, these two machines were still fitted with the fifth-wheel steerage.

We have now seen several of the main features of our modern engines appear: the steam-jacketed cylinder, the all-gear drive, the differential gear, the loco boiler, the attached tender with water tank below the footplate, steerage from the footplate, and the wrought iron (later steel) construction for wheels. But many of these improvements were not yet in common use, including especially the gear drive, the differential gear, and the footplate steerage; even Clayton's, pioneers of the wrought-iron wheel, were still using cast-iron rims on the front ones. There was still to be plenty of experiment and development, all of it highly interesting, before the industry really settled down. And we ourselves have still some very diverting machines to examine!

11

THE THOMSON ROAD STEAMERS

Those projects which abridge distance have done most for the civilisation and happiness of our species. MACAULAY

ASK THE AVERAGE PERSON who first invented the pneumatic tyre, and you would receive the wrong answer. The correct one would be R. W. Thomson, who took out a patent in 1845 for them to be fitted to ordinary carriages or to invalid chairs. However, at that time rubber was scarce and badly made, Thomson could not realise much on his invention, and so it was discarded because of the difficulties of production.

He then devoted his attention to solid rubber tyres of large cross section for larger vehicles and road engines, taking out a patent for these on October 24th, 1867, specifying that the rubber should be so soft that small obstacles or lumps on the road surface would press into the rubber so that the wheel would not rise in surmounting them.

Thomson was an engineer of considerable attainment and many ideas – he had invented such diverse articles as a fountain pen and a portable crane – and had been employed in developing collieries in Java. Here it was necessary to provide haulage for the coal to the port, and Thomson, returning to Edinburgh, set to work to design a road haulage engine in harmony with his own notions. This resulted in the first practical use of rubber tyres on a mechanically propelled vehicle, and also of his 'pot' boiler, of which more anon.

The first Thomson road steamer was tested in the Edinburgh district in December 1867, before being shipped to Java, and in the trials, hauling a large omnibus, speeds of 10 to 12 miles an hour were readily attained. Built by Tennant's of Leith, the engine had a single cylinder of 5-in. bore by 8-in. stroke, laid horizontally, and was mounted on three wheels on rubber tyres, those on the drivers being 12 in. wide and 5 in. thick. It was very similar to Fig. 63, which actually shows an engine built in 1868 for Ceylon. In both cases, the machines were intended for use alternatively for passenger hauling in omnibuses or with trains of goods wagons.

In 1869, some trials were made with two 6-horse engines, of which a contemporary account states: 'One of the 6-ton road steamers was harnessed to four wagons of pig iron – weight of iron and wagons, 34 tons – which it drew without an effort or any stoppage from the foot to the top of Granton Road, a distance of a quarter of a mile, with inclines of 1 in 18 . . . The other road steamer was attached to an omnibus which conveyed a party of gentlemen from Granton to Leith . . . at the rate of over eight miles an hour, that being the highest speed at which it was deemed safe to run through a town.'

Of another road steamer employed at Aberdeen to draw a 15-ton boiler on a 5-ton wagon, it was said: 'It is certainly a feat for a 5-ton engine to drag out a 20-ton load and climb gradients of 1 in 20 with single gear. We had all Aberdeen out as we passed. It was an unusual sight to see the infant 'Hercules' in front of the great boiler, 30 feet long and 7 feet in diameter, bowling along with it like a plaything at its tail, whilst the plaything itself shook the houses again as it danced over the rough causeway.'

Many foolish statements were made regarding the rubber tyres by people who should have known better, and many over-optimistic claims were made: in fact, a great deal of harm was done to the cause of india rubber tyres by such false claims as to durability and grip. The blunt truth is that without steel 'chain armour' to protect them, the rubber of the time was *not* up to the task which it had to do.

Thomson's original rubber-tyred wheel was constructed of wrought-iron plates, strengthened by angle-iron hoops and diagonal spokes, with flanges on each side to keep the tyres in place. Holes $\frac{5}{8}$ in. diameter were drilled all over the rims, the tyre being made less in diameter than the rim, to keep it in place and be gripped by the holes.

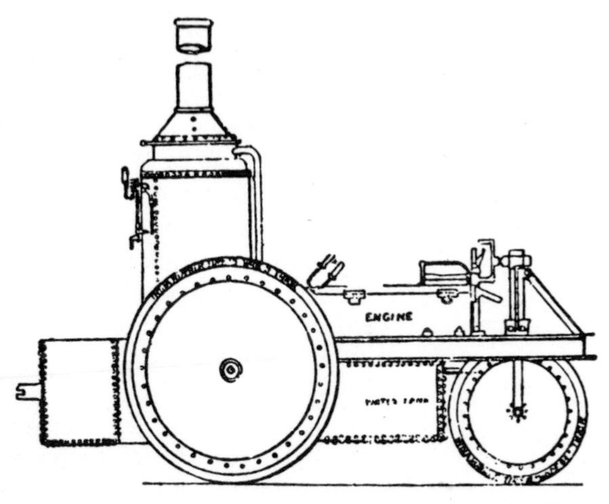

Fig. 63. Thomson-Tennant Road Steamer.
Steam Locomotion on Common Roads.

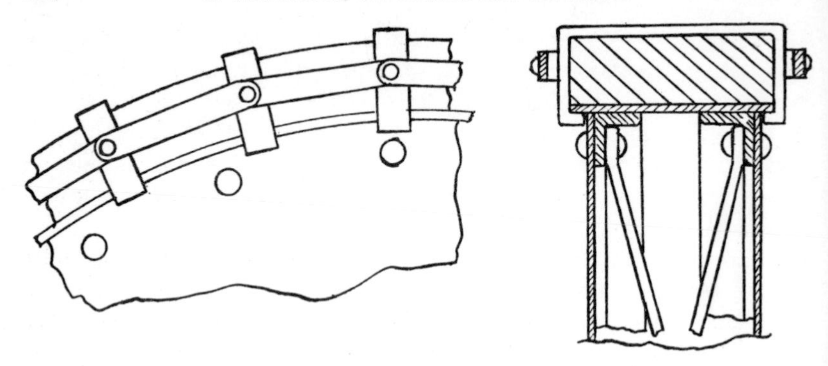

Fig. 64. Arrangement of the Thomson wheel.
Author's sketch

The first chain armour was as in Fig. 64, with narrow steel strips bent round, and joined together by flat malleable iron links. But the link pins broke frequently and annoyingly and, moreover, unless the shoes were very tight, the tyre was difficult to keep in place. The trouble was that the soft rubber being compressed under the load of the wheel, it 'bagged out' at the front when rolling, but was under tension at the rear. If heavily loaded, and without armour, there could be a gap of as much as 4½ in. between tyre and rim at the front.

This bagging out caused the tyre to work round the rim with a reverse movement, even when armoured, under ordinary circumstances about 1 revolution in 30 or 40, giving rise to considerable internal wear. On soft ground in wet conditions, the mud or clay acted as a lubricant, giving practically no traction at all, even with chain armour to help to hold the tyre in place. The wheels simply spun round inside the tyres.

Even so, under most conditions the rubber tyres were a success on good roads, and thus it was on the roads that the Thomson steamers gave the best account of themselves, not as agricultural engines.

At the time that Thomson was developing his ideas, there was a certain young Army lieutenant in charge of the Regimental Workshops at Rawalpindi in India. His name was R. E. Crompton, and later he was to become founder and head of the great electrical firm of that name. But as yet his interests were in mechanical transport, and though his means were very limited, he succeeded over several years of hard work in building a steam carriage.

Whilst testing this vehicle on the good, well-metalled roads of the Punjab, Crompton was much interested in the accounts in the engineering press of the trials of the Thomson steamers, and wrote to Thomson him-

Fig. 65. Robey's Thomson Steamer 'Advance'.
Steam Locomotion on Common Roads.

self. He also drew up and presented a scheme to the authorities showing that road motors could be used for the transport of troops, stores, mail and heavy guns, instead of the slow bullock trains which were the only alternative means where there were no railways.

The scheme being accepted (not without considerable argument!), a small department called the Government Steam Train was formed, with Crompton as its first Superintendent. A Thomson steamer was sent for, and was tried out in 1869. It was successful so far as haulage power, good adhesion, and freedom from vibration at speed were concerned, but it failed badly in that the firebox was not large enough to burn the wood fuel which was all that was available in the test area. The engine had to stop frequently to raise steam, so that its average speed was little more than that of a bullock train.

Crompton was many weeks at Simla persuading the authorities to give the experiment another chance, but in the end the Governor-General himself signed the authority for four improved steam trains to be constructed. Crompton was to go to England to discuss the design with Thomson in view of special Indian conditions.

On his arrival in 1870, he found that the latter was a severe invalid, unable to leave his sofa, though with a very keen and active brain. Several months were spent at Thomson's house, discussing and designing, and Crompton found already that an improved type of steamer was being built. Tennant's had been unable to cope with the demand from home and abroad, and Robey's were building a larger engine, *Advance* (Fig. 65), for Woolwich Arsenal.

A vertical double-cylinder engine, totally enclosed, was fitted to the Robey engine, and Fig. 66 gives its arrangement. The cylinders were 7¾ in. diameter by 10-in. stroke, with a crankshaft 3 in. diameter. A parallel countershaft was driven at a reduced speed in permanent mesh, and the water pump was driven from this shaft. At each end of both the crankshaft and the countershaft were spur-pinions sliding on splines, and either pair could be engaged with internal spur-rings bolted to the hind wheels. If, therefore, the crankshaft pinions were engaged, this gave high gear, whilst engagement of the countershaft pinions gave low gear. No compensating gear was fitted, but for turning sharp corners one pinion could be thrown out of mesh. The driving wheels were 6 ft. diameter, and leading wheel 4 ft., with 5-in. thick tyres in each case.

In December 1870, a brake and an omnibus were attached to the steamer, and with 45 passengers it proceeded along Canwick Road, Lincoln, at not less than 6 m.p.h., over a short and steep hump-backed bridge, to 1-in-9 Lindum Hill, which it climbed at 4 to 5 m.p.h. With its

Fig. 66. Engine and gearing of 'Advance'.
Steam Locomotion on Common Roads.

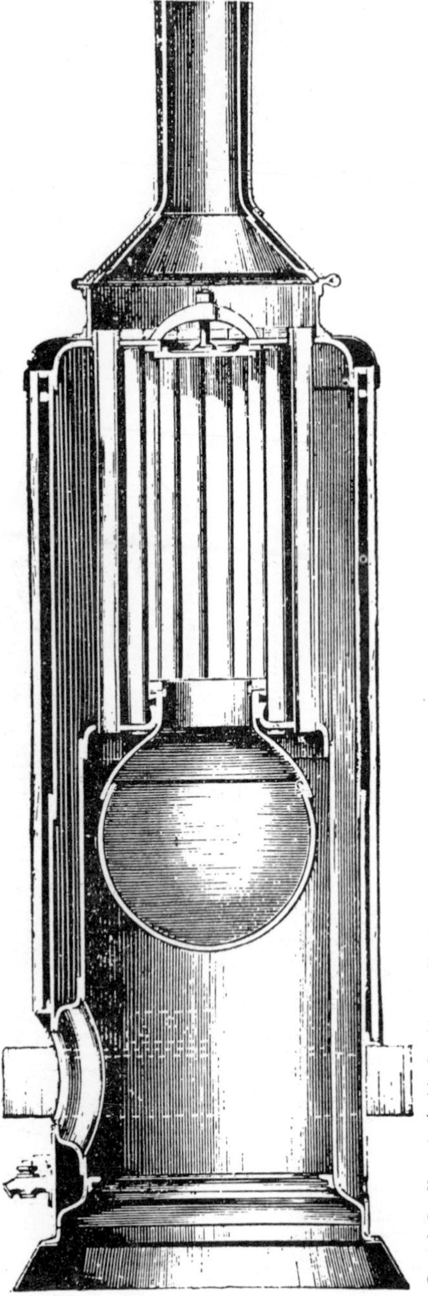

Fig. 67. The Thomson 'pot' boiler.
Steam Locomotion on Common Roads.

train it then turned in a circle of about 18 ft. inner diameter, and flew downhill at such a speed that runners could not keep up. From time to time it was checked and brought almost to a standstill, to show the braking capacity. The engine was then demonstrated for goods haulage, and also on soft ground where, despite sinking in from 2 to 5 in., it covered a measured mile in seven minutes.

However, on longer journeys the drawback was Thomson's pot boiler, shown in Fig. 67. The shell was of steel, $\frac{3}{8}$ in. thick, 2 ft. $9\frac{1}{2}$ in. diameter, and 7 ft. $9\frac{1}{2}$ in. high. The inner firebox was 2 ft. 3 in. diameter, containing the copper 'pot', 2 ft. inside diameter, and with a ring of tubes 3 ft. 4 in. long and $2\frac{1}{4}$ in. diameter. This pot, of course, cut down the combustion space enormously, and only allowed for one row of tubes for the gases to get to the smokebox, reducing the possible heating area badly. The result was that, even with good steam coal, the engine could not maintain pressure for a sustained period.

Moreover, Thomson did not at first appreciate the large grate area needed for burning wood fuel, and whereas Crompton wanted to use the Field type of boiler which had proved so successful in Merryweather fire engines, and in his own Indian-built road engine, the first two engines were fitted at Thomson's insistence with the pot boiler. They were built by Ransomes', who at this same time were building several smaller Thomson steamers for agricultural purposes.

By the middle of May 1871, the first engine, *Chenab* (Fig. 68), was ready for trials in the Ipswich area, but although coal was used for fuel, it became obvious that the boiler would never make sufficient steam on wood. In fact, the blast had to be sharpened so much that *Chenab* became a fire-thrower and set fire to the grandstand of Ipswich race-course, which the Government of India had to pay for.

But Ransomes wanted to show one of the new engines at the R.A.S.E. show at Wolverhampton, and off it went, still with the pot boiler. Meantime Crompton had arranged with Lewis Olrick to design and tender for the construction of different boilers of the same external dimensions, so as to be interchangeable with the pot boilers, and fitted with a sufficient number of Field tubes to give enough heating surface.

The bus shown in Fig. 68 had been built in Edinburgh to carry 130 people, 60 below and 70 above, but on the trip to Wolverhampton the lower deck was used as sleeping quarters, there being 15 or 16 people in the party. Crompton had recently married, and the group included his wife, the chief designer Oscar Bremme and his wife, a fitter, a fireman, and one or two boiler makers who had plenty of work on the eight-day trip! Irreverent people called this 'Lieut. Crompton's honeymoon trip'!

At the show itself, the engine was placed at the disposal of the judges, with the bus as their office, but the boiler constantly gave trouble, which gravely prejudiced the new vehicle's reputation. Moreover, the weather was very bad, with heavy rain and storms, and the cross-country trials course was reduced to a sea of mud, stiff in places, very liquid in others, in which loaded wagons sank to their axles, and even ordinary traction engines had difficulty with their spuds or paddles on. *Chenab* was not in for competition, but Ransomes' smaller Thomson engine *Sutherland* (Fig. 69) was, failing miserably. This was the agricultural type with horizontal engine in front of the boiler.

The Engineer's correspondent says fairly: '. . . many persons will at once and hastily jump to the conclusion that india-rubber tires are valueless . . . I never expected that india-rubber or other dry, smooth-surfaced wheels would or could traverse the ground actually run over. And no one would have expected any result but that which was actually obtained, if it had not been that the extravagant puffs which have appeared in *The Times*, and very many other journals, led people to believe that india-rubber possessed some mysterious powers . . .'

Burrell also had a Thomson engine there, but wisely declined to run it

Fig. 68. 'Chenab' and her omnibus.

Ransomes, Sims and Jefferies, Ltd.

through this quagmire, though his other 'orthodox' traction engine did quite well, through a very heavy rainstorm.

On the Thursday, when the traction engines were tried on a run of 16 miles to Stafford, and 16 miles back, *Chenab* was in sad disgrace. She was off after the slower engines, at 6.57 a.m., and after a stop of 6 min. to lower the funnel to pass under a railway arch, stopped at Coven, 5 miles out, to take water. 'This pump was dragged off the top of the omnibus, slid down a board, and planted in an old woman's garden . . . The hose was then popped into the old lady's well, without asking her consent. In a minute a good stream was pouring into our tank, and it was not till we

Fig. 69. Ransomes' agricultural engine 'Sutherland'.
The Practical Dictionary of Mechanics.

had got all the water required that our confiding hostess found that we had pumped her well dry. After this discovery it became expedient that we should proceed as quickly as possible . . . and after a slight difference of opinion between Lieut. Crompton and his boiler as to the pressure necessary to drive the *Chenab* had been settled in favour of the former, we started at 7.58. At 8.15 we passed Burrell's locomotive . . . and availed ourselves of the opportunity to extinguish the lagging of *Chenab's* boiler, which had taken fire at the smokebox. Thomson's pot boiler is the best I ever saw for burning off lagging . . . I may add here that the way in which Lieut. Crompton took his engine over heaps of stones by the roadside and into complicated holes and trenches when passing other engines was sufficient to startle weak nerves. I began to think that the *Chenab* had been designed *pour la chasse*.'

Further on, at Penkridge, water was again taken on, and '. . . there was a serious difficulty, indeed, between Lieut. Crompton and the boiler, which very nearly ended in the victory of the latter. The boiler would have it that 50 lb. pressure was all that was needed, Lieut. Crompton insisted on 75 lb. as a minimum. The contention was very sharp, but ended in the defeat of the boiler for the time'.

Sutherland had the fastest time for the 16-mile trip – 3 hrs. 35 min. exclusive of stops – among the official entrants, but *Chenab* made the trip in 2 hrs. 30 min.

The Engineer correspondent went off to watch the ploughing tackle at work 'for the amusement of the public', and then back to Stafford for the return journey where he found that Crompton had 'treated his boiler to a dose of red lead and oatmeal to stop a leak or leaks – let me say leaks. How the matter had been adjusted between the Lieutenant and his boiler I cannot pretend to say, but we had a fair pressure of steam on starting at 6 p.m., or thereabouts, and rattled along at a good pace along the wrong road: we smashed through boughs, and traversed paths unknown to the tire of india-rubber, for more than an hour . . . The mode of procedure was this: first we got up steam, and ran till it fell down again; then we stopped and pumped up the boiler; then we got up steam again as high as the boiler would let us: then we started and ran a little way, and repeated these operations over and over until we reached Four Ash's. Here the difficulty I have already alluded to as existing between Lieut. Crompton and his boiler assumed very serious proportions. Early in the day he had blown the spark catcher out of the chimney: now, here, far on in the evening, at Four Ash's, more than five miles from home, he discovered he had melted off the copper nozzle of his blowpipe. A contest now commenced between the boiler and everybody as to whether it would or would not make steam. In the end everybody was beaten, Lieut. Crompton went to bed *in* the Omnibus, his men went to bed *on* the Omnibus. Under the circumstances I thought I would walk on. I did so, and reached Wolverhampton after a walk of four or five miles, which I did not want, over a very pretty road which I did not wish to see; I amused myself *en route* by composing complimentary phrases concerning the *Chenab* and the pot boiler.'

Later there were trials on the high road of haulage power, and up an average gradient of 1 in 20.39 the 8 h.p. *Sutherland* easily distinguished herself by hauling three loaded wagons and a portable engine, gross weight hauled 26 tons 4 cwt., plus 10½ tons for the engine, comfortably and easily. Another try, with an additional load of 11 tons 4¾ cwt., could not be continued on the 1 in 20: five tons was dropped and she proceeded for a few minutes, but continuous slipping brought her to a stop.

The Aveling 10 h.p. with iron wheels was now tried, and hauled the *original* load, with tremendous slipping and great effort, up only two-thirds of the original course of 1,900 ft. in 29 min. as against 10 min. for the rubber tyres.

Meantime, *Sutherland's* hind wheels had been changed for smooth-surfaced cast-iron ones, but with an 18-ton load, slipping brought the train to a standstill on the 1 in 22. Reducing the load by dropping the 5-ton portable enabled her to continue easily over the remainder of the course. Thus on a good metalled road she was able to haul more than double the load with rubber tyres than she could on cast iron.

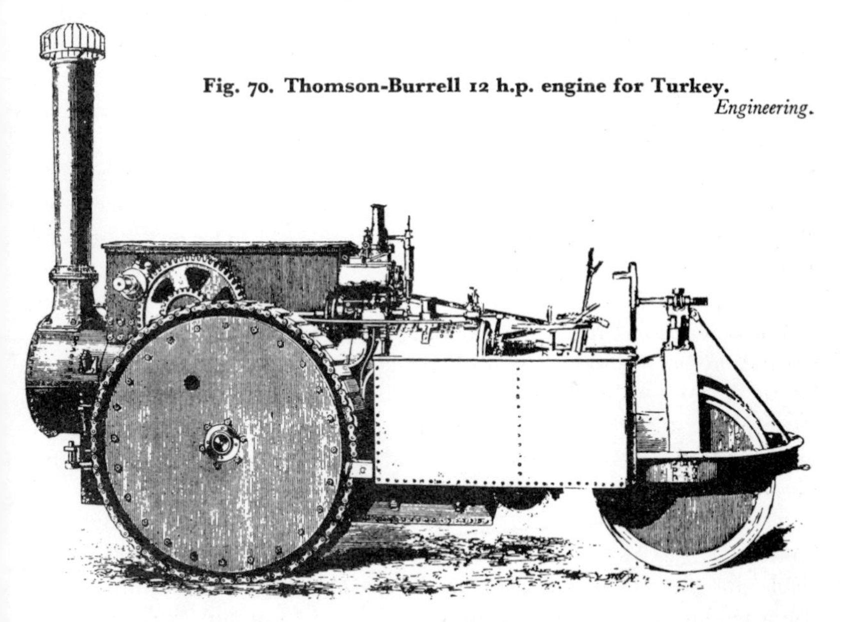

Fig. 70. Thomson-Burrell 12 h.p. engine for Turkey. *Engineering.*

Engineering pointed out, however, that cast-iron tyres were by no means as good for adhesion as wrought iron, especially with the cross ribs now coming into use: '. . . we nevertheless readily admit that on a hard macadamised road there is a decided advantage as far as adhesion is concerned, attendant upon the employment of the india-rubber tyres. But there is another and very important element to be taken into consideration, namely, the cost of these latter tyres . . . The price of the *Sutherland* with india-rubber tyres, is 750*l.*, while that of its competitor, Messrs. Aveling and Porter's 10-horse engine, is but 390*l.*, and in proportion to the capital invested, the latter therefore did by far the greater amount of work.'

This journal concluded 'that india-rubber tyres are quite unadapted for use on agricultural locomotive engines, but that if they could be manufactured at far less cost than at present, or if their endurance for a long period of years could be insured, they might be beneficially adopted in cases where the main work of an engine would lie over hard macadamised roads'. Nevertheless, a special medal was awarded to *Sutherland* for its excellent performance.

Crompton, in disgust at the pot boiler, sent *Chenab* back to Ipswich in disgrace, by rail, and pressed on with the preparation of *Ravee*, the second engine, and especially the fitting of the Field boiler. Meanwhile, Burrell was also extremely dissatisfied with the pot boiler, but his solution was to fit a locomotive type, with twin horizontal cylinders. For the last few days of the Worcester show this engine (Fig. 70) was exhibited, though not in time for the trials, and *The Engineer* pronounced it '. . . in our opinion, one of the best designed road locomotives yet constructed'.

Built for the Turkish Government, the engine was of 12 n.h.p., and the boiler was balanced about the driving axle, with a horizontal hand-wheel on the footplate to work a worm, worm-wheel, and a curved rack attached to the firebox side, so that on a long hill the boiler could be brought horizontal. *Engineering* comments: '. . . we expect that in practice the appliances for inclining the boiler will be very little used . . .' and this proved to be the case, though Burrell built several engines with this arrangement (originally used by Smith of Coven) before discarding it. The firebox door was in the side, but is hidden by the bunker, in the engraving which, by the way, was made before the boiler and smokebox lagging was fitted.

The double cylinders were 7¼ in. by 10 in., with valve chest between, working at 150 p.s.i., and dome with Salter safety valve on top – an extra 'lock-up' safety being fitted on the firebox top to prevent tampering by the attendants. It was not unknown for them to obtain extra power by screwing down the spring of the 'open' valve, and, regrettably, it was not unknown for the boiler to explode and blow itself, the engine and them to bits. Hence many portables and some tractions, especially for abroad, had the lock-up valve fitted.

The eccentrics were forged in one piece with the wrought-iron crankshaft, which carried a sliding pinion at each end to give two gear ratios on the steel countershaft below. Outside the spur wheels, at either end of the countershaft, a pinion engaged a spur wheel bolted to each hind wheel, giving double drive to the hind wheels. All gearing was of malleable iron. No compensating gear was fitted, but the drive could be disconnected at either side on sharp curves.

The driving wheels were shod with Thomson tyres, 6 ft. 1½ in. by 14 in., and there were two wrought-iron leading wheels, 4 ft. 2 in. diameter, placed close together on a short axle. A single vertical pin rose from the front axle, surrounded by a helical spring, the steering being effected by worm and worm-wheel. Normal speeds were 4 and 8 m.p.h., and the total weight was 8 tons.

A very similar engine was built by Burrell for passenger service in Greece, with an omnibus designed to carry 50 persons. Unlike Crompton's bus, this had four wheels, but it should be explained that Crompton had

Fig. 71. Burrell engine for Russia.
Steam Locomotion on Common Roads.

bought his two-wheeler second-hand as a bargain, and the steam trains actually used later in India had four-wheeled buses.

Still another Burrell engine, built in 1871 for Russia, is seen in Fig. 71, and there are several improvements. One of these is the new Burrell-Thomson chain armour, with the shoes now extended and bent in at the ends, to clip over the angle of the rim which, says Fletcher, 'answered well in practice'. The twin cylinders are at the smokebox end, and a flywheel is fitted. The single front wheel is 3 ft. 6 in. diameter, carried in a fork with eight helical springs at each side. The drivers are 5 ft. diameter, and the cylinders 6 in. by 10 in., with a working pressure of 130 p.s.i.

In this engraving, by the way, the steersman is George Fowell, Burrell's leading draughtsman, whose father had his own firm and produced some handsome engines. As the design necessitated, the firedoor is again in the side of the firebox, and the stoker is appropriately placed. He is seen grasping the handle of the boiler-levelling device, the curved racks of which, attached to the firebox, are well in evidence.

Fletcher describes trials in September 1871, witnessed by officers of the Turkish Service and others, in which the 12-horse engine, itself weighing 10½ tons, hauled a 37-ton load up and down the streets of Thetford (including a 1-in-8 slope) at 5 m.p.h. Later in the evening, 'men and boys swarmed over the 'bus like bees', and the engine drew the load uphill and down at from 9 to 12 m.p.h. After witnessing these trials, *The Engineer* said: 'No difficulty whatever exists in applying steam on common roads to the purposes of passenger traffic'.

Burrells' made a considerable number of these fast road locomotives for foreign governments – the law would not permit their proper use in the country of their origin! – and a good number of similar design for farm purposes in Great Britain. These all had the cylinders at the smokebox end, and many of the agricultural engines were on wrought-iron wheels shod with strakes instead of rubbers.

Meantime, Lieut. Crompton's second engine, *Ravee*, was ready for trials with the Field boiler (and an efficient spark arrester!). This made ample steam when using wood fuel, and it was necessary to block off the centre of the grate when using coal. There was also an adjustable cone on the blast nozzle, so that the opening could be varied to suit the fuel in use. The grate area was 11¼ sq. ft. for wood burning, and the heating surface 177 sq. ft. The arrangement of the boiler is shown in Fig. 72, though here the chimney is considerably fore-shortened.

Before Thomson would consent to the other engines being fitted with the Field boiler in place of his 'pot', he desired Crompton to give *Ravee* as extensive a test as *Chenab* had had. This would also allow continuous high-speed tests of the engines and tyres, which had not been possible with *Chenab* owing to the boiler troubles. Accordingly, Crompton decided on a run from Ipswich to Edinburgh and back, which would enable Thomson to see for himself what the engine could do.

This epic journey started at 3.40 a.m. on Friday, September 15th, 1871, from Ransomes, Sims and Head's yard at Ipswich. Loaded with 1 ton of coal and 375 gallons of water, *Ravee* weighed about 14 tons, and the loaded omnibus from 5 to 6 tons including tools, luggage, extra coal, etc. The driving wheels were 6 ft. diameter, the cylinders 8 in. by 10 in., and the gear ratios were 3¾ and 12 to 1 respectively. At 10 m.p.h. the crankshaft

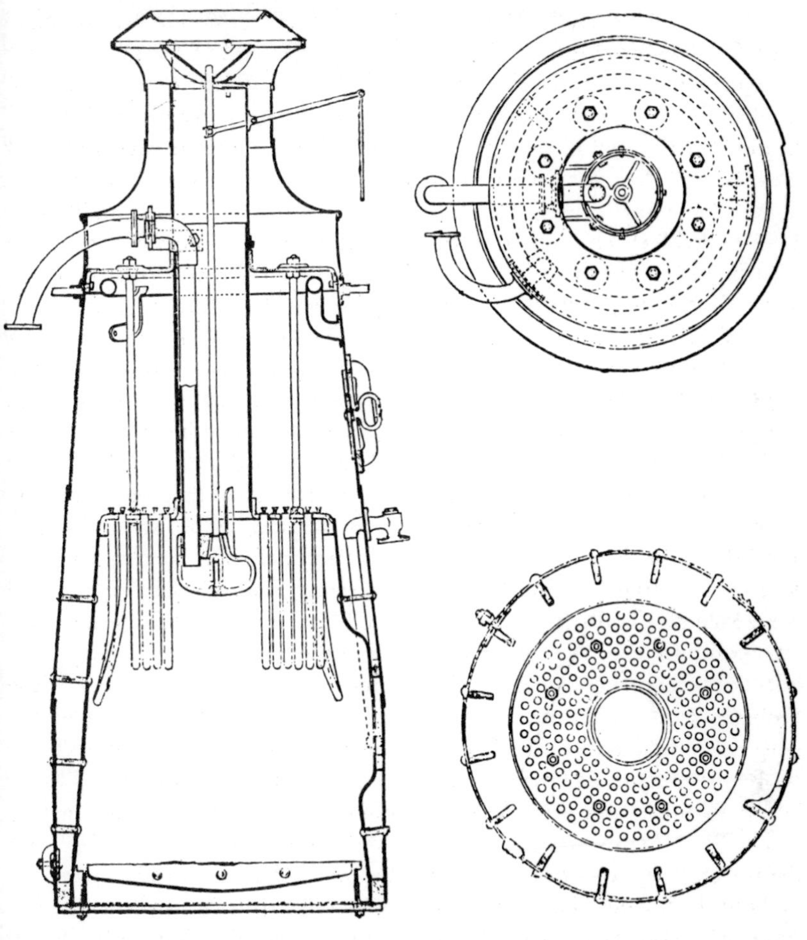

Fig. 72. Arrangement of the Field boiler of 'Ravee'.
The Engineer.

revolutions were 157 per minute. With the centre of the grate blocked off by firebrick, the area left was 7.6 sq. ft. The staff consisted of Lieut. Crompton, one fitter, one fireman, and a driver who was a lad of seventeen.

Water supply was often a problem – at Stowmarket only 250 gallons was obtainable, and another stop had to be made eight miles further on. At Newmarket, the crew had to turn to and fill up with buckets from a cistern in a pub backyard, since the hose would not reach. Ely was reached at 6.15 p.m., after ploughing along all day on a road 3 to 4 in. deep in dust and flints.

Crompton writes: 'We coaled at Ely, and got a guide for Peterborough – such a designing ruffian! his sole mission appeared to be to guide us into scrapes. Our troubles commenced about ten miles after leaving Ely. Our guide piloted us into a *cul de sac*, terminating in a triangular piece of ground, as boggy and treacherous as you please. As its greatest diameter was about 30 ft. it required some manœuvring to twist the train round and come out again. A few miles further on we crossed a very indifferent wooden bridge. The wooden bridges in the Fens are most of them built on this plan: The piers are of piles, and the roadway is laid on 14-in. square oak balks, untrussed in any way. When the spans are short this is all very well, but when they get to 18 ft. and 20 ft. as in the case with some of the bridges near Peterborough, traction engines had better go round. However, Meeple Bridge was judged to be safe. Shortly after crossing it, and a second one over the Forty Foot river, our guide insisted upon our turning sharp round to the left, and taking the road along the top of the bank of the Forty Foot. This road was tolerably wide at first, but gradually narrowed until it was only about 10 ft. at the top, with a steep slope on one side to the river, on the other to the Fen ditch. The surface consisted of a thin coating of metal laid on the springy Fen soil of the bank, and the whole rose and fell under the engine like the waves of the sea. It was an anxious time for the steersman, as he had only a margin of a few inches outside each driving wheel, and if he came within this margin ever so little the side of the bank immediately began to cut and slide away under the wheel. We had ten miles of this fearful road, but to the honour of the rubber tire, be it said, it never once failed us in a situation where a slip or failure to bite for one single instant would have been a very serious matter.'

The Forty Foot water was brackish, and caused bad boiler priming, and then eventually at 2 a.m. a Field tube burst, due to defective welding, and put the fire out. They had run 69 miles from Ipswich, in 12 hrs. 9 min. travelling time, at 5.67 m.p.h. After resting, and allowing the boiler to cool off, the burst tube was replaced, and the journey recommenced at 12.30 p.m. next day, heading for the Great North Road at Sawtry.

'After twelve miles of cross-country lanes we reached the much desired road, and found such a change in the rolling resistance! The engine appeared to leap forward directly we got on to its hard level surface.' The chain armour was removed from the wheels, and they went ahead 17 miles to Wansford in under two hours. Here they put up at Stebbington House, whose owner entertained them over the Sunday. The average speed was 6.8 miles per hour on this short run.

On the Monday, setting off at 6 a.m., the party reached Doncaster at 11.30 p.m., 83½ miles in 10 hrs. 25 min. running time: speed 8 m.p.h. 'We

IPSWICH TO EDINBURGH 15th-19th September and 1st-4th October, 1871	Ipswich to Edinburgh	Ipswich to 40-foot River	40-foot River to Wansford	Wansford to Doncaster	Doncaster to Azerley	Azerley to Darlington	Darlington to Wooler	Wooler to Edinburgh	MOST ECONOMICAL RUN—RIPON TO DARLINGTON	AVERAGE PERFORMANCE WITH CHAIN ARMOUR ON	AVERAGE PERFORMANCE WITH CHAIN ARMOUR OFF
Total fuel consumed in lbs.	29,148	7,392	1,792	4,704	3,052	2,016	5,488	4,704	1,568	18,696	10,552
Total water evaporated in lbs.	137,850	28,500	8,900	21,150	16,400	10,650	27,500	24,750	8,750	86,280	51,870
Total distance traversed in miles	422.5	69	29	83.5	53	40	78	70	35	229	193
Time actually travelling	77h. 26m.	12h. 9m.	4h. 19m.	10h. 25m.	9h. 28m.	5h. 22m.	18h. 45m.	16h. 58m.	4h. 17m.	51h. 1m.	26h. 55m.
Engine standing under steam	72h. 23m.	11h. 51m.	5h. 26m.	7h. 30m.	6h. 40m.	5h. 8m.	20h. 15m.	15h. 32m.	2h. 58m.	—	—
Average speed in miles per hour	5.45	5.67	6.8	8.016	5.59	7.453	4.16	4.11	8.5	4.4	7.1
Gross load in tons	19	19	19	19	19	19	19	19	19	19	19
Mile Tons	8027.5	1311	551	1586.5	1007	760	1482	1330	665	4351	3676.5
Lbs. of coal per ton per mile	3.631	5.638	3.25	2.96	3.00	2.65	3.70	3.53	2.36	4.29	2.87
Lbs. of water per ton per mile	17.17	21.739	16.15	13.33	16.28	14.01	17.9	18.60	13.1	19.8	14.0
Lbs. of water evaporated by 1 lb. coal ...	4.729	3.85	4.96	4.5	5.37	5.28	5.01	5.26	5.7	4.61	4.91

EDINBURGH TO IPSWICH 1st-4th and 7th-10th November, 1871	Edinburgh to Ipswich	Edinburgh to Kelso	Kelso to Morpeth	Morpeth to Darlington	Darlington to Tanfield	Tanfield to Doncaster	Doncaster to Grantham	Grantham to Wansford	Wansford to Ipswich
Total fuel consumed in lbs.	25,312	3,584	3,920	3,584	2,464	3,584	2,240	2,240	3,696
Total water evaporated in lbs.	144,300	18,400	20,550	20,850	14,300	21,150	13,250	11,650	24,150
Total distance traversed in miles	424	45	61	48	35	59	53	27	95.5
Time actually travelling	61h. 13m.	7h. 42m.	9h. 5m.	9h. 19m.	5h. 32m.	8h. 37m.	5h. 36m.	5h. 31m.	9h. 51m.
Engine standing under steam	42h. 3m.	6h. 33m.	5h. 28m.	6h. 11m.	3h. 13m.	5h. 58m.	2h. 49m.	4h. 47m.	7h. 24m.
Average speed in miles per hour	6.9	5.84	6.71	5.15	6.33	6.85	9.46	4.90	9.69
Gross load in tons	20	19.6	19.6	19.6	20	21.5	20.75	20.75	20.5
Mile Tons	8480	882	1195.6	940.8	700	1268.5	1099.75	560.25	1957.75
Lbs. of coal per ton per mile	2.98	4.06	3.27	3.80	3.52	2.825	2.03	4.00	1.88
Lbs. of water per ton per mile	17.01	20.84	17.18	22.16	20.43	16.67	12.04	20.79	12.33
Lbs. of water evaporated by 1 lb. coal ...	5.7	5.13	5.24	5.81	5.8	5.9	5.91	5.20	6.53

should easily have averaged twelve miles an hour, but for the frequent stoppages for horses, the slow speeds through villages, etc.' On this run, the tyre on the steering wheel proved defective, and it had to be removed the following day at Boroughbridge, 42 miles further on.

Wooden felloes, hooped with iron tyres, were substituted, but despite the front fork being sprung, it now proved impossible to travel at more than 5 m.p.h. 'without fearful jolting and fracture of the steersman's teeth'. That day's journey was concluded at Azerly Hall: average speed 5.6 m.p.h. Here they waited two or three days for the new tyre, and then several days for the exceptionally heavy rainfall to lift.

But this it refused to do, and Crompton set off again at 8 a.m. on October 2nd, making a good run to Darlington at 8.5 m.p.h. The following day, seven hours were occupied in straightening a connecting rod at Ferryhill, but *Ravee* reached Durham at 9 p.m.

Carrying on through the night, Newcastle High Level Bridge was reached at 3.10 a.m. but permission to cross was refused. They went down to the Low Level Bridge and then up the steep and greasy 1 in 13 gradient of Dean Street at 6 m.p.h. 'Coaled at Seaton Bourne colliery, at the very pit mouth, and reached Morpeth at 10.40. After breakfasting, and coaling, we set out across the bleak moorland road to Wooler, and not often before, I suppose, was such a road traversed by a traction engine. The road is one series of ascending and descending inclines, most of them long and steep. Outside Wooler we had an amusing passage of arms with the toll-gate man, who deliberately refused to open his gate. The head-lamp was removed, and the flange of the framing of the engine placed gently against the gate: it was wonderful to see how easily the gate opened, without a murmur, I should say – and the tollman's face!'

This run of 78 miles occupied 19¼ hours' travelling, plus 20¼ hours in halts for food, water, and coal, as well as for straightening the rod. The rain had been continuous, and there had been constant gradients, and frequent stoppages for horses, so the average speed was rather lower at 4.05 m.p.h.

The remaining 70 miles to Edinburgh were run in 16 hrs. 58 min., at an average of 4.11 m.p.h., in bad conditions of road and weather. At Lootray Hill, however, an incline about 3½ miles long, varying between 1 in 25 and 1 in 17, the engine made a fine ascent, finishing with both more steam and water than at the start.

Nearly three weeks were spent in Edinburgh, giving Thomson ample time to inspect the train, and for tests of haulage power to be carried out, both for his satisfaction and for that of Mr. Monteath, the Director-General of the Indian Post Office. One of these included a 26½-ton load, including wagons, being hauled up a 1 in 17 incline over a mile long – with the engine itself, a gross load of over 40 tons.

The return journey of 424 miles was accomplished in under nine days, in the actual running time of 61 hrs. 13 min., at an average of 6.9 m.p.h. The table (page 117) will be found interesting as giving all important data. It also shows how careful Crompton was in assessing the value of this epic trip – the first really long-distance journey undertaken by mechanical road transport which, had the authorities of the time been alert and far-seeing, could have pointed the way to developments of unparalleled importance.

The fastest speed yet attained on the public roads was made going north, on the way to Doncaster, when *Ravee* made more than 25 m.p.h., overtaking and passing several goods trains at points where the Great North Road and the Great Northern Railway ran parallel. Incidentally, through the influence of the Government of India Crompton had a special permit to exceed the speed permitted by the 'Red Flag Act', otherwise he would have collected a good crop of summonses in his 850 miles!

It was also after this fast run, without chain armour, that the engine and bus were first noticed to have acquired a high static electrical charge, so that anyone touching it received a startling shock! The cure, as with steam wagons later, was to suspend a wire or chain to touch the ground.

Soon after this, Crompton returned to India to prepare premises and make other arrangements for the steam train, leaving his assistant Muirhead to complete the other engines and to follow him when ready. This was in the spring of 1872, and from then on the engines did great service, until the spread of light railways caused the Government of India to decide that the road steamers were not longer necessary – despite a very favourable report from a Committee of Inquiry.

Nevertheless, this experiment, in its few brief years of existence, helped to solve many problems, including the use of rubber tyres, and the coupling and manœuvring of trains of as many as nineteen vehicles with over 70 tons' load. It was also directly responsible for the extensive use of steam transport in the Boer War, when Lord Roberts called in Crompton to organise it in 1899. In turn, his work so impressed the War Office that he was sent home to England to organise mechanised transport for the Army as a whole.

The Thomson road steamers and their rubber tyres undoubtedly became an unqualified success, and they did play a very valuable part in the development of road transport. How different that development could have been, if successive Governments had been alive to the possibilities not only of these engines, but of so many other equally valuable schemes!

12

INTO THE SEVENTIES

Oftentimes an Uncertaintie hindered our going on so merrily, but by persevering the Difficultie was mastered, and the new Triumph gave stronger Heart unto us. RALEIGH

BESIDES THE THOMSON STEAMERS, the 1870's saw the evolution of many ideas, some good and some not so good, as in the previous years. One of the most important of these was Aveling's invention of the horn-plate. Up to now, following portable engine practice, the crankshaft had been carried in cast-iron brackets bolted or riveted to the boiler top, and this gave rise to trouble when, with the to-and-fro working of the motion, the rivets or bolts became slack in their holes.

Aveling's patent specified that the sideplates of the firebox were to be extended upwards and backwards to carry the bearings of the crankshaft, countershaft, and hind axle. Fig. 73 is a photograph of the first engine to be so fitted, which was exhibited at the Royal Show at Oxford in 1870, and we now see the appearance of the modern engine becoming apparent in many ways. These 'hornplates' also relieved the boiler of much strain, and effected a material reduction in weight. They were used eventually by all other makers.

Another feature of this engine is the steerage, again as used on all modern machines, and this was the first Aveling to be fitted with a lever for engaging or disengaging the single gearing. We are fortunate that an engine of this type has been preserved by the Road Locomotive Society; it was completely restored by Aveling-Barford Ltd. in 1954, and the R.L.S. presented it to the Science Museum. This is engine No. 721, built in 1871; *Engineering* said of the same type: 'The gearing is very strong and simply arranged, and has a ratio of 17 to 1, while the driving axle is fitted with compensating gear . . .'

The wheel rims are still cast-iron, with the spokes cast into them as well as the hubs, but the familiar strakes are riveted to the rims. 'Old-fashioned' features still include the Watt-type governor, the Salter safety valves, and the cast-iron smokebox.

Aveling also exhibited an engine fitted with a crane at the Oxford show, and this, as shown in Fig. 74, was very similar apart from the crane

Fig. 73. The first Aveling 'hornplate' engine.

A. R. Dibben, Esq.

Fig. 74. The Aveling crane engine.

John L. French, Esq.

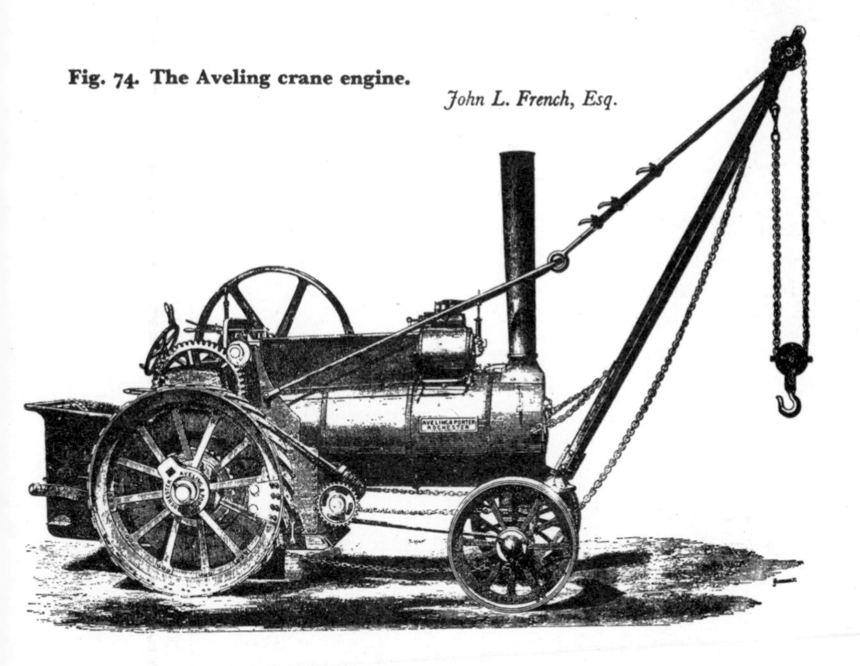

Fig. 75. The Aveling Steam Sapper.
A. R. Dibben, Esq.

fittings. The jib is built from T-iron, with a ball casting at the foot dropped into a socket cast on the perch bracket. The winding drum was mounted on the second shaft, and could be locked to it by a band brake, whilst the hoisting chain passed down and round a guide pulley on the hind axle, and thence forward as seen.

It should be mentioned that this was not the first Aveling crane engine, for *The Artizan* describes one at work in Chatham Dockyard in 1865, lifting and carrying 6-in. armour plating weighing 6½ tons for the frigate *Bellerophon*, and lifting and moving a propeller weighing several tons. Because of the danger of fire from shavings and chips, this engine was fitted with a spark catcher and a special ashpan.

The 1871 crane engine was fitted with the Bridges Adams' spring wheels, in which india-rubber blocks were sandwiched between an inner and outer rim, being held by an angle ring on each side riveted to the latter. The spokes were riveted to the flange of the inner T-ring, and the drive to the outer rim was taken by a drag link from the T-ring to the plate seen riveted to the outside angle. Fletcher says: 'This wheel is simple and has proved durable', but the cost of the india-rubber was too great to compensate for the advantages gained.

In 1871 Aveling introduced his 'Steam Sapper', specially constructed for the Government as a result of the deliberations of a committee set up to consider the advisability of using traction engines on military service. It was a light engine of 6 n.h.p., specially designed so as not to overload the pontoon bridges it might have to cross. The first of the class was at the Wolverhampton trials; it had a single cylinder 7¾ in. by 10 in., worked by a loco-type boiler at 115 p.s.i. The hind wheels were of wrought iron, 5 ft. diameter by 10 in. broad, and the front ones of wood, 3 ft. 6 in. diameter by 6 in.

The crankshaft was 2¾ in. diameter, and the hind axle 4¼ in. diameter; the drive was by pinion to a spur wheel on a stub-shaft, and thence by pitch chain to the hind axle, as in the Aveling of the previous decade, in fact. In full working order the engine weighed only 5 tons 4½ cwt., and it was priced at £300 or, with Bridges Adams' wheels, at £340. (Aveling's 10 h.p. engine at Wolverhampton cost £390.)

Both the Aveling engines did well in the trials: at one place the little engine 'took itself and its load (of 5½ tons) through a place literally knee-deep in stiff mud, in which the wagon sunk to the axles'. The 10-horse engine also took a load of 9 tons non-stop through a gap, in which 'such was the depth to which the wagon wheels sunk, that they could not revolve, and the wagons proceeded for six inches at a time with the front wheels not turning, but simply dragged through by sheer force'.

The Steam Sapper was still thought to be rather heavier than it should be, and more rigorous pruning brought the working weight down to just over 4¾ tons. On test, the engine drew up Star Hill at Rochester, a gradient of from 1 in 11 to 1 in 22, a gross load of more than 15 tons, 'without any slipping of consequence, but it is probable that on the steepest part of the hill she was loaded to the last ounce'. On the friction brake, running at 160 r.p.m., this 6 n.h.p. engine developed 36.7 *actual* horse power, and on the indicator showed 41.19 horse power. So much for 'nominal' h.p.!

In Fig. 75 we see a Steam Sapper specially equipped with Aveling and Greig's hind wheels. These had rubber tyres fitted in short segments, with a piece of angle iron riveted to the rim transversely between each segment. In this way, the tyre was prevented from creeping round the rim, and at the same time if a segment got damaged, it was quickly and cheaply replaced. Steel shoes were fitted to protect the rubber. Incidentally, the name 'Greig' associated with that of Aveling in this patent bears witness to the friendly relations between Fowlers' and Avelings'; David Greig had

been associated early with John Fowler, as we know, and the surname was to be prominent among 'Fowler' patents for years to come.

The wooden front wheels in Fig. 75 are also fitted with rubber tyres in segmental form: it would appear that the segments are held down by metal clips at each side, but the details are not clear, and I have not been able to trace any contemporary description, unfortunately.

Besides being used by the British Army, Steam Sappers were purchased by the French, Italian and Russian Governments. They were used for hauling guns and supplies, for pumping water for camps, and similar duties. We read of one engine, on a coal consumption of 6 cwt., pumping 35,000 gallons of water per day from a spring, through a main ¾ mile long with a head of 110 ft., into ten different camps on a hill. 'This effected a saving of at least 70 pairs of horses.' At least one engine was mounted on flanged wheels for shunting work on sidings.

To anticipate somewhat, the first use of mechanical transport under actual war conditions, as against manœuvres, occurred in 1876–8, when Russia was at war with Turkey. Russia purchased twelve traction engines, of which two were built in Russia at the Maltzef Works in Briansk, three were Clayton and Shuttleworth, one was a Fowler, and six were Aveling Steam Sappers. They were worked for less than half the time, but they paid for themselves outright and also saved £1,000 over the cost of animal transport in moving more than 9,000 tons.

Now back to 1871, to Fig. 76, and to further evidence of collaboration between Aveling and Fowler. For this unusual three-wheeled Fowler was not only shod with the already-described Aveling and Greig wheels, but also used Aveling's hornplate invention.

There were four examples of this class of Fowler at the Wolverhampton 'Royal', two being of 12 n.h.p., and two of 6 n.h.p. All were single-cylinder machines, with a shapely dome embodied in the steam-jacketed cylinder, and with the motion enclosed in side-plates, and flywheel plated too, 'so that no movable part is visible which could frighten horses, and thus cause accidents on ordinary roads'. One of each size of engine was on Aveling and Greig hind wheels, and the others were on wrought iron ones, as shown in the cross section (Fig. 77).

One of the engines also had a 'double' chimney, into the outer chamber of which the exhaust steam was discharged before going to the blast pipe. In this way, the exhaust was made much more silent, but it must have been correspondingly less effective for blast purposes; it does not seem that this experiment was very protracted, for we do not hear any more about it.

The 12-horse engine had a cylinder 10½ in. by 12 in.; the total heating surface of the boiler was 142 sq. ft., with a working pressure of 100 p.s.i.,

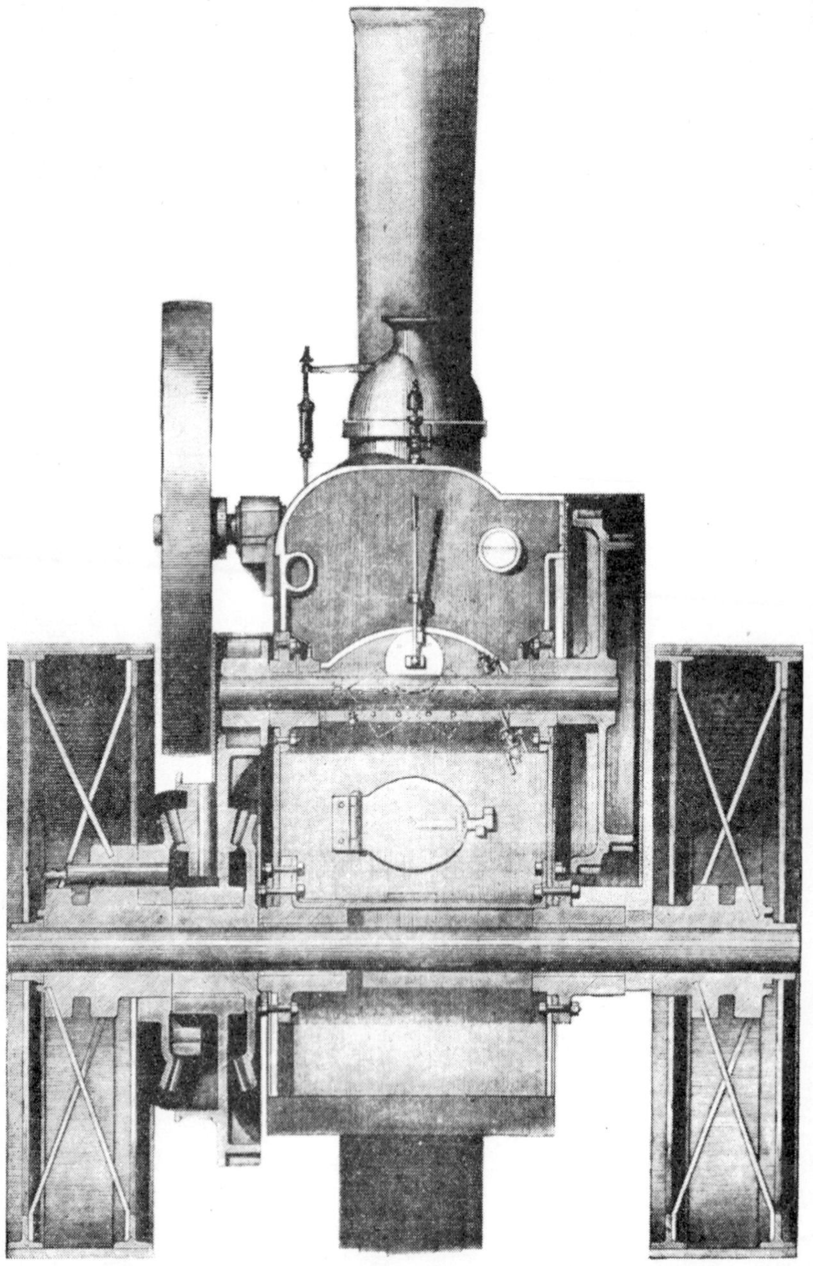

Fig. 77. Cross-section at hind axle of Fowler three-wheeler.
The Engineer.

the flywheel was 4 ft. 6 in. diameter, and the hind wheels were 6 ft. diameter by 18 in. wide. Total weight in working order was 11 tons. On the 6-horse engine the corresponding figures were 7½ in. by 10 in., 115 sq. ft., and 100 p.s.i.; flywheel 4 ft. diameter, and hind wheels 5 ft. by 14 in.; weight 7½ tons.

Both sizes had a belly tank as well as one in the tender, and the single front wheel turned in a ring or turntable, supporting the front end of the engine on balls or rollers. The steerage can be seen in the photograph, with a worm and worm-wheel, a vertical shaft mounted on the belly tank, and a chain-wheel at the foot of the shaft, with a pitch chain passing round and attached to the turntable rim.

Looking at the cross section (Fig. 78), the Aveling type hornplates may be seen, joined by a flanged transverse casting. The bearings for the three shafts are set in holes bored in the hornplates, and bolted in place. On the countershaft is a pinion, engaging a spur wheel which also forms the compensating centre. The latter carries three bevel-pinions (one of which with its pin may be seen under the flywheel), and these engage with the two bevel wheels, one at each side, thus forming the differential or compensating gear.

Note that the inner bevel wheel had an extended boss, on which the compensating centre revolved. This bevel wheel was keyed to the hind axle, and so also was the off-side hind wheel. On the other side, the bevel wheel was mounted on the extended boss of the hind wheel hub, and drove the wheel by means of the pin which passed through a hole bored in both the hub and the bevel wheel.

The object of this 'jack-in-the-box' gear – another popular name for it – was of course to allow the hind wheels to rotate at different speeds when cornering, whilst fully maintaining their propelling power. On soft or muddy ground, it possessed the disadvantage which the modern motorist finds in snow – namely, that if one wheel meets little or no resistance, it will spin madly (and dig itself in!), whilst the other wheel stands still. But the traction-engine men were smarter than car designers – they arranged for the differential to be lockable, so that *both* wheels were solidly driven. All that had to be done was to withdraw the driving pin from the hub and bevel wheel, and insert a longer one which passed through into a further hole bored in the compensating centre itself, so that they must all rotate together. Simple!

The advantages claimed for the single front wheel were 'a greater facility in turning, a safer position of the engine on narrow slippery roads, and a more quiet run, as a great number of the shocks received by a four-wheeled engine are avoided by the application of only three wheels'. At

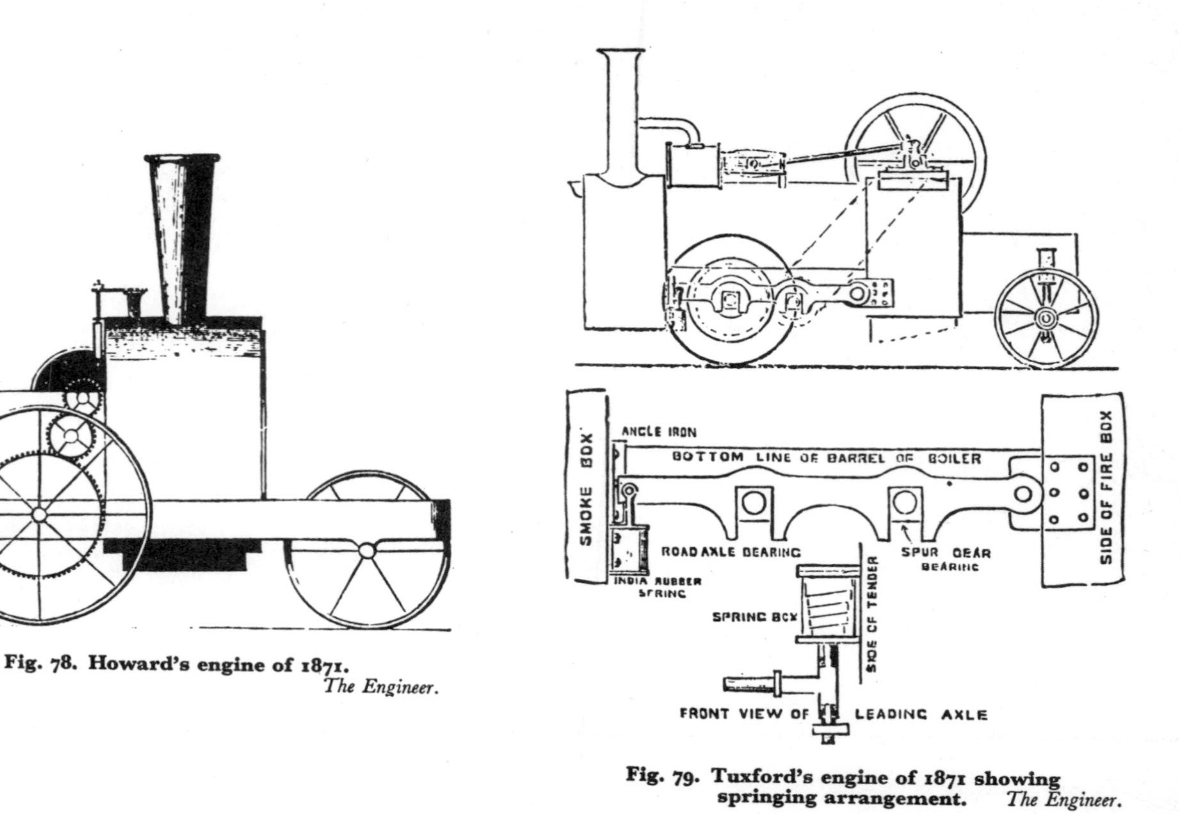

Fig. 78. Howard's engine of 1871. *The Engineer.*

Fig. 79. Tuxford's engine of 1871 showing springing arrangement. *The Engineer.*

the same time it was stated that four-wheeled engines could be supplied 'to work over more than ordinarily soft land, or for larger sizes'.

In actual practice, the three-wheeled engines were 'light on': the front of the engine tended to rear up when hauling a heavy load, thus losing steerage entirely. *Progress*, shown in the photo, was prone to this, especially when going uphill, and eventually was converted to four wheels to increase the weight and steering effort. She was owned by the Cheadle Carrying Company, used for general haulage in Staffordshire, though at the time of the picture being taken, *Progress* was on pleasure bent, pulling three wagon-loads of passengers on a Sunday-school outing!

Turning to other engines at Wolverhampton, J. and F. Howard of Bedford had two ploughing engines on show about which *The Engineer* correspondent made some rather caustic comments, on several counts. Firstly the appearance (Fig. 78) 'which reminds one at first sight of a miniature set of reversing rolling mill gearing, combined with a gipsy cart . . . One of the judges, I am told, cried out in the delight of his heart . . . that "a thing of beauty was a joy for ever".'

Secondly, both engines stripped a gear wheel simultaneously – 'just the sort of accident that used to occur in the infancy of steam ploughing'. And thirdly: 'Part of the afternoon was spent by a fitter in cutting off about three-sixteenths of an inch of lap from the slide valve. I think this kind of adjustment would be better done at home. It is certain that the valve must have either been very defective when it left Bedford, or else that it is very defective now. Cutting three-sixteenths of an inch off each end of a small valve is equivalent to cutting six inches off a man. Either the engine or the man will find the change effected to be enormous. The steering wheel . . . is worked from the footplate by a steersman, who cannot see where he is going except by taking a sight like a gunner along the side of the boiler. Possibly steersmen acquire in time an intuitive perception of the way they ought to go.'

Further criticism concerned the boiler, and the slenderness of the crank-shaft and hind axle. Finally, steam was got up for trying the engine on the brake. 'The preliminary canter had just commenced, when with a loud crash the flywheel parted in two pieces right across the diameter.' A solid disc wheel with a heavy rim, it burst as the result of contraction, and when the halves were laid together, they met at the rim, but were ½ in. apart at the centre.

Tuxfords were exhibiting a 10-horse engine (Fig. 79), and our lively correspondent found 'many good points about this engine . . . but the slide valve was wretchedly set, the cylinder scarcely getting any steam at one end'. He also complained bitterly about the firm's place in the show-yard,

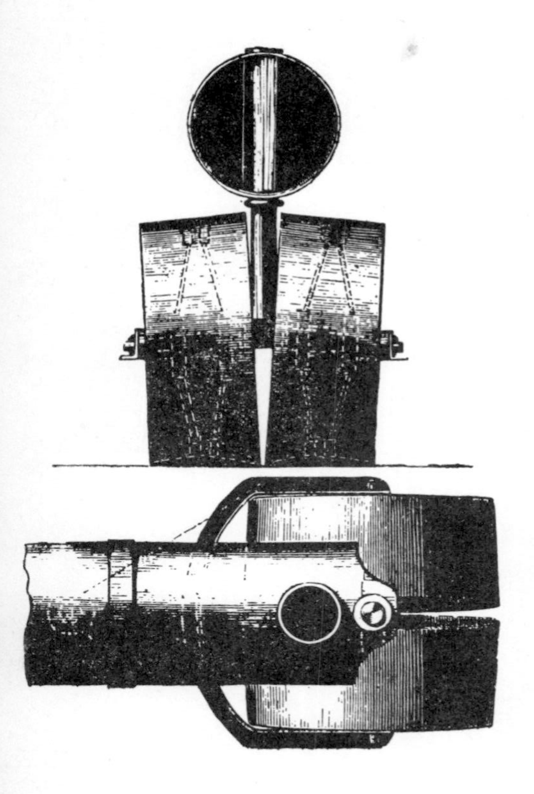

Fig. 80. The new design of Aveling roller.

The Engineer.

where '. . . it is impossible to move about except on planks, which go squash, squash, in the soft, slimy mud at every step. Rheumatism stares you in the face, catarrh peeps round the corner'.

It will be seen that Tuxfords had abandoned the steeple-type engine for tractions (though it was still used on portables) and were now using a steam-jacketed cylinder, which was 9 in. by 12 in., on top of the boiler. The firebox end of the engine ran first, and carried a round-fronted tender for the steersman and driver. Stub axles were still used for the front wheels, the vertical rods to which they were forged bearing on helical springs carried in the cylindrical casings. Fig. 79 shows the arrangement (at the bottom), and also that of the springing of the hind axle.

In this, two side frames were pivoted on brackets riveted to the firebox, being steadied by a pair of short angle irons attached to the smokebox, which end of the engine was hung from the frames by two rods, one at each side, bearing on india-rubber springs set in cast-iron boxes. These frames carried the bearings for the hind axle and the countershaft. The latter was driven at a 1 to 2 ratio by chain from the crankshaft, and drove the axle through spur gears with a 1 to 6 ratio.

Later in the year, at the Smithfield Club Show at Islington, there was an engine built by a firm named Ashby, Jeffrey and Luke, on which *Engineering* made the following comment: 'Engineers desirous to know how long a piece of overhanging shafting with a pinion at the end *can* be used for driving the wheels of a traction engine are recommended to examine this exhibit. When they see the distance which in this case exists between the driving pinion and the nearest bearing they will probably be surprised and delighted.' *The Engineer* contents itself by remarking that this engine 'is remarkable for little else than a boldness of design bordering on the foolhardy . . . the pinion being at least 14 in. distant from any bearing whatsoever'.

Aveling and Porter exhibited a 10-horse traction engine, and a 20-ton steam roller of similar design to that of 1865. They also announced a new design of steam roller (Fig. 80), much more like the ones we know today, but with the front rolls very ingeniously coned to allow of the vertical pivot shaft for the front axle to pass between them.

It may be that Howard's were discouraged by the adverse reports on their engines, or more likely by the poor performance, but in 1872 they introduced a completely new design, which they called the 'Farmer's Engine' (Fig. 81). It was quite orthodox in many ways, but not in the placing of the cylinder and motion in the tender. Like the Fowler three-wheelers, these engines were 'light on' due to poor distribution of weight, and reared like a frightened horse at the slightest provocation. The version

Fig. 81. The Howard 'Farmer's Engine'.

Ashley Butterwick, Esq.

Fig. 82. The straw-burning ploughing engine for Russia.

T. D. Walshaw, Esq.

built for cable ploughing was even worse, for it had the winding drums bolted to the back of the tender. However, this tendency was subsequently minimised by placing the hind axle further back.

The design proved quite popular, and in November 1931 *The Model Engineer* illustrated and described a Howard 8 h.p. double-drum farmer's engine which in 1928, after 51 years' service, was brought back to Bedford under its own steam. It is ironical that Howard's had bought it back to save it from having a final resting place in an American museum, for shortly afterwards the firm 'went under', and the engine was scrapped outright by the American-controlled firm who purchased the works!

Exports of British engines were greatly increasing year by year, and 1873 saw the fine pair of Fowler ploughing engines Nos. 1937 and 1938 among the many exported to Russia. Fig. 82 shows No. 1937 in the works yard. Her driving platform is at the front, with the steering column and all controls, because she is a straw-burner, leaving little room for anything at the rear but the necessary mechanism.

In the great granaries of Europe coal and timber were very scarce, whereas the straw left after threshing was of little or no value, for it was not required for animal bedding or fodder. So was born the Head and Schemioth straw-burning system, where the straw was fed into a hopper or trough as shown. Two belt-driven rollers then carried it into the firebox to be burnt. The system was first introduced at the Vienna Exhibition of 1873.

Straw had a poor thermal capacity, and the firebox had to be very large, with baffles to ensure adequate combustion. But the system was a godsend to countries such as Hungary, Russia, and the Argentine and North America, for ploughing by cable and by direct traction, and for threshing. Whilst steam was being raised, of course, the feed rollers had to be turned by a hand crank, but there was plenty of cheap labour about!

This particular pair of Fowlers was fitted also for auxiliary oil firing. At times steam ploughing could demand a sustained 'burst' of 80 or 90 brake horse power, and it was next to impossible to obtain so much from straw. The approximate consumption of straw per h.p. hour was 26 lb. *if dry;* if the straw was in poor condition, it could be much more, and it was just not possible to burn so much as was needed. In other words, the engine would stop for shortage of steam, because of insufficient heat. Hence the need for the auxiliary oil-burning apparatus, though of course the straw fuel would provide enough power for normal requirements.

The oil tank may be seen mounted over the boiler, behind the large spur wheel, with a gravity feed running to the burner, mounted directly over the straw trough. A steam pipe also passes to the burner, and when

Fig. 83. Lloyd Burr's Aveling of 1874.

F. Hal Higgins, Esq.

Fig. 84. The Fowler 'slanting shaft' crane engine.

T. D. Walshaw, Esq.

pressure is turned on, the steam jet injects oil into the firebox, in an atomised and partly vaporised spray giving an intense and highly efficient flame. Fowlers would fit similar oil-burning apparatus to any engine to order: in a later chapter we shall see oil-burning Fowlers which were built for the War Department.

Mention of North America a couple of paragraphs ago reminds me that in the *Pacific Rural Press* published in San Francisco, Aveling and Porter 'road and farm locomotives' were front-page news at least twice in 1874. On January 3rd, a large engraving appeared showing an Aveling engine hauling a four-furrow balance plough by direct traction, and the text stated that it could plough from 6 to 10 acres a day, according to the nature of the soil, or haul 15 tons up steep inclines. Mr. Dick, of Ross, Ohio, wrote to describe his Avelings being used for hauling coal, for threshing, for logging in the woods, and for drawing 12 to 15 tons of pork over boulder pavements in Cincinatti.

In August the same year, the newspaper gave another cut showing an Aveling hauling two wagons along a rutted road, past a second Aveling doing direct-traction ploughing. The engines were stated to be of 12 h.p. (American rating) with a cylinder 8 in. by 10 in. with a lagged and felted boiler having 120 feet of heating surface. 'The entire cost per day of running the engine, including fuel, labor, oil, etc., does not exceed six dollars', and

Fig. 85. Ransomes and Sims' engine.
The Practical Dictionary of Mechanics.

'The total cost in New York of a complete farm locomotive, four-furrow plow and all appliances ready for work, we are informed, does not exceed $3,600 gold, the engine without the plow costing considerably less.' Many other British makes also went to America in the years 1871–4, when Congress lifted the import duties for a short time. One of the Avelings exported to California in 1873 is seen in Fig. 83, during restoration by its present owner Lloyd Burr, who bought it for £50. The wooden front wheels and fore-carriage are copied from the originals, but the excrescence on the cylinder top is not, and is doubtless removed by now. The keen-eyed will also note that the 'prancing horse of Kent' on the smokebox door is of the modern pattern (supplied by Aveling-Barford), the original having disappeared long since.

Back in England, we can now examine an interesting Fowler crane engine (Fig. 84), converted from a ploughing engine. I have shown this partly for the drive to the crane winding drum, somewhat resembling that to the road wheels on the original 'slanting-shaft' engines. It will be noticed that the 'compensating gear' is similar to that seen already in Fig. 49.

This device was cheaper than the bevel type gear, of course, and was quite commonly used: it can be seen on Fig. 85 again, which shows a Ransomes and Sims' engine of the time. The two-speed arrangement here is interesting, with a pinion at each end of the crankshaft. If the off-side pinion was engaged with the spur wheel below, then the drive was direct, in fast speed. To engage slow speed, this pinion would be slid out of engagement, and the one at the offside end of the countershaft slid into mesh with the spur wheel. The drive then passed through the reduction gear on the flywheel side (which may or may not have been in permanent mesh), thus giving slow speed.

There are several interesting features about the Robey 6-horse engine shown in Figs. 86 (a) and (b), not the least being the two-speed gear, which is very similar to the three-wheeled Fowler of 1871, and which with slight variations, was to become almost universal on three-shaft engines (that is, engines with only one countershaft between crankshaft and hind axle).

There are two pinions sliding on keys or splines on the crankshaft to engage with one size or other of the double spur wheel on the second shaft. On this shaft a pinion is mounted, to drive the main spur wheel, which in this case is bolted to the hind wheel. (In the Fowler, it formed the compensating centre.)

Now, looking at the small plan view in the upper left corner of Fig.86 (a), and also looking at Fig. 86 (b), the small pinion is engaged with the large spur wheel, the engine being in slow speed. If, then, the small pinion is slid

Fig. 86(a). Side view of 1875 Robey engine.

The Engineer.

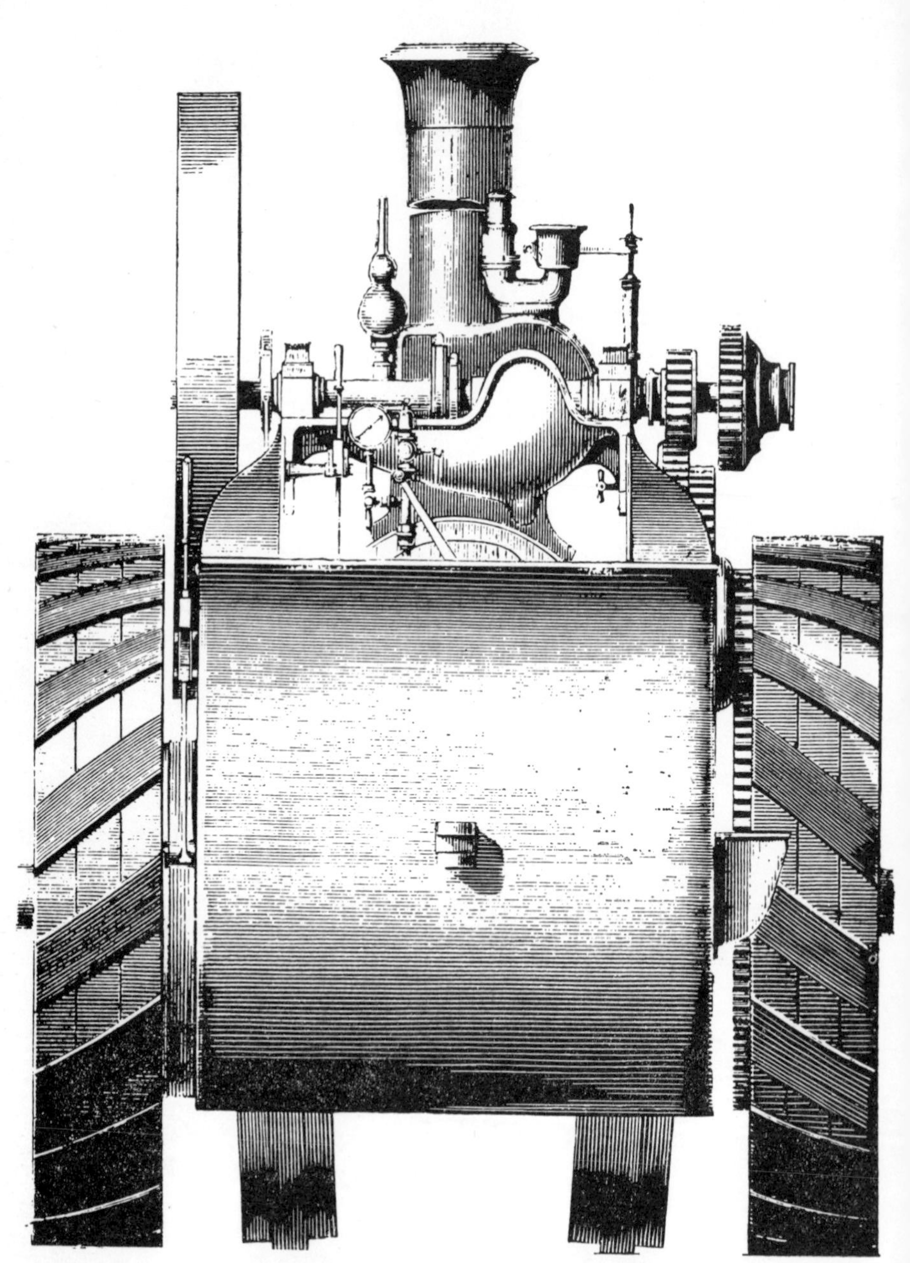

Fig. 86(b). Rear elevation of 1875 Robey engine.

The Engineer.

towards the off-side, the engine can run free, for stationary use as in threshing. The larger pinion is cast hollow, and can now be slid inwards to mesh with the smaller spur wheel, so giving fast speed. In this position, the larger pinion completely encompasses the smaller one: if this hollow casting were not resorted to, the pinion would have to be very far out from its supporting bearing, which is bad design. (See also Fig. 153.)

Robey's steerage arrangement is interesting, with the front wheels narrow-tracked and the steerage chains outside them. It was a feature they were to keep for many years, as also was the water gauge mounted on the boiler side. The motion layout is fascinating too, with the solid 'bed-plate' casting making a rigid connection between cylinder and crankshaft.

Marshall, Sons and Co. Ltd. are a firm who happily are still in business, which was opened in 1842 by William Marshall at Gainsborough, Lincolnshire. He started as a millwright and engineer, and the business prospered, becoming especially noteworthy for stationary and portable steam engines.

The firm started building traction engines in 1876 with the undertype depicted in Fig. 87. The double cylinders and motion were placed between plate frames, with the boiler above, and the drive to the hind axle was by spur-gearing. These engines were well designed and built, but cannot have

Fig. 87. The Marshall undertype of 1876.

Ashley Butterwick, Esq.

been too popular, for it was not long before they were superseded by the more orthodox (by now) overtype engine.

In the same year C. J. Fowell, father of the erstwhile designer for Burrell, built the traction engine shown in Fig. 88. It was a three-shaft engine with the crankshaft bearings carried by plates riveted to the firebox, and extended forward to be bolted to the cylinder block. Clayton and Shuttleworth, too, were using wrought-iron plates to carry the bearing brackets (Fig. 89). There were two speeds on the same principle that we have already seen, but the two-speed spur wheel was carried on a stub-shaft. As before, the countershaft carried the compensating gear, and a pinion at each end drove the hind wheels separately.

Another C. and S. feature of 1876 was the patenting of the rack steering gear (Fig. 90), which some customers preferred as late as 1896, though the firm also used chain steerage too as desired. The diagram shows that the steerage shaft carried a bevel wheel, meshing with another on the short

Fig. 88. Fowell's traction engine of 1876.

Ashley Butterwick, Esq.

Fig. 89. Clayton and Shuttleworth engine of 1876.
A Chapter in the History of the Traction Engine.

cross-shaft, which was carried in a bracket attached to the bottom of the boiler. A worm on the shaft then engaged the curved rack which was secured to the front axle. This was a good method of steerage, without backlash, but it was discarded eventually.

A very important invention of 1876 was that of Garrett's 'corrugated' firebox (Fig. 91 (a)), which completely obviated the need for staying the crown of the firebox. Thus the latter was free to expand and contract at will, which helped to keep it free from mud deposit and incrustation, and also rendered it easier to clean when washing out the boiler. From then on Garrett's used this type of box exclusively in all their portables, traction engines, road locos, rollers and steam wagons. Fig. 91 (b) shows the cruciform shape of the corrugations similarly used by Marshalls', later on.

Fowell built the unorthodox engine of Fig. 92 in 1877, to Box's patents. The countershaft extended across below the boiler, and carried another crank disc to drive the other hind wheel. The idea of the coupling-rod drive was to permit free vertical movement of the sprung hind wheels. Note that the final drive to the latter was by the friction-band method, by the way. Several of these engines were built by Fowell, and it is also known that Robey's built a Box engine in 1879.

A most unusual engine appeared from the Fowler works in 1877, with hind wheels no less than 12 ft. in diameter (Fig. 93). It was with the object

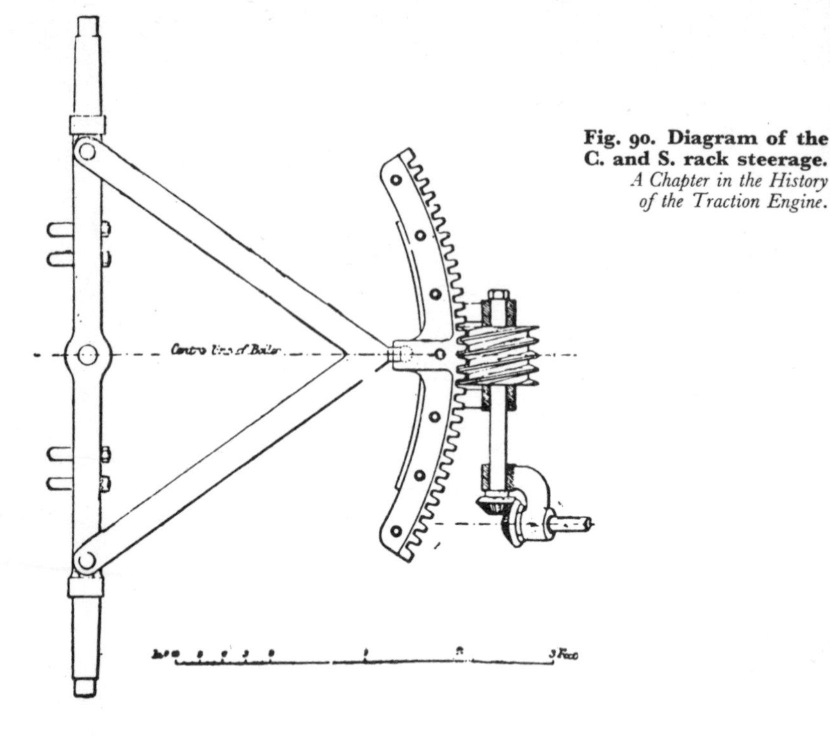

Fig. 90. Diagram of the C. and S. rack steerage. *A Chapter in the History of the Traction Engine.*

of giving as much contact with the ground surface as possible, and the engine was affectionately dubbed 'The Steeplechaser' by the workmen, for it would go anywhere.

The cylinders were over the firebox, driving forward to the crankshaft carried in a crankbox built of plate. A countershaft ran across the boiler top behind and below the motion, and it will be seen that orthodox two-speed gear with differential was fitted. At each end of this shaft was a pinion, engaging with a circular rack inside each hind wheel rim.

At the rear, the weight of the engine was not carried on the hind axle, but on a lower shaft running parallel with it. This shaft carried a double-flanged wheel at each end, in which ran the circular rail bolted to the hind wheel rim. Transverse leaf springs carried the weight of the engine on this shaft, which was coupled by compensating links to the upper axle to keep the two equidistant and parallel.

Only one 'twelve-footer' was built, for it proved too cumbersome, but in 1879 came a nine-footer (Fig. 94), which was of 8 n.h.p. and fitted with Church's patent circular slide valve. It was No. 3811, and supplied to Lord Amherst, of Didlington in Norfolk. The drive was somewhat similar to that of the larger engine, except that the final circular rack inside the rim had internal teeth instead of external.

A fitting now coming into common use was the water-lifter, seen on top of the belly tank with hose coupled up. It was a simple kind of steam injector, used for filling the tank from a roadside stream or other source of supply, and it gradually became a standard fitting on all makes of engine. The cylindrical chamber protruding from the base of the chimney was a feed-water heater.

At this period, Fowlers were also building engines with 8-foot and 7-foot drivers, and the latter size was to prove popular with many makers for road locomotives.

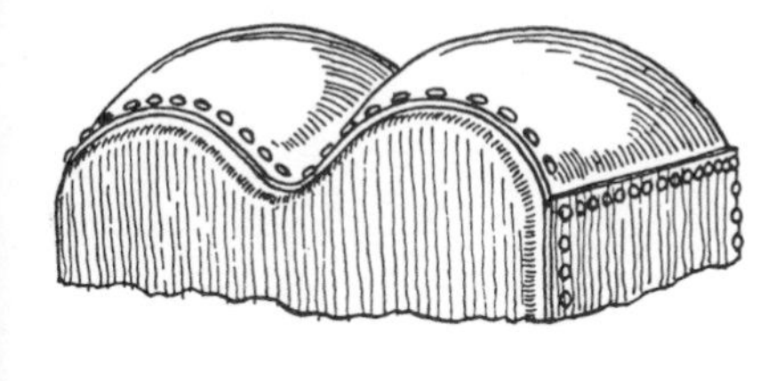

Fig. 91(a). Garrett patent corrugated firebox.
Fig. 91(b). Marshall patent corrugated firebox.
Author's sketches

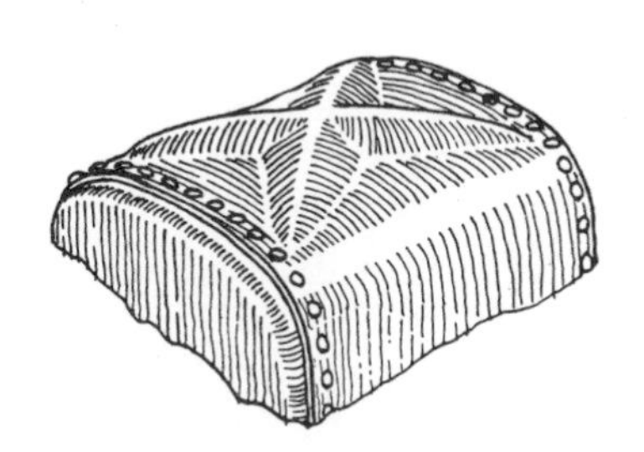

Meantime, another highly important development had come from the Aveling and Greig 'stable', for in 1878 they introduced a 'four-shaft' design with the change-speed gearing between the hornplates. It is, of course, much more satisfactory to do this than to have the gearing outside: the bearings are more fairly worn, there is far less vibration (especially when some wear has taken place!), and there is less stress on the gear teeth and the shafts.

Another point where traction engines were concerned was that it enabled better gear ratios to be chosen; with the three-shaft system, the fact that the fast speed pinion had to be hollow to encompass the slow speed one, more or less settled their relative sizes. And it was found in practice that if a suitable slow speed ratio was chosen, then the fast speed ratio was too high – or vice versa.

The first Aveling and Greig four-shaft system is shown in plan in Fig. 95 (a), and in cross section in Fig. 95 (b). It will be seen that the crankshaft carries two small pinions of equal size. The second shaft is actually fixed in its bearings, and acts also as a stay for the hornplates. On it revolves a sleeve which carries a spur wheel, and the fast and slow pinions. The third shaft carries the fast and slow spur wheels, and also the pinion for the final drive, which is outside the hornplates. In the position shown, fast speed is engaged; if the lever is moved to the centre of the quadrant, this gives neutral; if the lever is taken over to the right, slow speed is engaged.

Looking at Fig. 95 (b), the final drive is taken through compensating gear, with the compensating centre running on the extended boss of the inner bevel wheel, which is keyed on to the hind axle. (It should be noted that with cast gearing, the gear teeth are cast on an outer ring which is fitted on and bolted to a separate centre.) The outer bevel wheel in this particular design is bolted direct to the hind-wheel hub, and in normal running there would *not* be a pin passing through the hub into the compensating centre. As we already know, with the centre thus locked to

Fig. 92. Fowell engine built to Box's patent.

Ashley Butterwick, Esq.

Fig. 93. The Fowler 'twelve-footer'. *T. D. Walshaw, Esq.*

Fig. 94. The Fowler 'nine-footer'.

T. D. Walshaw, Esq.

one of the bevel wheels, the differential would be out of action and both wheels must revolve together, at the same rate.

At the flywheel side of the engine, a winding drum is mounted on and keyed to the hind axle, the hind wheel being driven from this by a pin (not shown) passing through a hole in the hub into one of the holes in the boss of the drum. When it was necessary to use the winding rope, the procedure was first to chock securely both hind wheels and then to remove the driving pin and, if fitted, the differential locking pin.

If now, say, slow speed is engaged, and the regulator opened, the hind axle will rotate not only in its bearings, but in the hind-wheel hubs as well, carrying the winding drum with it. Moreover, because the outer bevel wheel is not rotating, being bolted to the hub of the chocked hind wheel, the inner bevel wheel (and so the hind axle and winding drum) will be revolving at *double* the normal speed. A moment's thought will show why this is so.

The winding drum was a fitting which was now being fairly extensively used, and was to be universally adopted on British machines. It enabled a bogged down engine to haul itself out, and then to pull its wagons out, of awkward places. It could be used as a winch or windlass, and was widely used for such purposes as grubbing out tree stumps.

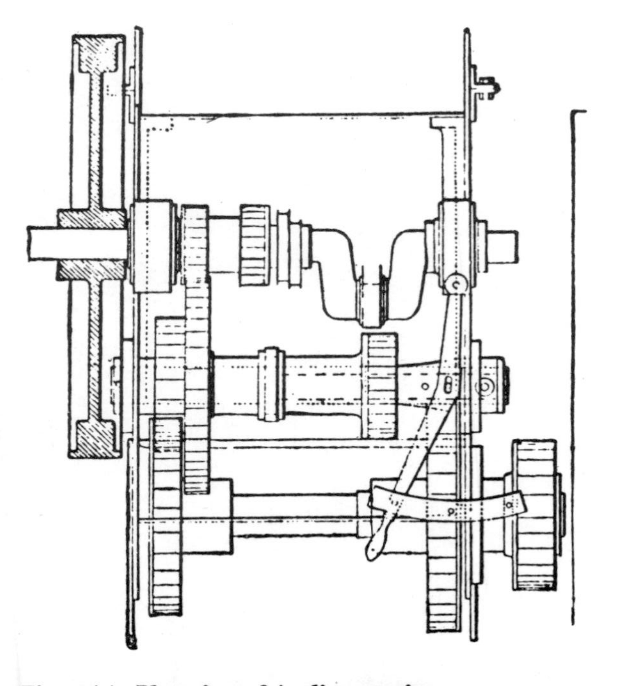

Fig. 95(a). Plan view of Aveling gearing.
Steam Locomotion on Common Roads.

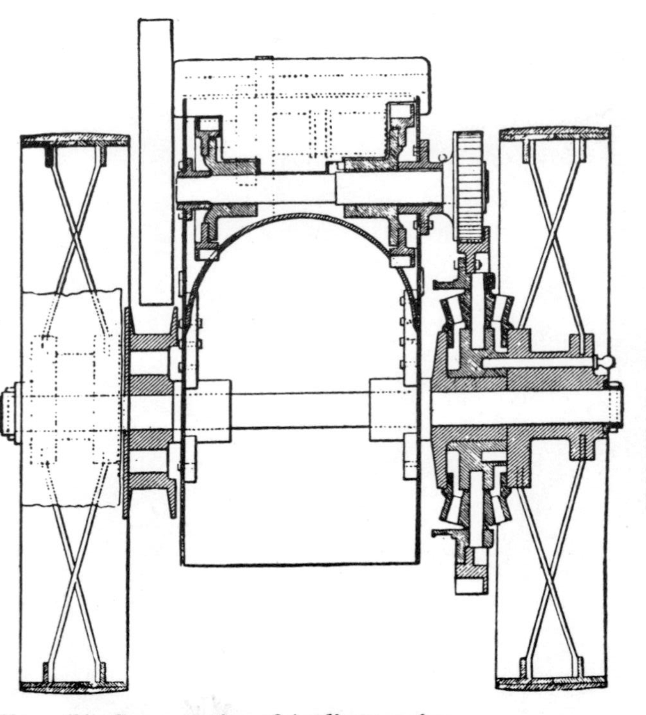

Fig. 95(b). Cross-section of Aveling gearing.
Steam Locomotion on Common Roads.

Fig. 96. Ransomes' traction engine of 1878.

The Engineer.

A very fine Aveling road locomotive, using this new four-shaft system, was shown at the Bristol Show of the R.A.S.E. in 1878, and another at the Paris Exhibition of that year. These engines had hind wheels 7 ft. diameter by 16 in. on the face, and the boiler was intended to work at 150 p.s.i. Fowlers also had four-shaft engines under the same patent, of course, at the same shows.

As a further example of the way in which design was settling down may be seen Fig. 96 showing Ransomes, Sims and Head's engine of 1878. In this case, the bearings are carried in separate plates rivetted to the firebox sides, thus achieving the same result as Aveling hornplates without infringing the patent. The cylinder is rather like Fowlers' with the built-in dome and Salter safety valves, and the two-speed gear is as we have already seen before. The handle below the steering wheel, on the side of the tender, operates the brake, which is a band working on a drum on the hind axle, probably in one with the winding drum. (On Fig. 95 (b) the brake drum may be seen machined inside the compensating centre.)

But however much design was crystallising, there was still room for experiment and improvement, and we shall see plenty of both as we look at the 'eighties in the next chapter.

13

DEVELOPMENTS OF THE EIGHTIES

Steam, mighty steam ascends the throne
And reigns Lord Paramount alone!
WILLIAM HARRISON

WE START IN 1880 with another unusual Fowler engine, which was designed for the Government by J. A. C. Hay of the Ordnance Department. It was of 8 n.h.p., and was called the Artillery Siege Train Traction Engine (Fig. 97). The boiler was vertical, and the engine between plates at the back, which carried the gearing and shafts too. There were coal bunkers at each side of the footplate, and a tank below. The engine was, of course, designed for use in military establishments.

In the following year, at the Derby Show of the R.A.S.E., Fowlers introduced a pawl mechanism on the winding drum, so that it was free to pay out the rope as the engine was travelling forward, but could be brought into action at once when required. They were also using steel exclusively for their boilers, instead of wrought iron, and their gears and bearing brackets were cast in steel too.

But the most important Fowler innovation was the use of compound cylinders for the first time in a traction engine (Fig. 98). This was not ready in time for exhibition in the show-ground itself, but was shown on the trial ground where Fowlers also exhibited their cultivating machinery in operation. The engine was of 8 n.h.p., with cylinders 6 in. and 10½ in. in diameter, and 12-in. stroke. (At the Smithfield Club Show later in the year they had a 10-horse compound, with cylinders of 6½ in. and 11¼ in. diameter by 12-in. stroke.)

The cranks were at right angles, with machined cheeks to which balance weights were fixed, and the valves were between the cylinders. (It was not long before the design was altered to bring the valves overhead, so making them more accessible.) There was a 'simpling-valve', operated from the footplate, whereby high-pressure steam could be admitted to the low-pressure cylinder, in case the high-pressure cylinder had stopped on dead centre, or to give extra power on starting.

With compounding, of course, the steam is admitted first to the high-pressure cylinder, from where it emerges at a lower pressure, but by no means fully expanded and still containing a fair amount of energy which in a single cylinder engine would now go straight up the chimney. However, in the compound, this steam passes into the low-pressure cylinder, where the piston is proportionately larger in diameter so that each cylinder does approximately the same amount of work. From the L.P. cylinder the steam emerges, much expanded, at a pressure of a few pounds only, but sufficient to work the blast necessary for the combustion of the fuel.

The net result of obtaining so much more work from a given amount of steam was that a great saving in both fuel and water – up to 30 per cent – was effected, a point of particular value where coal was expensive or water scarce. Moreover, the wear and tear on the motion was reduced, the exhaust noise was considerably lessened, and the smaller blast was kinder on the boiler tubes.

This was a most important innovation, and *Engineering* was right when it said: '. . . we expect to find that they will be largely adopted for both traction and steam cultivating purposes'. But, apart from one other example

Fig. 97. Fowler siege-train crane engine. *T. D. Walshaw, Esq.*

to be noted in a moment, the other traction-engine builders held aloof, and it was not for a few years that any other makers turned to compounding in a serious way. By this time Fowlers had turned out an appreciable number of compounds, particularly in engines for road haulage and for cultivation, and had thus gained the advantage of experience over their competitors.

The one exception just mentioned was built by Burrell, and also exhibited at Derby. It was a peculiar arrangement which does not seem to have been much good, and was quietly dropped. Briefly, the two cylinders were in tandem, with the L.P. nearest the crank. This piston had a trunk which practically formed the crosshead, the little end of the connecting rod working on a gudgeon pin within it.

The stroke from the crank was worked by admitting steam to the crank end of the H.P. cylinder. During the return stroke H.P. steam was admitted to the other end of the H.P. cylinder and the steam from the crank end, now partly expanded, was passed into the L.P. cylinder to exert pressure on the area of the L.P. piston. Distribution of steam to both cylinders was effected by a single valve. It will be seen from this description that in effect the arrangement gave little more power than a normal single cylinder, and it possessed the grave defect that one stroke was more powerful than the

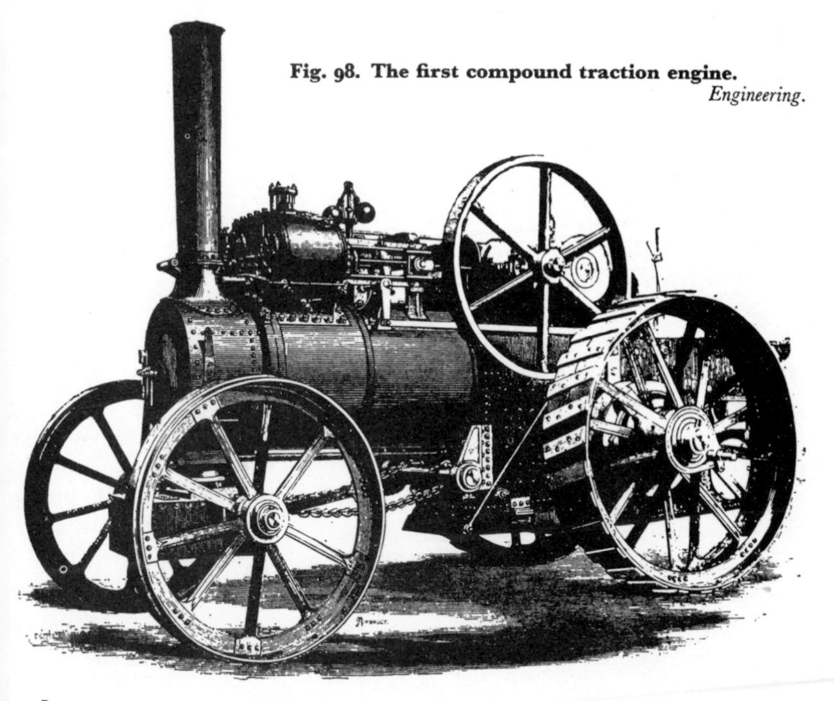

Fig. 98. The first compound traction engine.
Engineering.

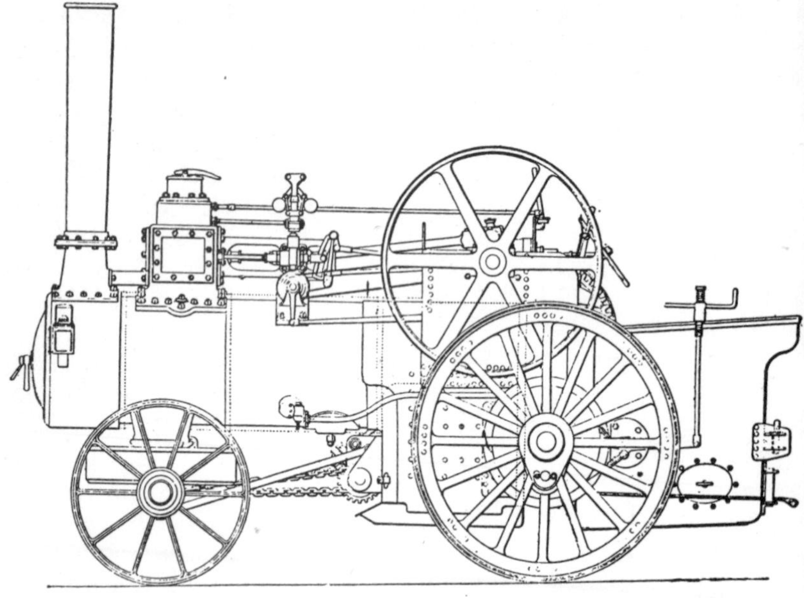

Fig. 99. Marshall traction engine of 1881. *Engineering.*

other, which must have led to vibration and wear and tear, with an uneven exhaust which could have an unhappy effect on the boiler tubes. Little wonder that we hear no more about it!

On a 10-horse engine at Derby, Burrell fitted Joy's valve gear instead of the almost universally used Stephenson gear. *Engineering* commented that the details were well worked out, but here again the firm does not appear to have taken the design further. This engine also was fitted with steam steering gear, worked by a beautiful little two-cylinder engine with a rotary valve, but once more the idea did not 'catch on'. After all, hard-headed farmers and road-haulage contractors were not likely to pay out good money for such devices; they would only make steersmen soft, and what were muscles for, in any case?

A very good Burrell feature which *did* become popular was to drive the feed pump at a reduced speed, instead of direct from the crankshaft, for with the increasing r.p.m. of traction engines the direct-driven pump tended to be inefficient. Like Fowlers, Burrells were using steel in their boiler work, but the fireboxes were still of wrought iron.

The Marshall traction engines were now of a very modern appearance (Fig. 99), though like many others of the day they still had the perch bracket for the fore-carriage secured to the first ring of the boiler shell.

This was a relic of portable engine days which gave the engine a short wheelbase, and thus added manœuvrability in a confined space, but which gave trouble when the inevitable leaks began to appear round the rivets. In due course, then, the perch bracket's position invariably became the bottom of the smokebox, which was easy to get at when necessary.

A further relic of portable design on this Marshall was the construction of the front wheels: light in weight, but not too strong. Good features were the bored trunk-guide for the crosshead, supported by a single casting which also served as governor-stand, weigh-bar spindle bracket, and valve-rod support. The trunk-guide also incorporated the front cylinder cover and piston-rod stuffing-box or gland: at the opposite end was a small inside flange to keep oil from flying off the wearing surfaces, and there was also a small trough to collect surplus oil, which could be emptied away at leisure. These were all features which were to become popular with, or were already being used by, other makers.

The brake drum was cast in one with the driving boss on the left-hand hind wheel, and a winding drum was keyed to the hind axle on the left-hand side. A very good fitting was the high-speed cross-arm governor working an equilibrium valve, both of which were much more sensitive than the heavy slow-speed Watt-type governor with its butterfly valve, which was still widely used however.

Barrows and Stewart of Banbury exhibited a traction engine (Fig. 100)

Fig. 100. Barrows and Stewart's engine.

Engineering.

with some unusual features, most of them good. For instance, the feed pump was of the long-stroke type, worked directly from the crosshead, and contained in the base of the cylinder, where it acted as a feed-water heater, too. There was also an injector for boiler feeding – an appliance which was gradually coming into favour among designers. The wheels were formed of two plates cut out as shown, and connected to the tyre by angle rings, which gave a neat and strong wheel. The hind wheels were 5 ft. 4 in. by 14 in., and the leading wheels 3 ft. 4 in. by 8 in.

All gearing was of crucible steel, and the winding drum, though mounted on the hind axle, was separately driven by a pinion on the countershaft. The cylinder was 9½ in. by 13 in., and the crankshaft was 3 in. diameter, rather small for the power.

In December 1881, at the Smithfield Club Show, there were many engines by many makers, but with few novelties. Burrell and Aveling both received commendation by *Engineering* for increasing the wearing surfaces of their valve gear, and Aveling exhibited a model of Allan straight-link gear which they proposed to use instead of Stephenson motion. But, as with Burrell's Joy valve gear, we hear no more of this proposed change.

Allchin and Sons of Northampton, who had started to build traction engines a couple of years previously, exhibited an example fitted with a new arrangement of gearing, as in Fig. 101. Here the slow gear was at the left, and the fast gear on the right, which the firm claimed enabled the overhang of the gear to be reduced, rendered the gear castings less complicated, and distributed the wear and tear more equally between the bearings of the two sides of the engine. One drawback not mentioned was that the flywheel had to be considerably overhung because of the sliding pinion between it and the bearing.

It was at about this time that Mark Twain, writing his *Life on the Mississippi*, described the Fowler steam plough (though not by name) at work on the rich soil of a sugar plantation near New Orleans. 'The traction engine travels about on its own wheels, till it reaches the required spot; then it stands still and by means of a wire rope pulls the huge plough towards itself two or three hundred yards across the field, between the rows of cane. The thing cuts down into the black mould a foot and a half deep. The plough looks like a fore-and-aft brace of a Hudson river steamer, inverted. When the Negro steersman sits on one end of it, that end tilts down near the ground, while the other sticks up high in the air. This great see-saw goes rolling and pitching like a ship at sea, and it is not every circus rider that could stay on it.' The steam plough, of course, was especially valuable in helping to replace the slave labour freed by the Civil War, and also in getting the ravaged plantations into order again.

Both at home and abroad, the use of steam traction by haulage contractors was growing rapidly by now, and Fig. 102 shows a typical example, although with a weight of less than 17 tons the bell was not a particularly heavy load. It was *Great Paul*, on its way from John Taylor & Co.'s foundry at Loughborough to be placed in the tower of St. Paul's Cathedral. The velocipede in the foreground also has a point of interest as another means of transport of the age!

In 1880, John Whittingham of Nantwich had patented (No. 3860) a four-wheel drive for traction engines, but without compensating gear. Four years later, he, with Alfred Greig and Richard Shaw of Fowlers, took out a similar patent but including differential gear, and this gave rise to the building of the engine shown in Figs. 103 (a) and (b).

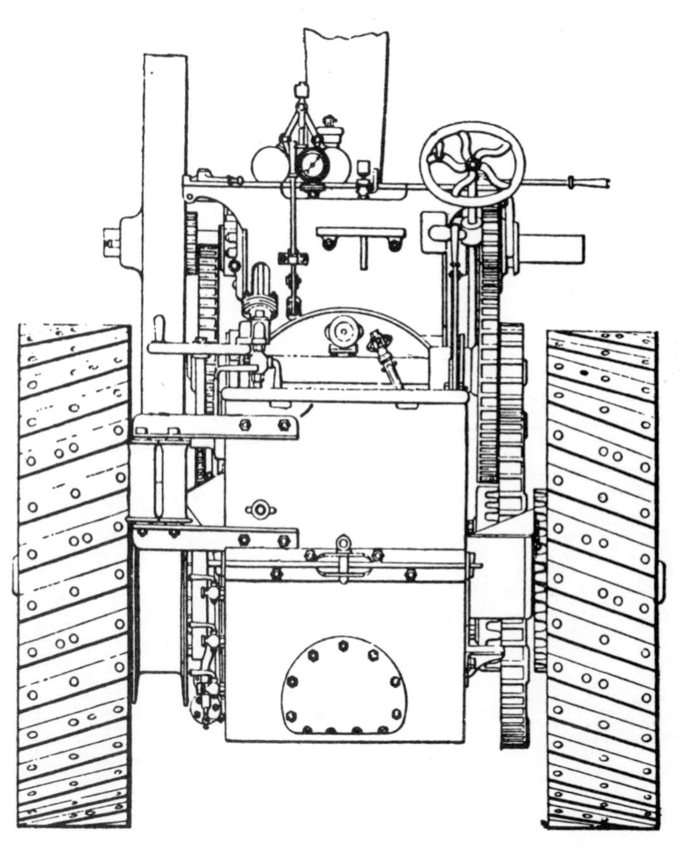

Fig. 101. Allchin's two-speed gearing. *Engineering.*

Looking at the former first, if we ignore the drive to the front, this might almost be a conventional four-shaft engine with all-gear drive on the off-side. But turning to the near-side, we note that on the extended end of the third shaft there is a chain sprocket, driving forward to the countershaft just below the motion work.

Back to the off-side, and from the countershaft a second pitch chain drives to a further countershaft under the front of the smokebox. From here the drive is taken to the front axle through gearing and a kind of gimbal motion, also incorporating the compensating gear.

Another four-wheel drive Fowler was built with the cylinders and motion underneath, with all-gear drive to both axles, the layout being shown in Fig. 104. Both these engines looked and were ungainly. They were, in fact, too heavy and too wide for ordinary use, and so no more were built. But it was an important and worth while experiment.

J. and H. McLaren of Leeds are a firm who are still very active, and whose engines have always borne a well deserved good reputation since they started building traction engines in 1877. A fine road loco for heavy

Fig. 102. 'Great Paul' en route to London.

John Taylor and Co.

Fig. 103(a). Near-side of the four-wheel drive engine.

T. D. Walshaw, Esq.

haulage, with crane attached, is seen in Fig. 105: a good solid job which obviously meant business and, indeed, was very capable of it, according to *The Engineer*.

Built in 1884 for a Liverpool firm for such tasks as moving heavy marine boilers, and lifting ships' propellers out of barges, the engine was of 12 n.h.p. – 'believed to be the most powerful haulage engine extant' – and had twin high-pressure cylinders of 8-in. bore by 12-in. stroke. It was guaranteed to haul 60 tons, which was partly achieved by lower gearing than normal – at 150 r.p.m. the road speeds in slow and fast gears were 1.04 m.p.h. and 1.9 m.p.h. respectively. The hind wheels were a special McLaren design, (not to be confused with the McLaren and Boulton wheel referred to later), with cast-iron blocks set into the sockets cast into the rims, and *forced* outwards by powerful springs of which the pressure could be adjusted. At no time were less than five blocks 'biting' the ground, and even on a level hard surface the wheels had a bearing two feet long.

In 1885, McLarens built a road locomotive for use in India for hauling a bus, and designed for a speed of 8 m.p.h. (Fig. 106). It was a compound, with cylinders 6½ in. and 10 in. diameter by 12-in. stroke, and the boiler, worked at 150 p.s.i., had a steel shell with wrought-iron firebox. The crankshaft was 3½ in. diameter, and the main axle 5 in. The large cab covered the crankshaft and gearing, the remaining motion work outside being neatly boxed in to protect it from the dust and the weather.

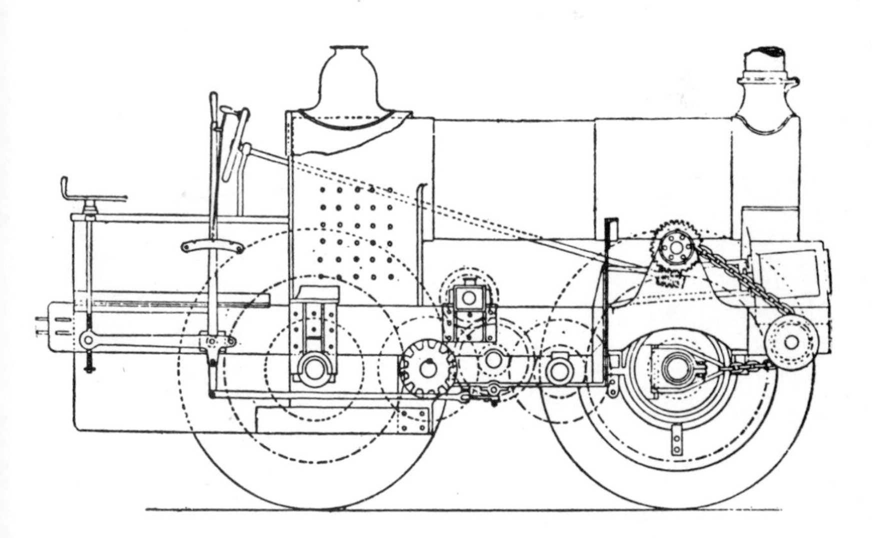

Fig. 104. Fowler undertype four-wheel drive engine.
English and American Traction Engines and Steam Cars.

Six-foot hind wheels were fitted, with rather elaborate looking spring spokes, and the front of the engine was carried on coil springs. There were three speeds, with ratios of 6, 12 and 22 to 1, and the change levers were interlocking so that a careless driver could not engage two speeds at once. This was usual with other makes, too.

Sectors were fitted to the front axle outside the wheels, and the steerage chains worked in these, with no backlash. The front wheels had chilled bushes running on case-hardened axle ends.

Of a test run near Leeds, over country roads, an eye witness said: '. . . we had some steep hills – plenty of them one in ten – to go up and down . . . However, the inspector was well pleased . . . After leaving the village of Harewood we had four miles of straight road wide enough, but with some long rises of one in twenty. We passed the first milestone in five minutes; the second in seven minutes – having to let a trap pass; the third in six minutes – eased to let carts pass; the fourth in less than five minutes. Running the four miles in twenty-three minutes'. The load was only three tons, but of course the loco was built for speed, not heavy work.

The next year saw three magnificent high-speed road locomotives built by McLarens for the *Fourgon poste* service in the south of France. This was a service which carried parcels from one town to another, and was run by contractors in opposition to the railways, who made excessive charges for quick delivery, and whose slow deliveries were *very* slow indeed. In fact, the carriers did a large business, even with horse transport.

These three locomotives (Fig. 107) were compounds, of 12 n.h.p., with a working pressure of 175 p.s.i., and were run regularly between Lyons and Grenoble, about 70 miles apart. Goods were collected during the day and packed in the wagon, which held up to six tons, and then one engine started out from each town every evening and delivered its load at the other end next morning. One engine was kept in the shed, in rotation, so that they could be washed out properly and kept in good running order.

Gradients up to 1 in 11 were common for forty miles of the journey, and there were some very long hills too, including one of four miles at an average of 1 in 40. For several miles the road ran on a shelf cut in the mountainside, so that a moment's carelessness might result in a drop of 500 feet for engine and crew.

A powerful steam brake was fitted which could pull the engine up with full steam on, and which by means of a chain operated the brakes on the wagon. The very brilliant head-light burnt gas, which was compressed into a receiver, one charge sufficing for the round trip of 140 miles. Both axles were sprung, and in thousands of miles 'there has never been a single breakage in connection with the springs. The roads are not good even

Fig. 106. McLaren road locomotive for India.
Steam Locomotion on Common Roads.

Fig. 107. McLaren road locomotive for France.
Steam Locomotion on Common Roads.

where level, as they are full of great holes, and many open drains run across them without any covering'. Moreover, it was common for the engines to hit, and run over, stones as big as a man's head.

Each engine weighed about 15 tons in working order, and averaged about 15,000 miles per year, often at 8 m.p.h. for hours on end – though it is said that a speed of 20 m.p.h. was not unknown. That these splendid locomotives could keep up the strenuous work like this was a great tribute to British engineering in general, and to McLarens in particular.

The general run of agricultural engines was from 6 to 8 n.h.p., but in 1884 Fowlers were producing the rather pretty little 4 n.h.p. *Sutherland* 'to supply a want which has long been felt by the users of our heavier engines for agricultural purposes. While heavy engines have been proved to do the heavier work economically, they have been found badly adapted for the lighter operations, such as rolling, reaping, and carting on the farm . . .'

This light engine (Fig. 108) could pull 6 tons on the road, and it could be converted into a land roller by attaching widening rings to the hind wheels, to cover a breadth of 8 to 10 feet; it could roll 30 acres a day. It could be used as a reaper, with a knife-bar and delivery reel driven off the crankshaft without disengaging the roller rings, reaping up to 3 acres per hour and rolling at the same time.

But versatile as it was, the *Sutherland* could not drive the average threshing machine, designed for a 6- or 7-horse engine, without strain, and it does not seem to have gained much favour.

Spring wheels were now being tried out extensively and Fig. 109 shows Fowler compound road loco No. 5165, built in 1885, fitted with Aveling spring wheels. In these an inner ring or rim was attached to the spokes, and connected to the outer rim by means of the springs, one end of the latter being attached by eyebolts to the spokes, and the other end similarly to the outer rim. Thus the springs effectively damped out the shocks of starting a load, and also many of the road shocks. These wheels cost £20 each as an 'extra'.

This photo also shows the later arrangement of the compound cylinders which was to remain virtually unchanged until the last of the Fowler compounds. The valves were now set over the cylinders, the faces being inclined inwards so as to obtain close centres for the valve rods, to avoid cranked eccentric rods, the four eccentrics being between the crank dips. The valve faces were also inclined obliquely the other way, so that (as can be seen) the valve rod centre-lines were in line with the crankshaft centre-line.

Other points to notice on this fine engine are the large wheels, the spring links in the steerage chains, the toolbox on the side of the tender and the

Fig. 108. Fowler 'Sutherland' light traction engine.
Text-Book of Farm Engineering.

Fig. 109. Fowler No. 5165 of 1885, with Aveling wheels.
T. D. Walshaw, Esq.

fairlead for the wire rope below it, by means of which the rope could be led off to haul at an angle. There is a belly tank for extra water – always a fixture on an engine used principally for haulage – and a pipe running between the two tanks to equalise the water level in both. The cock in the pipe near the bend could be closed before ascending or descending a steep hill, so that water would not be lost from one tank or the other.

Two spring wheels of Fowler design are shown in Figs. 110 (a) and (b), and in both cases it will be seen that whilst the weight of the engine is supported on the spring spokes, there is an arm projecting from the hub, connecting to the rim by springs, to absorb driving stresses.

A fourth type of wheel, which proved very popular indeed, was the McLaren and Boulton wheel, patented in 1887. (Isaac Watt Boulton, co-patentee, was a direct descendant of Matthew Boulton, partner of James Watt.) It was not only manufactured by McLarens, but also by Fowlers and Avelings. (See Figs. 170 and 174.)

The wheel rim was cast, with deep square sockets in the face, into which were fitted iron-bound blocks of wood, end grain outwards, and bedded on india-rubber or felt. Each block was retained by a bolt, with a coil spring inside the rim, held by locknuts. Being set with one row half a space in front of the other row, there were always three blocks, and often five, giving a very good grip. As each block made contact, of course, the spring absorbed any shock, and then the pad further deadened it.

They were very quiet in use, and were often called 'elephant's foot' wheels for obvious reasons. They were kind not only to engines, but also to road surfaces: in fact, Fletcher writes '. . . certain local authorities, who, by virtue of special powers had practically prohibited the use of traction engines within their districts, have waived their restrictions in favour of engines mounted upon these wheels'.

Sprung axles too were coming to favour, more especially for road haulage, and whilst the front axle presented no difficulty, the hind axle did. The trouble was to arrange that the up-and-down movement of the axle did not affect the correct meshing of the gear-teeth, and Fig. 111 gives the Burrell solution, which was introduced at the Newcastle Show of the R.A.S.E. in 1887.

From the crankshaft A, motion was given to the double spur wheel C by means of one or other of the two-speed pinions. C revolved upon the outer boss of the steel tube D which was fixed to the hornplate, and to the box G on the other hornplate. Countershaft B, passing through the steel tube (often called the 'cannon-bracket'), was connected to C by means of a universal joint at E, and at the flywheel side it carried the pinion M, meshing with spur wheel N on the hind axle. The bearing F carried the

Fig. 110 (a) and (b). Two types of spring wheels by Fowler.

A. R. Dibben, Esq.

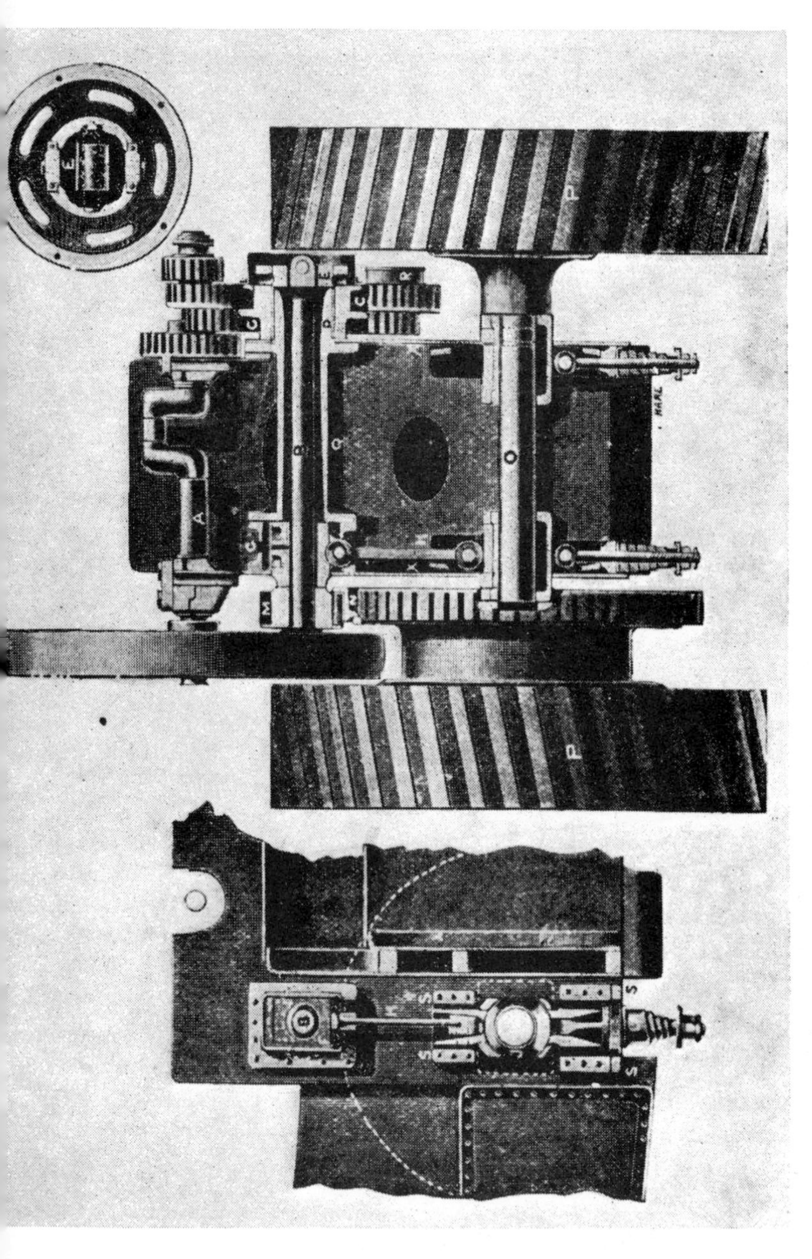

Fig. 111. Arrangement of Burrell springing.

Official catalogue.

countershaft at the flywheel side, and was free to slide up and down in the box G, bolted to the hornplate.

The bearing F was connected by the link H to the axle box J, thus retaining the correct centres of the final drive, and the axle box was free to slide up and down in the guides S, as was the axle box on the other side. The weight of the engine was taken on the two volute springs which were attached to their respective axle boxes. It will be seen then that the hind axle and the main drive end of the countershaft were free to move up and down, without disturbing the mesh of either set of gears.

Another important Burrell patent (No. 3489) was taken out early in 1889. It was for the famous 'single-crank compound', to which hundreds of engines were subsequently built, and it was first shown at the Windsor 'Royal'. The layout is shown in Fig. 112, where it will be seen that the H.P. cylinder is placed diagonally above the L.P. one, as is the H.P. valve.

Now, looking at the side elevation, the two valve rods are joined by a single crosshead, to the centre of which the valve slide, worked by a single set of Stephenson link-motion, is attached. The two piston rods are similarly attached to one crosshead (directly behind the governor-stand in the side view), from which a single connecting rod passes to the single crank. The crosshead has inside flanges bearing on the four guide-bars, presenting a large wearing surface.

The steam after leaving the H.P. cylinder passes into the L.P., of course, and then, almost fully expanded, to the blast pipe. In some ways this was not as good a system as the side-by-side compound: there were only two power impulses per revolution, which was not so kind on the working parts and the hornplates and boiler. Moreover, as with the ordinary single-cylinder engine, if the engine stopped on a dead centre, the flywheel had to be pulled round by hand before a start could be made. Nevertheless, it was a really good system which worked well.

Fodens Limited of Sandbach are a prosperous firm who celebrated their centenary in 1956, and those who were present on that occasion will never forget the magnificent procession of traction engines and other vehicles from the Elworth Works and through the streets of this small Cheshire town. It was in 1880 that Fodens built their first traction engine and right from the start they established the principles of economy and efficiency.

In 1884, the Royal Manchester and Liverpool and North Lancashire Agricultural Society offered a gold medal for the best traction engine, and fourteen engines were entered for the competition. The trials were not conducted entirely satisfactorily, nor were all the competitors satisfied, but *The Engineer* commented: '. . . Mr. Foden . . . has, it will be seen, fairly beaten . . . the most eminent firms in the trade. Messrs. Fowler, Aveling

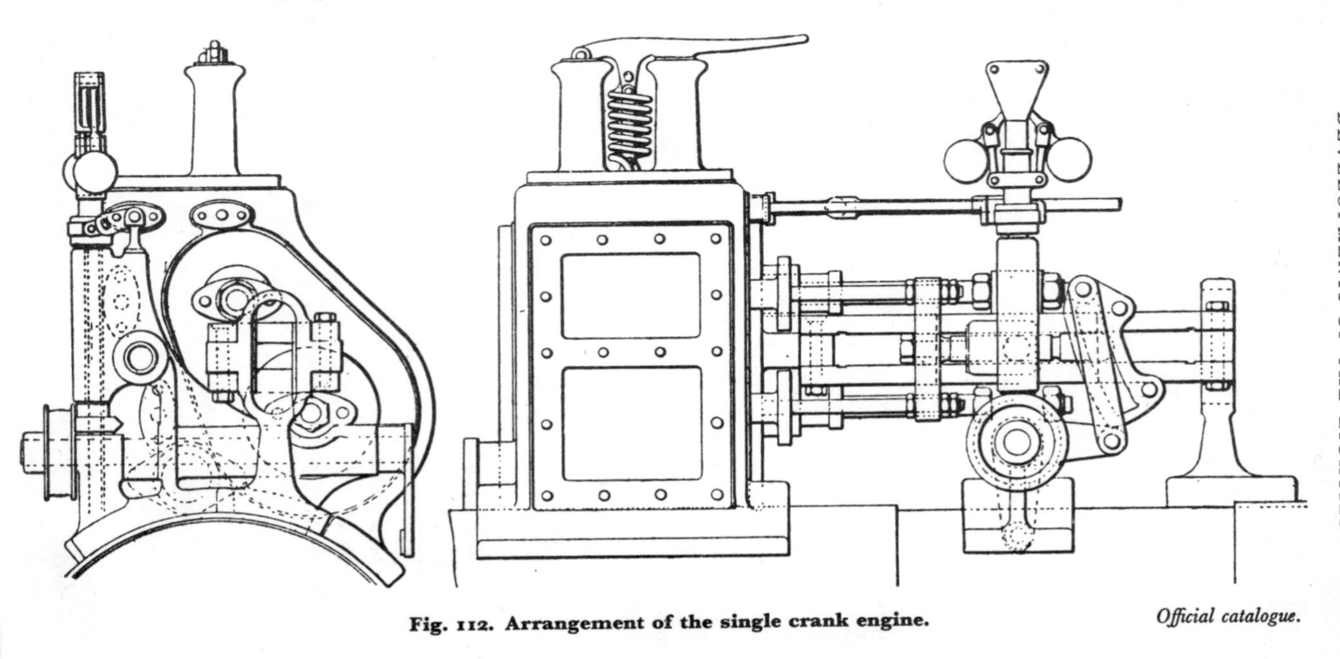

Fig. 112. Arrangement of the single crank engine. *Official catalogue.*

and Porter, Burrell and Marshall can none of them equal him in economy'. This particular engine had double cylinders 5¾ in. diameter, and even so beat the compounds!

The R.A.S.E. held trials at Newcastle in July 1887, for which Foden entered a single and a compound, the former with a cylinder 7½ in. by 10 in., and the latter 4¾ in. and 9½ in. by 10 in. The single worked at 120 p.s.i., and the compound at the unprecedented pressure of 250 p.s.i., with valves set to blow actually at 300. Again *The Engineer* noted: '. . . the boiler and all its fittings were perfectly tight, not a breath of steam or drop of water being apparent', and, once more, '. . . concerning the design and workmanship of this engine we can say that both are as good as that of any other builder of traction engines, and the perfect way in which both boiler and engine dealt with the enormous pressure carried – 250 lb. on the square inch – is sufficient assurance that there is nothing gimcrack about this engine'. The coal consumption for the single was 2½ lb. per b.h.p. and in the compound only 1 lb. 13½ oz.!

The latter appeared as in Fig. 113 (which is Engine No. 174), and the reader will be struck at once with the large diameter of the wheels and the large number of spokes in them. These two factors were a recognisable feature of all Fodens from first to last: the hind wheels of the 6 n.h.p. were never less than 6 ft. 4 in., and the larger sizes up to 7 ft., with some of the 10 h.p. engines even 7 ft. 4 in. The reason was the same as with the large-wheeled Fowlers, of course. The spokes were more numerous because Foden used a lighter cross section, to give a much more springy wheel.

All Foden engines from 1882 onwards, even agricultural types, were on springs, and on No. 174 they were coil springs: the hind ones were contained in the cylinders (looking rather like a pair of screw-jacks) projecting above the hornplates. Note that the latter, by the way, are separate plates riveted on. Later engines had leaf springs carried above the hornplates.

The Foden springing is shown in Fig. 114 where A is the third shaft, B the hind axle, and EE their respective bearings, connected by a link F at each side, so as to keep the main drive gear teeth correctly meshed, and also to keep the two shafts parallel. The bearings can slide in the cast horn-cheeks C, on top of which the boxes D for the springs are mounted. To accommodate the gearing between the moving third shaft A and the second shaft, which cannot move up and down, the latter is on a horizontal centre-line only very slightly above the former, so that the movement is more or less radial to the gearing, and has very little effect on the depth of mesh.

It should be explained that in the Foden springing, as in many others, the maximum vertical movement was only about ¼ in. each side of the

Fig. 113. Foden compound traction engine.
Steam Locomotion on Common Roads.

centre-line, whereas with Fowler, Burrell and a few other firms, it was at least 1 in. each side of centre, that is, a total of 2 in.

A very good reason for Foden economy was the large number of fire-tubes, there being no less than fifty-six of $1\frac{3}{4}$ in. diameter in a 6-horse boiler, giving a large heating surface ensuring quick generation of steam without excessive stoking, and making full use of the heat in the gases. In the Newcastle trials, the heat units left in the waste gases were analysed, and Fodens' single was ten times better, and Fodens' compound nearly four times better, than the nearest respective rivals.

Added to the economical boiler design was that of the slide valves. These were very long, and the inlet ports were very close to the ends of the cylinders. Thus the passages were very short, too, and this meant proportionately less 'live' steam blown to waste at each exhaust beat.

In discussing the Fowler compound cylinders, we touched on the 'simpling valve' which could pass H.P. steam into the L.P. cylinder if desired. Fodens had an extremely good design to take care of this (Fig. 115). From the exhaust port of the H.P. cylinder, the curved passage leads up to a three-way cock, from which a further passage leads to the L.P. valve chest on the left.

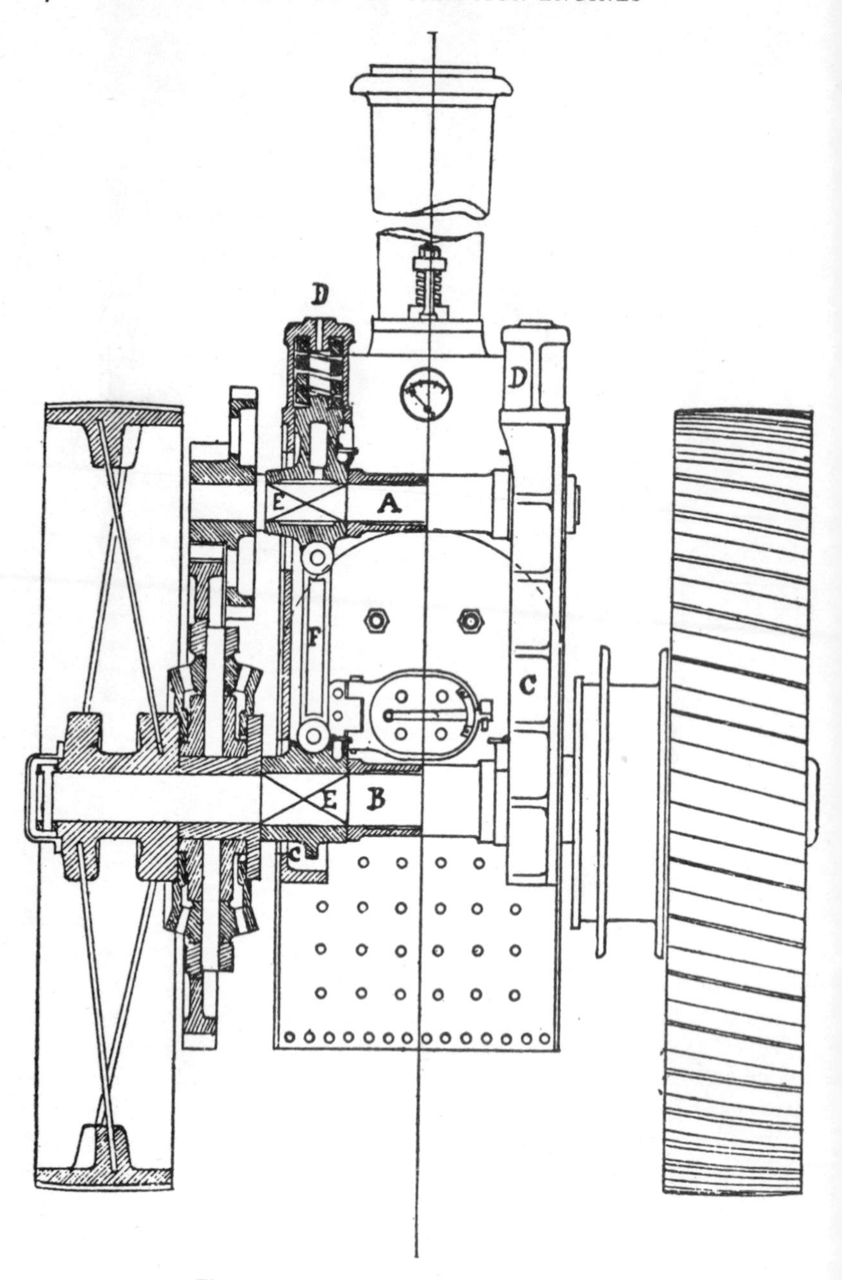

Fig. 114. Arrangement of Foden springing.
Steam Locomotion on Common Roads.

When compounding normally, the steam passes through the H.P. cylinder, where it is partly expanded, and then through the curved passage, the three-way valve, and the straight passage to the L.P. valve chest. From here it passes through the L.P. cylinder where it is further expanded, and then through the exhaust passage to the blast pipe. But when working 'double-high', the three-way cock is opened, and firstly the exhaust from the H.P. cylinder passes direct into the chimney, which relieves that cylinder of the back pressure due to working the L.P. cylinder, thus increasing the power on the H.P.

Secondly, the three-way cock admits live steam direct from the dome into the L.P. cylinder: but because this cylinder is so much larger than the H.P. one, the live steam is 'throttled' by means of a reducing valve so as to equalise the power of both cylinders – otherwise the engine would run very unevenly. (The Fowler simpling valve also throttled the H.P. steam to the L.P. cylinder for the same reason).

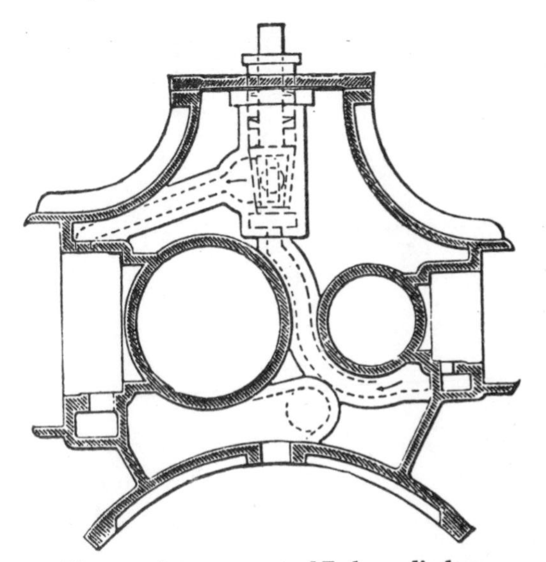

Fig. 115. Arrangement of Foden cylinders.
Steam Locomotion on Common Roads.

By this system the engine can be run as an ordinary double-cylinder engine, giving greatly increased power when required. Again, in case of accident – say an eccentric rod broke on either the H.P. or L.P. side – it would only be necessary to uncouple the eccentric straps on that side, set the valve to centre, and open the three-way cock, when the other cylinder would run as an ordinary H.P. single cylinder.

In Fig. 113, the auxiliary exhaust pipe may be seen emerging near the top of the cylinder, and going downwards to discharge into the ordinary blast pipe: on later engines it went straight into the chimney. Note, by the way, the small auxiliary tank beneath the boiler barrel, with the pump mounted on it: this tank, too, is a Foden recognition feature, though in many cases the pump was mounted on the boiler barrel.

Besides single cylinder and side-by-side (sometimes called 'cross') compounds, Fodens also built tandem compounds (with cylinders in line, that is), and twin high-pressure engines. In fact, I have a catalogue of *circa* 1903 in which it is categorically stated that the firm still built all those classes, as required, but exactly what demand there was at this date either for double-cylinder engines or for tandem compounds, is open to doubt.

In a later chapter, by the way, we shall read something of the more than half-a-century record of a Foden in Australia—and she's still going strong!

14

THE HEYDAY OF STEAM TRACTION

Now, a'together, hear them lift their lesson – theirs an' mine:
'Law, Orrder, Duty an' Restraint, Obedience, Discipline!'
Mill, forge, an' try-pit taught them that when roarin' they arose,
An' whiles I wonder if a soul was gied them wi' the blows.'

RUDYARD KIPLING

IT WAS THE PERIOD from 1890, and for forty years after, that was the heyday of steam road traction. True, during and after the First World War, the i.c.-engined unit began to make headway, but even in the 1930's there was nothing to touch the steam-powered road loco for the real hard work. Timber hauliers, furniture removers, heavy haulage contractors, showmen and many other trades, all used steam traction, which together with the engines in use by farmers for general purpose work and for steam ploughing, as well as all the steam rollers owned by road contractors and local firms, must have totalled many thousands.

There was quite a difference between the engines built for the different jobs, of course: those of the steam roller and the steam ploughing engine are more or less obvious, but not so those of the traction engine, the road locomotive and the tractor. To an inexperienced eye, these three all look very much the same.

The general purpose traction engine was a machine of from 5 to 8 n.h.p., and as the name indicates, it was used for any job that might arise. Its chief use was on the farm for threshing or other agricultural tasks, but some were owned by local councils or by building or road contractors, quarry owners and others. These engines were not designed for continuous road haulage, and only two speeds were fitted, as a general rule.

A majority of general purpose engines was single cylindered, but most builders also supplied compounds. A representative single cylindered 8 n.h.p. machine would be 17 ft. 6 in. overall length, 7 ft. 3 in. overall width, with a cylinder 9 in. by 12 in. The hind wheels would be in the region of 6 ft. 4 in. diameter, and the flywheel (usually spoked) 4 ft. 6 in. Normal revs. per minute would be 180 to 250, and average weight empty, 10½ tons. An 8 n.h.p. compound would have cylinders of 6½ in. and 10½ in. bore by 12 in., developing 40 to 50 b.h.p. Again, as a general

Fig. 116. Aveling road locomotive of 1890.
Steam Locomotion on Common Roads.

Fig. 117. Aveling road loco No. 2465 with dynamo.
Steam Locomotion on Common Roads.

rule, traction engines were not fitted with a canopy or awning for the driver, nor with sideplates to conceal the motion.

Road locomotives *were* built primarily for road haulage, and were of generally heavier construction, with shafts of larger diameter, wider gearing, and larger wheels. In later years, road locos almost invariably were compounds, mounted on rubber tyres, and with springing on both axles. Three speeds were used. A belly tank was fitted to give increased road mileage, there was usually a canopy to keep the worst of the weather off the driver – and a seat for his comfort, too.

The flywheel was of the disc pattern (or in earlier days the spokes were covered with a plate), and sideplates were fitted to conceal the motion work. This was 'to avoid frightening horses', which is a point made in all the early catalogues and literature. Hard-headed farmers would not pay out good money on such unnecessary gew-gaws, so that their Suffolk Punches and Percherons had perforce to be less neurotic than the high-spirited animals which drew the smart turnout of the young blood, or the carriage of the local J.P.!

A typical road loco, the Fowler 'Big Lion' of 8 n.h.p. was capable of developing some 70 b.h.p., or even up to 100 for a brief effort. The cylinders were 6¾ in. and 11½-in. bore by 12-in. stroke: the overall length was 19 ft. 9 in. (extra for the showman's engine, of course) and the overall width 7 ft. 11½ in. In working order the weight was 16¾ tons, and quite an ordinary load would be 40 tons – in fact, we shall see later that this was often exceeded by a good margin. The 'Super Lion' of 10 n.h.p. would take up to 120 tons, in case of extreme need.

Steam tractor was the name given to small machines of 3 or 4 n.h.p., which were really miniature road locos, and used for the same purpose. There were a few 6- or even 7-tonners, but most of the class were built to a 5-ton limit under the Motor Car Act of 1903. These, like their larger brethren, were almost invariably compounds, had belly tanks, sideplates and disc flywheels, and were spring-mounted and rubber-shod in later years.

Typical dimensions could be 14 ft. length, 6 ft. width, 4 ft. 6 in. to 5 ft. hind wheels, and flywheel 2 ft. 9 in., with cylinders 4½ in. and 7½ in. by 9-in. stroke. Tractors were used by furniture removers, timber fellers and merchants, brewers and, of course, showmen, haulage contractors and other classes.

By 1890 there had been a settling down in design and appearance, and from now on the majority of improvement was in points of detail. Even so, there was still plenty of experiment going on, and from time to time we shall see examples of this. But in Chapter Three we have examined already the points of a typical 'modern' engine of the general purpose class.

An orthodox road locomotive of 1890 is shown in Fig. 116, which is an engraving of an 8 h.p. Aveling and Porter – a magnificently proportioned engine which has the appearance of wanting to get on with the job. Readers will note the points made in an earlier paragraph, but on the Aveling we might mention their massive one-piece steel castings to carry the bearings of the crankshaft and the two countershafts. These castings not only were riveted to the hornplates, reinforcing them greatly, but also had right-angle flanges at front and rear, so that the transverse plates forming the rest of the crankbox were bolted to these. This made a more rigid structure than the usual construction, with the transverse plates riveted to angles riveted to the hornplates. (Alternatively, the transverse plates could be flanged, and riveted to the hornplates, on other makes.)

The transverse plates, by the way, were known as the front plate and spectacle plate, the former being that nearer to the footplate, and not, as might be imagined, that nearer to the chimney. To a traction-man, too, the 'front' end of the cylinder was that nearer the footplate, and the 'boiler-

Fig. 118. Early Burrell single crank compound showman's engine.
The Engineer.

front' was the one with the fire-hole in it, which a railwayman would call the backhead. This is due to the influence of the portable engine, of course.

Electric lighting was now beginning to come into favour, and both the military men and the showmen were not slow in realising that it could be of inestimable value to them. Fig. 117 shows an Aveling of 1890 with dynamo over the crankshaft, driven by a gear-ring bolted to the flywheel. Several of these engines were built for military use, being used for searchlights, for lighting camps and similar purposes.

We have already noted that Jim Myer was the first showman to use steam traction, back in 1858, but it was Jacob Studt, the famous showman of Pontypridd, who had the first dynamo equipped engine. This was a Burrell single-crank compound, built in 1889, and it appeared very much as in Fig. 118, though this is actually an engraving of a 10-horse loco built in 1894, without dynamo.

There are not twisted brass standards or other fancy work of the modern showman's engine, but it was not long before they made their appearance. The dynamo had been moved to the now accustomed place in front of the smokebox; the position over the crankshaft had not proved suitable, because of oil flung up by the motion.

Of course showmen had other engines in the early days, without dynamos; in fact, before the dynamo became commonly fitted to the haulage engine, it was often mounted on an ordinary portable engine, which the loco hauled in its train along with the rides and the caravans.

And what trains some of those were! I have a photo (which unfortunately is not fit to reproduce) of Jacob Studts' Galloping Horses *en route*, where there are at least nine vehicles behind the engine before the end of the train is lost in haze. The haulage engine here was No. 1457 *Monarch*, a single-cylinder Burrell, and the first vehicle in the train was the centre engine of the roundabout. Another photo of about the same date – early 1890's – shows Twigdon and Son's single crank compound (usually shortened to S.C.C., by the way) hauling nine vans. This engine has a dynamo platform, but no dynamo on it, in the picture, and the 'spectacle plate' similar to loco practice, as in Fig. 118, to support the front of the canopy.

The handsome engine seen in Fig. 119 is a Fowler 8-horse which was exhibited at the Darlington 'Royal' in 1895. It was fitted with Marshall and Wigram's patent valve gear, where the cylinders, of $6\frac{1}{2}$ in. and $11\frac{1}{4}$ in by 12 in., were controlled by a single piston valve between but above the cylinders. This necessitated only one set of link motion, of course; it had not been exhibited before, but Fowlers said that similar engines had been at work for four years.

The Engineer mentioned that several users spoke of these engines as running very quietly on the road, using less fuel and grease, pulling heavier loads, costing less to maintain, and much liked by the men in charge. From a series of tests, it was found that with a pressure of 150 p.s.i., there was no difficulty in pulling 32 tons in *fast* gear upon a heavy gradient. The engine indicated 65 horse power.

In the engraving the motion covers have been removed to show the valve gear which, it will be noticed, is inclined to line up with the crankshaft. Note too that the twisted brass standards have now appeared, but not yet the full-length canopy.

The engine was also fitted with Fowler's new patent spring gear (Pat. No. 14,242 of 1892); they had taken out their first patent for springing as far back as 1876, but this was the culmination which was to remain unaltered in principle (though not in detail) up to the very last spring-mounted Fowler. It was of the 'large movement' type which allowed up to 2 in. vertical movement, and was compensated or equalised so that any vertical motion on one side of the engine was also transferred to the other side, which did away with any rocking tendency of the engine itself.

Fig. 119. Fowler showman's engine with Marshall and Wigram valve-gear.
The Engineer.

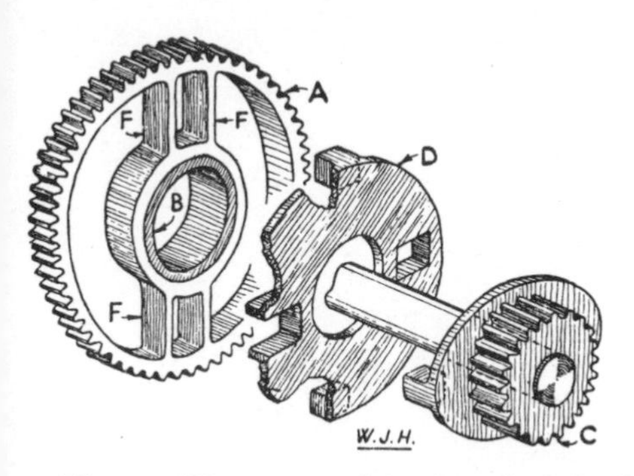

Fig. 120. Diagram to show the principle of the Fowler universal joint.
Traction Engines Worth Modelling.

The method of coupling the moving countershaft to the fixed gearing is shown diagrammatically in Fig. 120. Spur wheel A is driven from a pinion on the second motion shaft (not shown), and revolves on the hollow boss B which is firmly secured to the horn-plates. The driving frame D (shown partly broken away for clarity) carries two lugs which engage with the webs F formed in spur wheel A. Similar lugs on the pinion C engage with slots in the driving-frame D, and C is keyed to the third shaft M. Thus, since both pairs of lugs are free to slide in their respective slots, we have a universal joint which allows pinion C and shaft M to move vertically, while not affecting spur wheel A even though all are rotating.

Turning now to Fig. 121, we see that the third shaft M and hind axle N are connected by two rigid cast steel brackets or links OO, which have bearings in each end to carry the shafts. The brackets OO can slide freely in guides formed by the horncheeks SS and TT, which are bolted to the horn-plates GG. (The boss B is formed on the upper part of the off-side horncheek, and projects through a hole bored in the hornplate.)

Now, because M and N are kept rigidly parallel by the links, then pinion C and spur wheel P are kept evenly and constantly in mesh.

The weight of the engine is taken through the hornplates on the ends of twin transverse laminated springs, one of which is seen at H. Between the springs passes an eyebolt J, its lower end passing through a hole in the spring-buckle connector, both buckles being formed in one piece. Tension of the springs is adjusted by locknut K.

Through the eye of J passes a pin which carries the two equalising levers LL, of each of which one end rests in a slot cut in hornblock and hornplate, with the other end suspended by a hook R from the bottom of the link O. Thus, any 'scissor action' at either side must be balanced at the other side, so that *both* ends of hind axle and third shaft *must* move vertically together, and both shafts *must* keep at right angles to the hornplates.

Now, back to our early showmen's engines, in May 1896 *The Engineer* showed a single crank compound (Fig. 122), which it stated was one of

Fig. 121. Arrangement of the Fowler hind axle springing.
Block loaned by J. and H. McLaren, Ltd.

thirty-five supplied by the firm to leading showmen in Britain 'It will indicate 50 horse power, and is capable of hauling 50 tons through any part of this country.'

The hind wheels were 7 ft. diameter by 20 in. wide, shod with oak blocks, end-grain out, supported by angle rings at each side and with rivets from side to side to secure the overlapping blocks together (Fig. 123). The

Fig. 122. Burrell single crank compound with wood-rimmed hind wheels. *The Engineer.*

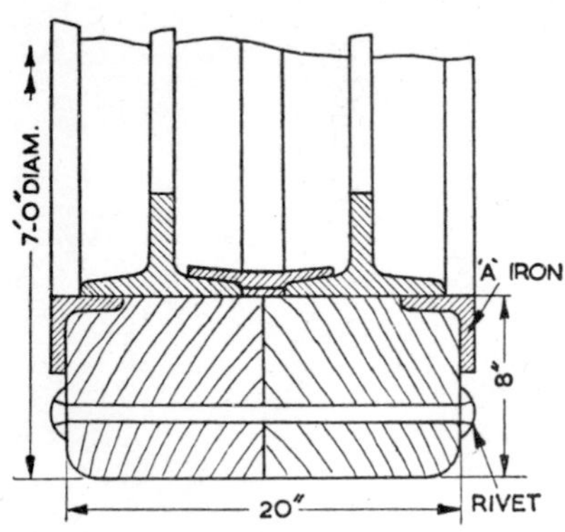

Fig. 123. Cross-section of wood rims.
The Model Engineer.

engine was spring mounted, and it was stated that Burrell's system had now been applied to more than 300 engines. 'The brass fittings shown in the engraving are in accordance with showmen's requirements.'

But not all makers were thus embellishing their engines. At the Leicester 'Royal' in the following month, Ransomes exhibited the single cylindered showman's engine shown in Fig. 124, which appears to be merely a heavy haulage engine with dynamo and platform added – it hasn't even a belly tank for extra water capacity. Incidentally, it is a fact that showmen did not 'go' for Ransomes engines, and very few were produced by the firm for them. This particular example was mounted on volute springs at the firebox end, and a leaf spring on the front axle.

The Aveling and Porter engine in Fig. 125 also has no fancy work, but it does possess a full-length canopy. The dynamo platform too has an appearance of austerity, and it cannot have been too easy to sweep the boiler tubes! Here, again, this make of engine was never really popular with the showmen.

Not all Fowler early showmen's engines had 'gilt and gingerbread' either, for a catalogue of 1896 shows a single cylindered example (Fig. 126), which is described as for 'travelling showmen, bioscope operators, etc.' Note the large flywheel to give steadiness and freedom from flicker on the dynamo, which the single cylinder might not otherwise give. The engine, by the way, was specified not as a road locomotive, but a 'heavy haulage traction engine', which Fowlers and some other makers built as a kind of in-between – more robust than a general purpose engine, but not as much so as a road locomotive. The latter was specified as 'for heavy haulage *and continuous road work*' (my italics).

Now see the magnificent 10-horse Burrell in Fig. 127, taken from a catalogue of 1897. This engine was actually No. 1980 *Her Majesty*, a double-crank compound mounted on springs. Not everyone liked the single-crank system, with the difficulties previously described, and Burrells had commenced to build the D.C.C. engines in 1896. From this time on no showman ordered another S.C.C. engine, though plenty of S.C.C. types were still sold, of course, for other purposes.

Fig. 124. An early showman's engine by Ransomes, Sims and Jefferies.
The Engineer.

Her Majesty had cylinders 7 in. and 11½ in. by 12 in., and she was fitted with a steam brake. A cylinder bolted to the off-side of the tender contained a 7-in. diameter piston which, when steam was admitted, pushed on a lever mounted on a shaft passing across the tender. This shaft carried long brake shoes which acted on turned steel angle rings (nearly as large as the rims) bolted to the spokes.

Fig. 129 shows an interesting development of the showman's engine – the 'traction centre'. The particular example, *Empress*, belonged to the Cambridgeshire showmen Barker and Thurston Ltd. (later Thurston and Abbott), and had been built in 1898 by Savages of King's Lynn. She was a compound of 6½ in. and 11¼ in. by 12 in., and on what appears to be the dynamo bracket there is actually a small vertical steam engine for driving the organ of the roundabout.

It will be seen that plate frames were extended upwards from the sides of the engine, and these carried the turret on which the roundabout was erected, thus doing away with the separate centre engine of the ordinary roundabout. The turret was driven by bevel-gears from the crankshaft, with dog-clutch interposed. From about half-way up the chimney an extra flue branched backwards and upwards, so that when the 'ride' was mounted, the chimney was blanked off above the branch, and the gases passed up the branch and through the centre of the ride.

Several traction centres were built by one firm or another, but were very cumbrous. In the long run most of them were converted to conventional engines – *Empress* was so altered in 1920, and a dynamo was substituted for the organ engine.

Turning back a few years, at the 1893 Royal Show Aveling and Porter exhibited the sturdy roller seen in Fig. 129. They had by now turned to compounding with valves overhead rather like the Fowler arrangement, and they exhibited a handsome compound traction engine, too. Both these machines now possessed an appearance very little different from those of thirty years later.

It must not be thought that Avelings were the only firm building steam rollers, of course. By now the whole business was highly competitive, and practically all makers would build any type of engine required. The

Fig. 125. Aveling and Porter showman's road loco No. 7051 of 1896.
A. R. Dibben, Esq.

Fig. 126. Fowler showman's engine of 1896.
A. R. Dibben, Esq.

Fig. 127. Burrell double crank compound No. 1980, 'Her Majesty'.
Official catalogue.

Fig. 128. Savage traction centre showman's engine No. 730, 'Empress'.
B. H. Maycock, Esq.

'convertible' was catalogued by most makers: it is not clear who first had the idea of building an engine which could be traction engine or roller at will, but Figs. 130 and 131 show the Burrell version. In the former a normal fore-carriage is attached to the perch bracket, and normal wheels are mounted on the hind axle. In Fig. 131 a heavy casting to take the front roll stirrup is bolted to the smokebox extension, and rolls have been substituted for the hind wheels.

Another offshoot of the traction engine was the railway shunting engine with a similar layout, sometimes chain driven but usually with gear drive, and made by several firms. Most of these are outside the scope of this book, but Fig. 132 from the 1896 catalogue shows a Fowler traction engine which was specially built for London County Council. It was not only convertible to a steam roller, but also to a railway loco, as shown. Details are not available, but it certainly proves the versatility of the traction engine.

This same catalogue also shows a Fowler compound with two parallel steel arms pivoted on a pin on the fore-carriage and projecting forward almost like horse-shafts. In one engraving a centrifugal pump, driven by belt from the flywheel, is mounted between these arms, pumping water from a stream or river and delivering it into an irrigation flume.

In the second engraving, a saw similar to a very large hand-saw projects forward from the arms, and a steam cylinder mounted between them gives it reciprocating motion, the cylinder taking steam by flexible pipe from the base of the compound cylinder block. A third picture shows the arms lifted into a nearly vertical position out of the way, whilst the engine is used for direct ploughing, hauling a four-bladed gang plough.

Haulage contractors had been quick to realise the value of a road loco equipped with a crane, and in the 'nineties several firms were building them. The engraving Fig. 133 illustrates 'Fowlers Class B Compound Crane Engine mounted on springs, recently supplied to Messrs. Cattermole & Sons, Haulage Contractors, London. It was used by them at the Bath and West of England Agricultural Show at St. Albans, and also at the Royal Agricultural Show, Leicester, this year, and was found of immense service to the Society and Exhibitors, in removing and transporting all kinds of heavy machinery and other exhibits'.

The engine was of 10 n.h.p., and the drive for the crane hoist was taken by a bevel wheel sliding on the crankshaft to engage with a pinion on the nearly vertical shaft near the off-side hind wheel, with a worm and worm-wheel to drive the hoisting barrel. The weight limit was five tons.

Because of the extra weight thrown on the engine, the hind wheels were made wider on the rim; the front ones were also extended, and made vastly

Fig. 129. Aveling compound steam roller of 1893.
The Practical Engineer.

Fig. 130. Burrell convertible as a traction . . .

Official catalogue.

Fig. 131. . . . and as a steam roller.

Official catalogue.

Fig. 132. Fowler convertible as a railway locomotive.
A. R. Dibben, Esq.

stronger with double T-rings instead of the normal single one, and with extra and stronger spokes. The extra price for the 5-ton crane was £80 to £95, on top of a price for the road loco of £635, plus £65 for the springing.

Other Fowler prices of 1896 were, according to horse power, from £360 to £530 for single-cylinder traction engines, and from £415 to £630 for compound tractions. Single-cylinder road locos were £490 to £650, and compounds £550 to £635. Springing cost from £50 to £65 extra. To give some idea of the extent of Fowler exports, at this time they had branches at Berlin, Magdeburg, Prague, Budapest, Bucharest, Sydney, Calcutta, Kimberley, Johannesburg and Buenos Aires, and, of course, agents in very many other cities and towns in the world.

Burrell prices were rather higher, with single-cylinder tractions costing from £420 to £595; double-crank compound tractions were from £50 to £100 dearer, but the single-crank system cost only £50 extra on any horse power. Springing was £60 extra on the hind axle, and another £10 on the front, on any size. Parts to convert to a roller cost from £120 to £175 extra.

Single-cylinder road locos were from £540 to £700; compounding and springing were charged at the same rates as on the tractions. A polished copper top to the chimney cost £5, and crane fittings were from £70 to £95.

The Burrell 1897 catalogue also shows the very handsome 'Devonshire' light traction engine of 6 n.h.p., which became very popular indeed. It was a single-crank compound, and was stated to be 'designed to meet the requirements of thrashing machine proprietors in the west and other hilly parts of England, who want a small, light and powerful Engine to drive a 4 feet 6 inch thrashing machine, and haul it from place to place, with the greatest economy of fuel, and capable of climbing the steepest hills with ease'.

This engine (Fig. 134) was double geared on the last motion: that is, the second shaft carried the differential, and a pinion at either end of the shaft drove each hind wheel separately through its own spur wheel. Thus there was only half the wear on the teeth of the last motion gearing, and only one-sixth of the normal strain on the compensating gear.

The 'Devonshire' was only 6 ft. 3 in. wide overall, and would do a full day's thrashing on from 3 to 3½ cwt. of coal. It sold in 1897 for £475.

In 1899, the Boer War broke out, and Lord Roberts, remembering Lieutenant Crompton's experiences in India with the Government Steam Train (see Chapter Eleven), put him in charge of the small instalment of steam transport which had been taken to South Africa by Colonel Templer as part of the equipment of the Balloon Corps. For the past several years the War Office had been experimenting with road locomotives of various

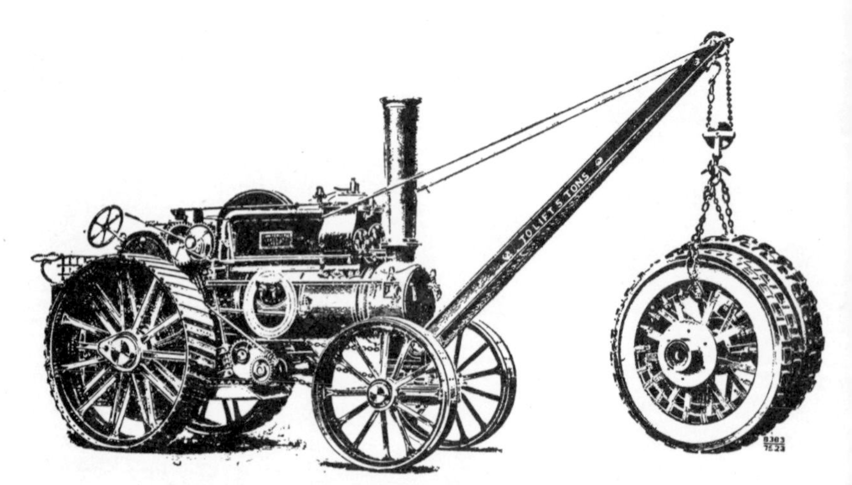

Fig. 133. Cattermole's five-ton Fowler crane engine.
A. R. Dibben, Esq.

makes but, as always, they had much less equipment available than they should have had in time of real need.

However, Fig. 135 shows part of this 'small instalment' crossing a drift in the Transvaal, with a Burrell road loco in the foreground and a Fowler actually hauling the train. Crompton's work in this field so impressed the War Office that he was called home to organise mechanical transport for the Army.

Several showmen's engines had been purchased and altered to suit military needs, and the War Office had ordered many new engines, too. These included some Fowler armour-plated road locos complete with armoured wagons for carrying 4.7 howitzers and ammunition, as well as Fowler special road locos with machine-cut gears, and shafts and axles of special steel. All these were to the express orders of Lord Roberts himself.

The armoured road loco and train appeared as in Fig. 136, though actually in a complete train there were two howitzers, and provision was made for carrying them in the wagons. To load them, steel channels were placed sloping from the wagon floor to the ground, and the guns hauled up into the wagons by means of the loco's winding rope.

It must have been very torrid in that steel-plated cab (Fig. 137), with the heat from the boiler and firebox added to that of the African sun. The

Fig. 134. Burrell 'Devonshire' S.C.C. light traction engine.
Official catalogue.

driver only had two narrow slots facing forward for vision, and could see through the left-hand one of these only by means of a mirror! The total weight of the engine was 22 tons, of which the plating accounted for 4½ tons. The cylinders were 6¼ in. and 11½ in. by 12 in. (10 n.h.p.), and the working pressure was 180 p.s.i. The hind wheels were 7 ft. diameter by 2 ft. wide, the water capacity was 400 gallons and the coal bunker held 15 cwt. The wagons were 15 ft. 6 in. long and 7 ft. 8½ in. wide, weighed 5 tons each, and each could carry 12,000 lb. of ammunition for the guns.

Following the Boer War, Fowlers built a number of special road locos for the War Office, in 1902–03. These had copper fireboxes and brass

Fig. 136. Fowler armoured road loco and train.
T. D. Walshaw, Esq.

tubes, and the water lifter could discharge into a trailing service tank as well as into the enlarged belly tank. A Worthington steam pump was fitted besides the usual injector and feed pump. To test adequately these special road locomotives (Fig. 139), they were sent from Leeds to Aldershot with 60-ton loads, and then tried with loads of more than 60 tons, which they handled comfortably up hill and down dale. Built to burn coal, wood, or oil fuel alternatively, the engines were tested on all these, and the illustration shows an oil tank wagon in the train, immediately behind the foremost engine. The other wagons were loaded with scrap iron mostly, to make up the weight. It should be mentioned that these test loads were excessive – a normal 'everyday' load for these fine engines would be, perhaps, 35 to 40 tons, to avoid excessive strain, wear, and tear. However, as already mentioned, road locos could and did, single-handed, move loads well in excess of 60 tons, when necessity demanded it.

Fig. 137. Cab view of the Fowler armoured loco.
T. D. Walshaw, Esq.

Fig. 138. Testing the special road locos for the War Office.
T. D. Walshaw, Esq.

15

THE EXPORT TRADE

Steam, that great civilizer. . . . FREEMAN HUNT

A VAST INCREASE IN the export of British traction engines, rollers and road locos took place in the 'nineties, and in the remaining years preceding the First World War. On page 191 I gave a list of places in which Fowlers had branches, and of course other makers had similar foreign depots and connections, though in most cases not so extensive as Fowlers. Makers were alive to the special needs of foreign and colonial customers, and designed special engines to meet them. It is the purpose of this chapter to discuss such engines, though the reader should understand that besides the 'specials', large numbers of more or less standard types were also exported.

A quite typical early example of a 'colonial' road locomotive is seen in Fig. 139; it was exhibited by Burrells at the 1893 show of the R.A.S.E. A single-crank compound, the engine is spring mounted, and has an extra large firebox for burning wood – the increased capacity being necessary because of the inferior calorific value of wood as compared with coal, of course. The smokebox, too, is larger than standard, and fitted with baffle-plates and screens so as to check all sparks without checking the draught. (Other wood-burners sometimes had a spark-catcher mounted on the chimney, as did some straw-burners.)

Our Burrell's tender is longer than standard, and fitted with a rack for wood carrying: the road wheels are extra large, and the gearing has somewhat smaller ratios. The engine is considerably higher from the ground than usual, for clearance when travelling over rough ground or through water splashes, and the ashpan is constructed to hold water, so as to prevent sparks being dropped and thus setting fire to long and possibly parched grass or bush. For ploughing by direct traction, hind wheels of extra width could be fitted or, alternatively, extension rings could be bolted to the outsides of the rims. Burrells also stated that they 'will be pleased to forward complete specifications of special engines', and that they 'can supply their agricultural general purpose traction engines with the above features, at extra cost.'

Fig. 139. Burrell wood-burning colonial engine of 1893.

The Engineer.

From the same firm's catalogue of 1897 comes Fig. 140, showing the kind of light straw-burning traction engine which was very popular in all the great granaries of the world. In these areas portable engines had been widely used for thrashing, but were displaced often by the light traction which, besides its other obvious advantages, could also be used for light direct traction ploughing work.

The mechanical arrangement of such engines was often different from that of a conventional traction engine, apart from such necessities as the enlarged firebox and the apparatus for straw-burning, previously described. On the Burrell there are no hornplates, the crankshaft bearings being carried in triangular shaped plates riveted or bolted to the firebox. The gearing arrangements are different, too: the two-speed spur wheel is carried on a stub-shaft mounted on the crankshaft bearing-plate, and from here the drive is taken to a countershaft passing under the boiler barrel just in front of the firebox throatplate. At either end of this shaft a pinion drives each road wheel separately through an internally toothed gear ring bolted to lugs cast on the wheel rims.

The hind wheels have round spokes cast into both hubs and rims, on to which the traction bars or strakes are also cast. They rotate on stub axles riveted to the firebox sides. A driving platform is bolted on at the rear, with the footplate for the driver raised over the straw feeding apparatus, of which can be seen the feed handle used when raising steam. There being no conventional tender, the water tank is carried beneath the boiler.

In later years, when competition from American makers was becoming very keen – especially in South America – ways and means had to be found of cheapening the export types. One of these was an abandonment of some of the traditional British classical 'finish': in fact, the Marshall 'Gainsborough' engines were stated to have no high finish or polish or bright parts 'which do not add to the mechanical effectiveness of the engine'. This meant, for example, that such parts as eccentric rods and connecting rods were left straight from the forging hammer, with only a lick of paint to minimise the roughness.

A post-war 'Gainsborough' is seen in Fig. 141; this is the light pattern, and readers familiar with American outline will notice a considerable likeness though at the same time there is a sturdiness which frequently was not so evident on the American counterpart. Entirely unconventional to British eyes, the cylinder is not supported underneath, being merely bolted to the trunk-guide which is supported on the boiler top.

The trunk-guide forms part of the bedplate of the engine, with an arm joining it to the crankshaft bearings, all being contained in a single casting of course. An overhung balanced crank is fitted to the shaft, with the

Fig. 141. Marshall 'Gainsborough' light traction for export.
D. N. Wright, Esq.

crankpin outside. The flywheel carries a friction clutch, and this, though foreign to our practice, was quite a usual feature of these export engines. One reason was that when threshing, it was customary with a straw-burner to use a very long belt to keep the engine well away from the unthreshed grain, and also to give a good drive. With the clutch, it was possible not only easily to 'set' the engine just right for the correct belt tension, but also to move back to tighten the belt as it stretched, without stopping the threshing machine. Moreover, when direct ploughing, which gave a heavy starting load, the clutch made this easier. Almost all these 'Colonial' engines were single speed, by the way.

In our Marshall, there is a separate dome, with two Salter safety valves on top, and the regulator valve on the side of the safety valve stalk. From here the steam passes through a pipe to the governor valve, and so to the valve chest. Stephenson link motion controls the slide valve, and the exhaust steam passes through a feed water heater on the boiler side before passing to the blast pipe. An independent steam driven feed pump is mounted on top of the belly tank, with the water lifter close by.

The drive again is by gearing to separate spur-rings bolted to each hind wheel; though this engine does have hornplates of a kind, the hind axle is not live. Medium sized and large 'Gainsborough' engines were built, and in general appearance these were much more English, with conventional cylinder saddled to the boiler, and normal hornplates and crankshaft bearings. But there was still the friction clutch, the straw-burning gear, and those flimsy looking hind wheels.

Ransomes made what they called a 'special light type agricultural traction engine' (Fig. 142), and several of these engines were used on the Western Front in World War I, where, it was stated, '. . . in the soft condition of the ground generally prevailing they were able to haul their loads across country which heavier Engines could not deal with'. The War Department also ordered a new engine of this type in 1940, but it is not known for what purpose it was used.

These single speed engines at normal r.p.m. travelled at 2 m.p.h. A friction clutch was used, and a pinion on the boss of the clutch drove an idler spur wheel on a stub-shaft. The idler drove a spur wheel on the countershaft, with compensating gear incorporated, and a pinion on either end drove the hind wheels as before. An unusual feature was a foot brake, working on a drum on the countershaft. The clutch could be locked by means of a pin, incidentally.

The cylinder casting had a flat base, and was bolted to a cast steel

Fig. 142. Ransomes' 'Type R.C.T.' light traction engine.
Ransomes, Sims and Jefferies, Ltd.

Fig. 143. Ransomes' 60 b.h.p. straw-burning engine. *Ransomes, Sims and Jefferies, Ltd.*

seating riveted to the boiler. This idea, now in fairly common use, not only made it easier to line up the cylinders and motion in erection, but did away with bolts passing through the boiler shell, which was often a source of trouble. The governor was of the Gardner high speed type.

Working pressure was 180 p.s.i., with a boiler test pressure of 280, and a larger firebox for burning inferior fuels could be fitted at extra charge, as could straw-burning apparatus. The engine was made in five sizes, of 15, 18, 25, 30 and 35 brake horse power, which sizes correspond approximately to 5, 6, 8, 10 and 12 nominal horse power. Further particulars are in the table following:

	15 B.H.P.	18 B.H.P.	25 B.H.P.	30 B.H.P.	35 B.H.P.
Weight empty ..	5 tons	5¾ tons	6¾ tons	7¾ tons	9½ tons
Weight with coal and water ..	5¾ tons	6⅝ tons	7¾ tons	8¾ tons	10¾ tons
Cyl. bore and stroke	6 in. × 8 in.	6½ in. × 8 in.	7 in. × 9 in.	7½ in. × 9 in.	8 in. × 9 in.
Flywheel dia. and and width ..	3 ft. × 6 in.	3 ft. × 7 in.	3 ft. × 8 in.	3 ft. × 9 in.	3 ft. × 9 in.
Hind wheels: dia. and breadth ..	5 ft. × 12 in.	5 ft. × 14 in.	5¼ ft. × 14 in.	5¼ ft. × 18 in.	6 ft. × 18 in.
Approx. gross load on normal roads	8 tons	9 tons	10 tons	11 tons	15/20 tons

The 35 b.h.p. size was stated to be very suitable for direct traction ploughing.

A very imposing engine of 60 b.h.p. (Fig. 143) was also built by Ransomes, and this was arranged for burning straw as standard, though it could be fitted with a grate for burning wood or coal, and with bunkers as illustrated. This, too, worked at 180 p.s.i., and the huge compound cylinders were 8 in. and 12 in. diameter by 12-in. stroke. Again the cylinder casting had a planed flat seating, and a Gardner governor was fitted.

The transmission through friction clutch and compensating gear was arranged as described for the lighter engines, with all steel gearing. The steel hind wheels were 6 ft. by 2 ft. 2 in., and for direct traction ploughing or on very soft ground, could be fitted with extension rings to make them up to 3 ft. wide, the rings being bolted to the angles seen on the outside edge of the rim. Different patterns of cleats could be fitted according to requirement. The front wheels were 4 ft. 7½ in. by 12 in.; notice the construction, with two angle rings instead of a single T-ring. A steam feed pump was fitted besides the usual eccentric driven one.

Fig. 144. Marshall heavy-duty colonial road locomotive. *D. N. Wright, Esq.*

For continuous direct traction ploughing or road haulage work, it was recommended that a specially strengthened version of the engine be employed, with larger diameter crankshaft, countershaft and hind axle, wider gearing, specially strong drawbar, and larger water tank.

As a matter of interest, Ransomes show in their post-war catalogue their machines at work in North and South Russia, Siberia, Italy, Asia Minor, Australia, Bulgaria, France and South Africa.

Of the engine shown in Fig. 144 I have not much technical information, It is a Marshall compound built in 1913, and reputed to be of 100 b.h.p. Apart from its great size, it is much more 'conventional' in arrangement than the 'Gainsborough' engines, and intended more as a road locomotive, though I possess another print of the same engine showing it attached to a large gang plough. The very long firebox and the rack on the tender indicate that it was a wood-burner, probably for Australia.

As we have already seen, McLarens were early in the export trade, and they developed some massive engines of which Fig. 145 is a fair example, known as their 'Hungarian' engine. The steam roller shown is probably a ten tonner of normal size, and this will give an idea of the other's dimen-

Fig. 145. McLaren Hungarian engine compared with an ordinary roller.
R. G. Pratt, Esq.

Fig. 146. Foden 8 h.p. No. 1143 moving part of an hotel.
Ian Sinclair, Esq.

sions! Once more technical detail is lacking, but the engine is a cross compound, with flywheel clutch. The apparatus between chimney and cylinder block is a feed water heater, through which the exhaust steam passes.

Unfortunately, the original print of Fig. 146 is not perfectly clear, but I am including it as showing a typical job of work done by an ordinary traction engine in Australia. She is a single-cylinder Foden No. 1143 of 8 n.h.p., weighing 10 tons. Imported into Australia in 1906, she was purchased by the late Alexander Sinclair, and is now owned by his son Ian, who works her quite frequently on his own and neighbours' farms, for chaff cutting, log sawing, and similar duties.

When she was purchased, many of the engine men with whom Mr. Sinclair was acquainted said she wouldn't last more than three years on the hills and rough roads of the area, being too light. However, she was in regular use on all sorts of contract work, including road haulage, saw milling, threshing, chaff cutting and hay baling, for more than 30 years, before being taken for private use on the Sinclair farmstead. Even then, and since, she has been worked steadily and hard, but is still in excellent condition. Not bad for sixty-four years! How many infernal combustion engined contraptions would last half as long, one wonders? And in all that time her only replacements have been a new hind axle and two new sets of tubes!

She used to haul and drive a Robinson threshing machine with a 5 ft. wide drum through a large area in Victoria, between Lancefield and

Melbourne and in the Gouldburn Valley. This 'tour' usually lasted from 12 to 15 weeks, and then a week or two later off she went with chaff cutter and hay baler for another 3 or 4 months. Other work included hauling heavy logs to a sawmill, and then driving the mill to convert the logs to building timbers.

Between whiles she tackled any sort of job which came along, such as the one shown, where she is about to move a section of a country hotel to a new site, having already taken the other half. No. 1143 has always had a reputation for reliability, and will always keep a full head of steam in any circumstances that require it. Her 53 tubes and long slide valve with short clearance passages are of inestimable value here, of course.

Friend Ian remembers one occasion when he had a bad fright with her. The contract work involved journeys on all kinds of roads and back tracks, and often crossing old wooden bridges. On one occasion, taking a heavy load across one of these, he heard the frightening sound of falling timbers. With a glance at the deep drop into the stream, he pushed the regulator wide open, and made it to the other side with only his nerves damaged. As he says, he was then 'young and foolish': he would have done better to take the engine across alone and then use the winding rope to pull the load across. Later, the man who repaired the bridge said that he 'gave the only unbroken support three blows with his axe, and the whole bridge fell to the bed of the stream'.

No. 1143 works still at 160 p.s.i.; the boiler shell is $\frac{7}{16}$ in. thick, and fire-box $\frac{3}{8}$ in., with the two tube plates $\frac{1}{2}$ in. The cylinder is 9-in. bore by 10-in. stroke, her flywheel is 4 ft. 6 in. by 7 in., hind wheels 6 ft. 10 in. by 20 in., and front wheels 3 ft. 10 in. by 10 in. Her long canopy was fitted by the Melbourne agents, and so was the rack on the tender for her wood fuel.

Mr. Sinclair remembers seeing Marshall, Burrell, Ransomes, Ruston and Proctor, McLaren, Clayton and Shuttleworth, Fowler, Aveling, and Foden engines in his time. Fowlers and Fodens were the most numerous, and McLarens were well liked, too. And when one thinks of all that multitude of engines at work, and especially of old No. 1143's sixty years and more, one cannot help but feel rather proud of the British brains and engineering ability which gave her and her sisters to the world!

16

TWENTIETH-CENTURY DEVELOPMENT

While pent within the iron womb
Of boiling caldrons, pants for room
Expanded Steam . . .
DALTON

MEANTIME, OF COURSE, DEVELOPMENT of the basic engines was still going on. Details were improved, and new ideas were tried out – and sometimes discarded. Such a one was introduced by William Fletcher when working for Clayton and Shuttleworth in 1900, for after he left them his version of Joy valve-gear was not used again, by Claytons, or by him, or, apparently, by any other firm.

Yet it was well designed and efficient, and it was a good and logical gear to use (Fig. 147) in a compound engine with the valves overhead (Fig. 148). Since it allowed the slide valve faces and valve rods to be parallel with the cylinder centre lines, it made it much more easy to set up accurately the block for boring the cylinders, planing the valve faces, and boring the stuffing boxes. The work was further facilitated by the base of the cylinder block being planed flat, to fit the separate saddle.

Still another advantage was that the four eccentrics were entirely

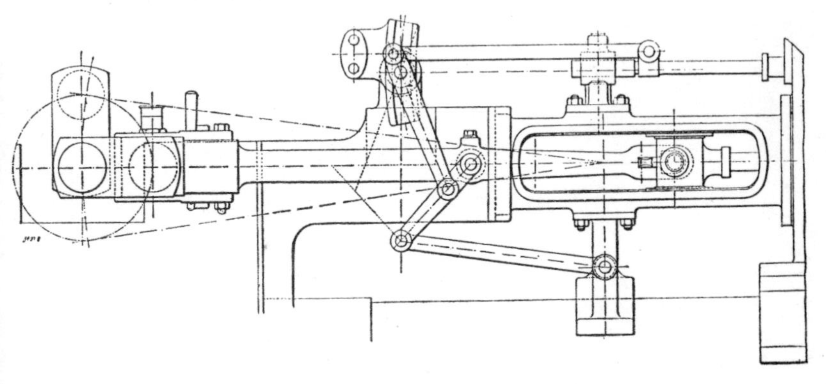

Fig. 147. Clayton and Shuttleworth's Joy valve-gear.
English and American Traction Engines and Steam Cars.

dispensed with, as the plan view shows (Fig. 149). This allowed room for wider crankpins and thicker crankwebs, and there was ample space for the two change speed pinions between the hornplates. In turn, this meant that exactly the same gearing could be used as on the single cylinder of equal n.h.p. – a 'standardising' feature of importance.

The first of these Joy-geared agricultural locomotives was exhibited at the York Show of the R.A.S.E. in 1900. It worked at 160 p.s.i., with cylinders 6½ in. and 10 in. by 12 in.

Early in 1902, Aveling and Porter, among much other correspondence, wrote a letter to an enquiring Dundee firm which to them would be a routine matter, but which more than fifty years later is rather more interesting to us. It was a quotation for a traction engine convertible to a steam roller, and ran as follows:

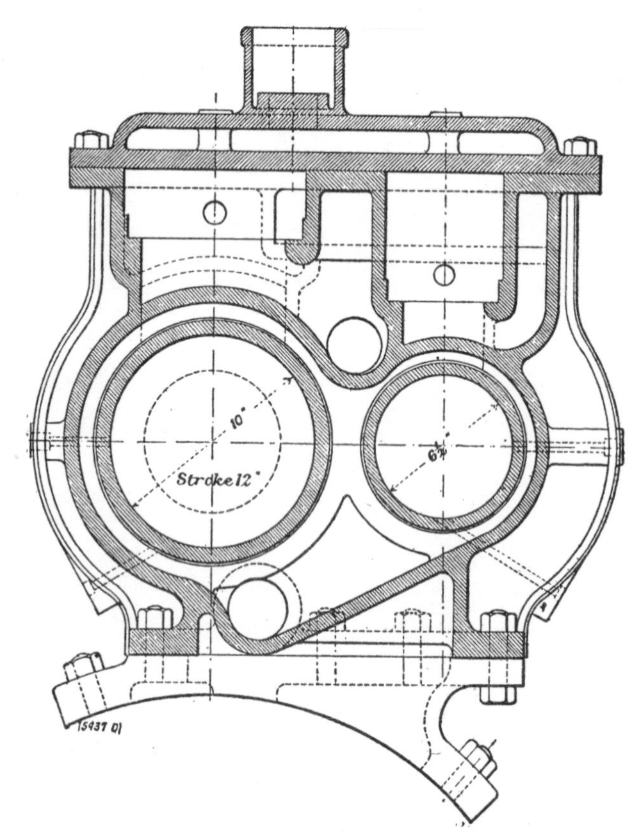

Fig. 148. Compound cylinders to suit the Joy gear.
English and American Traction Engines and Steam Cars.

'Rochester,
25th February, 1902.

Gentlemen,

We beg to offer you an Engine suitable for your work at the Quarry at Maryfield, and are pleased to place you upon our very best terms.

One 8 h.p. Traction Engine adaptable for a Steam Roller and capable of working a Rock drill as well as driving a Stone breaker. Such as already fixed.

The price of this engine is as a Traction	£520	0	0
Fitted for Injector	£10	0	0
	£530	0	0
Less 10 per cent	£53	0	0
	£477	0	0
Less 2½ per cent for cash ..	£11	18	6
	£465	1	6

Delivered free at Dundee.

If fitted for Roller with extra set Roller wheels ..	£175	0	0
Less 10 per cent	£17	10	0
	£157	10	0
Less 2½ per cent for cash ..	£3	18	9
	£153	11	3

also delivered free Dundee.

We are the largest makers of these Engines in the World, and in fact make these engines exclusively so that we can generally supply in two or three weeks after receipt of order.

We should much value your order and will send you the very best engine we can make.

We are, Gentlemen,
Your Obedient Servants,
(Sgd) Aveling and Porter Limited
H. Pitts
Director.'

It is pleasant to report that the firm secured the order for this convertible engine.

From time to time through the years attempts had been made to build 'go anywhere' engines, as we have seen, and at the beginning of 1902 some interesting experiments were being carried out with Diplock's 'Pedrail' engine (Fig. 150) – in fact, they were carried on for several years with different engines and with the 'feet' of developing design.

The particular engine under notice, built by Taskers, was *very* unorthodox, for besides having the Pedrail wheels, it had four-wheel drive, and *all* wheels were steerable (Fig. 151). I have no exact knowledge of the method of transferring the drive to the axles, but it must have been a gimbal arrangement similar to the Whittingham one.

The compound cylinders and motion were under the boiler, and at the rear a jib crane was mounted. But the feet are the real point of interest. They were mounted on ball joints round the rim, and inside the drum-like wheel was a complicated system of springs and compensating levers which on flat ground allowed three to four feet to rest on the floor together.

But when an obstacle, such as the wood baulk in the picture, was encountered, the engine could, as it were, pick up its feet and walk over it. At a demonstration at the R.A.S.E. show at Park Royal in 1904, the Pedrail Tractor, says *Engineering*, was asked to walk up a few steps which had been prepared for it. These it successfully mounted, stepping down again on the other side.

However, the wheels were very complicated, with a great many moving parts, and thus were expensive. Despite some simplification and improvement, they were not acceptable to the people who mattered – the customers!

In passing, the same volume of *Engineering* records that in January 1904 the weight of agricultural steam engines forwarded to foreign countries

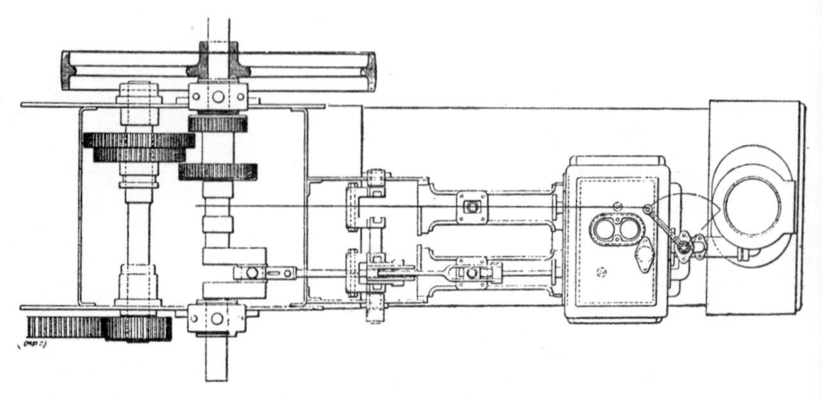

Fig. 149. Plan view of the Joy valve-gear.
English and American Traction Engines and Steam Cars.

Fig. 150. The Pedrail engine surmounts an obstacle.

and British colonies was 958 tons, valued at £42,674, compared with £33,762 in January 1903, and £16,481 in January 1902 – which goes to reinforce our last chapter.

It was at this stage that the light tractor began to make its appearance in increasing numbers. First introduced following the Heavy Motor Car Act of 1903, the tractors were, as we have previously mentioned, miniature road locomotives, designed principally for continuous haulage work, and mounted on springs, with compound cylinders for economy and belly tanks for longer journeys without replenishment.

Quite typical is the Clayton and Shuttleworth *Little Hercules* (Taskers called theirs the *Little Giant*) which had cylinders 5 in. and 8 in. by 8 in. worked at 180 p.s.i. The cast-iron flywheel was 2 ft. 9 in. in diameter, with a hand-brake working on its rim. In addition, a hand-brake worked blocks inside each hind wheel rim, as may be seen in Fig. 152.

All gearing was of crucible cast steel, with the first and second motion wheels machine cut. A section through the gearing is given in Fig. 153, and it can be seen that the slow-speed pinion slid on the crankshaft, with the fast-speed pinion sliding on a sleeve cast in one with the slow-speed pinion. Note the hollow fast-speed pinion, to envelope the other, as described before. The hind wheel springing somewhat resembled the Burrell arrangement, with a universal joint at the right-hand end of the countershaft, and a link connecting the latter and the hind axle at the left-hand side.

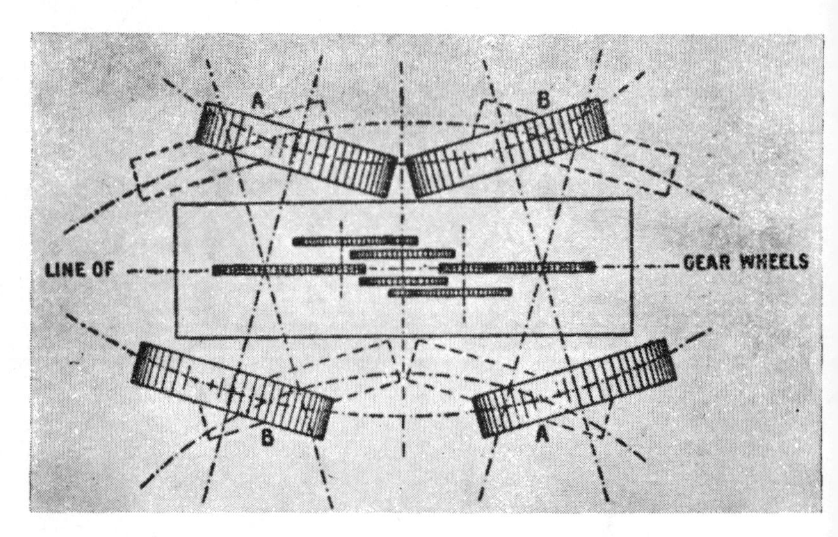

Fig. 151. Four-wheel drive and turning scope of the Pedrail.

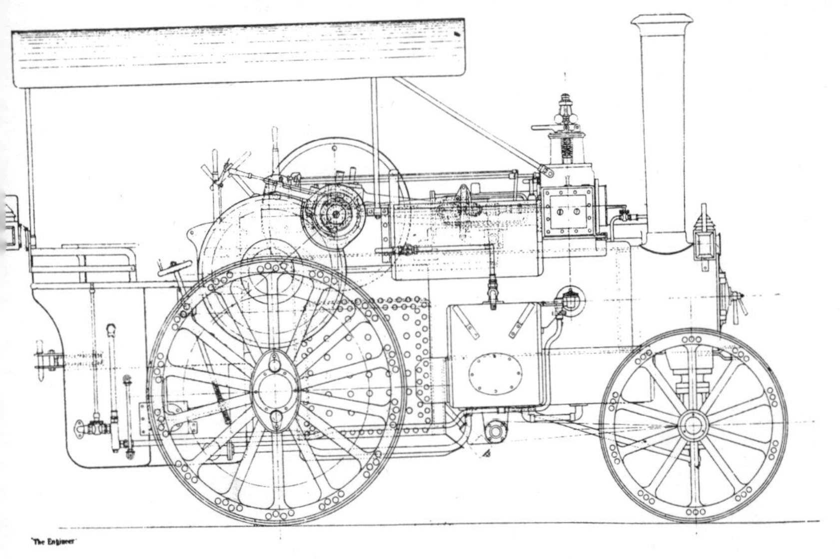

Fig. 152. The Clayton and Shuttleworth light tractor.
The Engineer.

The winding drum revolved on a boss machined on the compensating centre, and could be allowed to run free, to pay out the rope, by releasing the spring catch at the top. To lock the compensating gear, the upper driving pin on the left-hand side would be removed, and a longer one inserted, as described on the Fowler.

Another handsome tractor was the Ransomes (Fig. 154) which, though only of 4 n.h.p. ($4\frac{1}{2}$ in. and $7\frac{1}{2}$ in. by 8 in.), actually developed 20 b.h.p. when belt driving at the normal 230 r.p.m. The flywheel was 3 ft. by $5\frac{1}{4}$ in., hind wheels 4 ft. 9 in. by 12 in., and front wheels 3 ft. 1 in. by 5 in. Overall length was 13 ft. 9 in., and breadth 5 ft. 3 in.; weight empty, $4\frac{3}{4}$ tons, but a ton heavier in full working order. A normal gross load, in fast gear on a good level road, would be 8 tons, and she would comfortably haul the same in slow gear up an incline of 1 in 12.

Like their big brothers, many tractors in later years came out on solid rubber tyres, or were fitted with them, and typical sizes were on the hind wheels twin tyres 1,530 mm. (external) by 140 mm. wide, with 950 mm. (external) by 140 mm. on the front.

We have seen in previous chapters that the Fowler Company was never short of ideas, and was never afraid to build engines to try them out. Fig. 155 shows one of a small batch of tractors built for the War Office as a result of their Patent No. 19,690 of 1903, for a three cylindered compound engine.

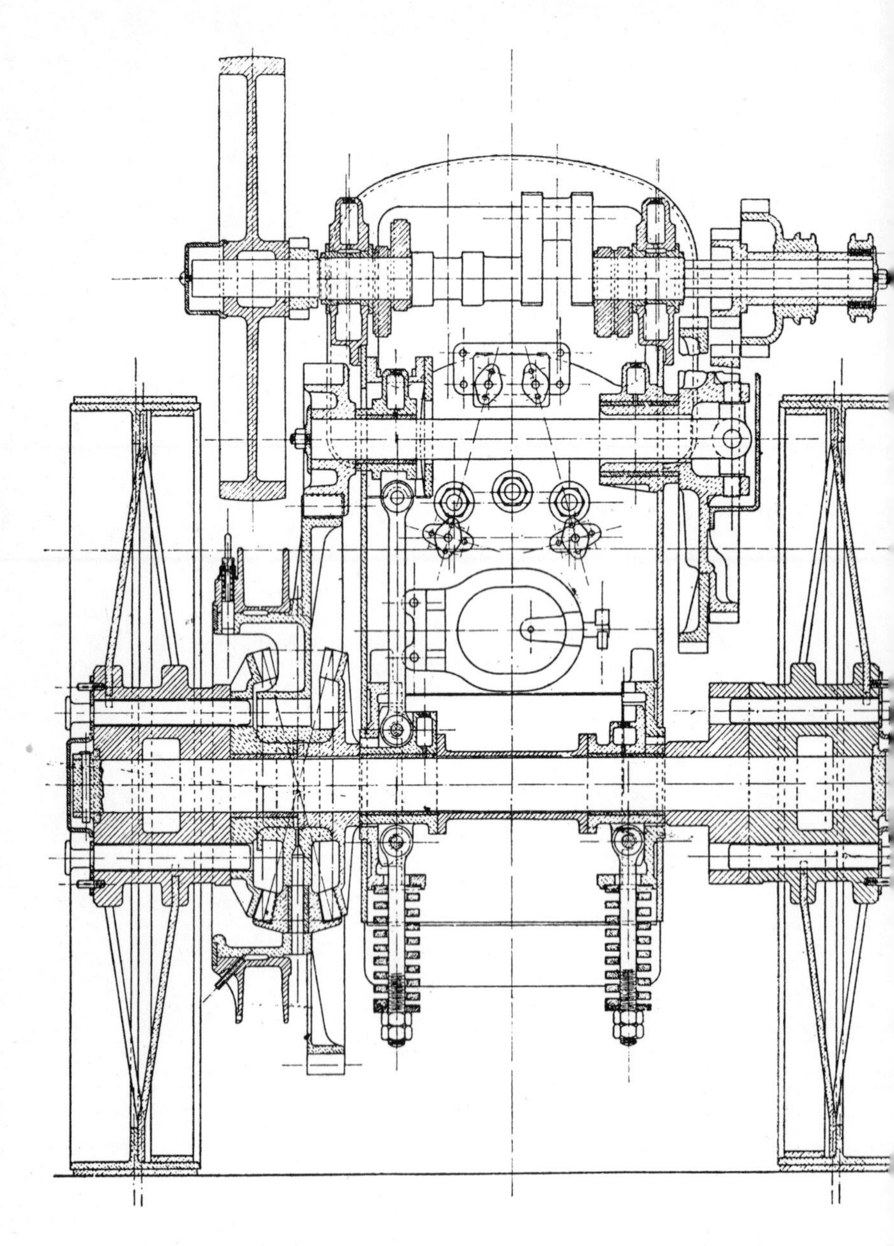

Fig. 153. Gearing and springing of the C. and S. tractor.

The Eng

In this patent, the steam passed into the H.P. cylinder in the ordinary way, and from there was exhausted into the valve chest of a L.P. cylinder at the side of the H.P. A pipe joined this valve chest to that of a second L.P. cylinder placed in tandem with the H.P., so that in effect the two L.P. valve chests took steam together, the second one acting as a receiver.

The cranks were at 90 deg., as usual in a compound, and, of course, the H.P. and auxiliary L.P. cylinders being in tandem worked the same piston rod. Their valves were also worked together. The patent specification states that '. . . the diameter of cylinders . . . is limited, and since high boiler pressures have come into common practice it has been impossible in compound engines . . . to maintain the proper relative diameters of the low- and the high-pressure cylinders required to secure the economic expansion of the steam'.

The auxiliary L.P. did, in effect, enable the L.P. cylinder diameter to be increased, and it also allowed equalisation of the effort transmitted to each crank, by correct proportioning of the two L.P. cylinders. Further, the arrangement gave four exhaust beats per revolution, instead of the two given by the normal compound: this gave a more equal draught

Fig. 154. Ransomes' light tractor of 4 n.h.p.
Ransomes, Sims and Jefferies, Ltd.

Fig. 155. Fowler three-cylinder compound tractor for the War Office.
T. D. Walshaw, Esq.

Fig. 156. Fowler 'Botrail' engine on test at Redcar, Yorks.
John Fowler & Co. (Leeds), Ltd.

(which was, incidentally, kind on the boiler tubes) and helped to deaden the exhaust. A simpling valve was fitted, to allow H.P. steam to pass to the L.P. cylinders if desired, as in normal practice.

This 'E' Class was named the 'Baby' type, and weighed 6 tons 15 cwt. The cylinders were 4 in., 5 in., and 7 in. in diameter, and Walschaert's valve-gear was used. All the motion work was enclosed, and worked in an oil bath – even the steerage worm and wheel did! There were disc cranks, and the steel gears were machine cut throughout. A steam feed pump was mounted on top of the belly tank.

Only the one batch of engines was made to this patent, and eventually they were converted to normal compounds, with auxiliary cylinder removed. One of the class, thus converted, is still in existence in Sussex. She is No. 11799, and is fitted with the dynamo, full-length canopy, and other equipment of the showman. In this guise she attended the great Old Time Steam Fair at White Waltham in 1964, but I would warrant that few who saw the engine there would realise her origin.

Another Fowler experiment, which lasted for a few years with moderate success, was with the 'Botrail' equipment, seen in Fig. 157 being tested at Redcar sands in Yorkshire. Superficially it resembled the Boydell endless railway, but the shoes were fixed to the wheels with steel cables, allowing much more flexibility.

It was in 1909 that an enterprising engineer in the Yukon wrote to Hornsby's of Grantham, having seen an account of their oil-engined chain track tractor, which David Roberts, Hornsby's Managing Director, had developed in May 1908 for a £1,000 War Office prize. It created great interest in both the technical and the lay press, but the generals were not enthusiastic – their inclination was rather for the 'glory' of the cavalry-charge than the mechanical horse.

Nor did the public enthusiasm at home and abroad result in the spate of orders which Hornsby's anticipated; in fact, the machine was a financial failure. But the Yukon engineer, reading his belated report of its wonders, thought it might well solve the problem of transporting coal to Dawson City from his mine forty miles distant, over rough virgin country. And could Hornsby's please build him a *steam* caterpillar tractor?

They could and did, with the assistance of Fosters' of Lincoln who supplied the engine and boiler, for Hornsby's had not built any steam engines for some time. The combined result was the forty-ton giant seen in Fig. 157, which though it accidentally demolished a house in its first trial run at Grantham, gave great satisfaction to its owner in the Yukon when it reached him in 1910. Like Grew's ice locomotives of 1861-2, it was fitted with protection against the cold on reaching its destination.

Fig. 157. Hornsby-Foster caterpillar engine for the Yukon.
Ruston and Hornsby, Ltd.

Fig. 158. The Fowler 'Snaketrac' built in 1923.
John Fowler & Co. (Leeds), Ltd.

Fig. 159. Tasker 'Little Giant' tractor No. 1778, 'Marshal Foch'.
A. R. Dibben, Esq.

It is interesting to mention in passing that in order partly to recoup the financial loss on the caterpillar tractor, Hornsby's sold the American and Canadian rights to the Holt Caterpillar Company of New York, who persevered with the idea and reaped their due reward. And it is ironical that when in 1915-16 the 'blimps' were forced to yield to pressure, Holt tractors had to be imported for experimental purposes – and it was Fosters' who built the 'tanks' which resulted from Mr. Churchill's brainwave!

Later on, in 1923, Fowlers' conceived and built the remarkable vehicle seen in Fig. 158, and in 1929 even put a ploughing engine on endless tracks. Because of the rope drum beneath the boiler, this was not easy, but the problem was solved by having separate tracks in place of the hind wheels, with a kind of tracked bogie in place of the normal fore-carriage. The 'Snaketrac' of 1923 was a 'go-anywhere' vehicle, of course, but like the four-wheel drive vehicles of half-a-century before, it was too heavy and cumbrous to prove of real value.

I have earlier remarked that Taskers of Andover called their steam tractor the 'Little Giant'. Fig. 159 shows one of these dressed up in show-

Fig. 160. Re-designed in 1920, the 'Little Giant' with chain drive.
A. R. Dibben, Esq.

man's livery, but without the dynamo mounted. The engine was *Marshal Foch*, works number 1778, and the photo was taken outside the works in 1918. For many years a Little Giant was kept in a shed near the Crystal Palace, and used by the R.S.P.C.A. to help horses to pull heavy loads up the steep hills of the district. Carmen could phone for this aid. This tractor was bought by Taskers in 1956 for their private museum, but the latter now being dispersed, it will be eventually on public view in Hampshire.

In 1920, the firm brought out a re-designed Little Giant, with the final drive by roller chain (Fig. 160) – a far cry to the pitch chain drive of older days. But this chain drive allowed the hind axle to be set on plain leaf springs at each side, the weight of the engine being transferred to the springs by lengths of steel channel fixed to the hornplates. Radius arms, one of which can be seen, were employed to keep the chain in tension.

At about this time, too, Garretts built a small number of the unconventional but well thought out 'Suffolk Punch' tractors (Fig. 161) which it was thought would counter the steadily growing menace of the i.c.-engined tractor. But it seemed that customers who wanted steam preferred

Fig. 161. The 1919 design of the 'Suffolk Punch' tractor.
Author's photograph.

the appearance they were accustomed to see, and few of the new design were sold. At least one of the clan still survives, and it is a very fast and manœuvrable little engine, with chain drive and motor-car type controls, including the steering arrangements. It is seen at many of the rallies in the southern half of the country – my photo was taken at Appleford – and invariably creates great interest.

About ten years later Garretts introduced another Suffolk Punch (Fig. 162) of even more unconventional appearance, with its engine under the bonnet, and its boiler and tanks in the 'body'. Drive was by chain to the leading rear axle, and again by chain to the other axle, so that the vehicle had four-wheel drive. These, too, were handy engines, well designed and built, and I have photos of one hauling a couple of light boilers, and of another one log hauling somewhere.

But Garretts also built large numbers of the very fine tractor shown in Fig. 163; it was rather heavier than most, the unladen weight being 6 tons 16 cwt. The overall length was 14 ft. 10 in. and width 5 ft. 11¼ in. and many of them were mounted on rubber tyres. Several examples of this excellent design are currently preserved, one of them by my old friend

Sam Breedon of Sheffield. Sam spent many years of his life in driving showman's engines, tractors, and other steamers, and is at his happiest when on the footplate. He spent nearly two years in overhauling, re-building and re-painting his Garrett, and she is now in perfect trim once more, though sadly no longer in his own possession.

In the 'twenties, increasing attention was being paid to detail improvements, and among these were higher pressures, piston valves and super-heating. In some cases plain crankshaft bearings with siphon lubrication were superseded by ring oiled bearings. Superheaters were of the smokebox type, and this entailed a longer smokebox. A steam pipe ran down from the steam dome on top of the cylinder to the superheater, and after passing through the latter, the steam passed back via another external pipe to the cylinder again. The superheated engines were not much in demand in this country, but were much more popular on the Continent.

We may quote prices of the 1920's from a catalogue of William Allchin Ltd., of Northampton, whose single-cylinder traction engines cost £801 for the 5 n.h.p., to £948 for the 8 n.h.p., the corresponding prices for

Fig. 162. The 'Suffolk Punch' as re-designed c. 1930.
R. G. Pratt, Esq.

Fig. 163. Garrett seven-ton tractor of conventional appearance.
R. G. Pratt, Esq.

compounds being £896 and £1,068 respectively. Extras were an injector at £17, enlarged firebox £15 to £21, spark arrester £6, short awning or canopy £21, long awning £26, coal rack £9 and front tank £29 to £42.

Standard equipment included two speeds, winding drum with 50 yards of steel wire rope, water lifter, 26 ft. of suction hose, Pickering governors, and 'outfit'. The outfit comprised '1 set of stoking tools, tube brush and rod, 1 set of spanners, 1 screw wrench, 1 hand hammer, 1 flat chisel, 1 caulking tool, 2 lamps, 1 waterproof cover, 1 set of spuds, 1 set of spud bolts and cotters, bucket, filling funnel, spare fusible plug, 2 gauge glasses, india-rubber washers, 1 gallon can of oil, oil feeder, &c.' (What the '&c' included is anyone's guess.) Working pressure was 140 p.s.i. Allchins made either three- or four-shaft engines to suit customers' wishes, but the prices were the same for either class.

Road locomotives had 75 yards of rope instead of 50, the injector and front (belly) tank were standard fittings, and side covers were fitted to the motion; brakes acting on both hind wheels, an extra large coal bunker, and a driver's seat were also included in the prices. These were £887 for the 5-horse to £1,122 for the 8-horse, or £938 to £1,261 for the compounds. Extras were priced as for the traction engines, but with additional ones – copper pipes cost £9 extra, a third speed was £42, flywheel brake £9, hind axle springing £65, and a sprung fore-carriage £17.

Road rollers had pump, injector, and copper pipes as standard, but no compensating gear (which was common practice by other makers, too), no governors, no winding drum and rope, and no water lifter and hose. Roller prices were £719 for a 6-tonner, up to £934 for the 14-tonner, with £798 to £1,021 as compounds. Governors cost £17, water lifter and hose £15, compensating gear £23, and winding drum and rope £19.

Allchins also made a cylinder boring machine and a valve seat planing machine, which could be clamped to the cylinder block and worked by hand, for re-machining damaged bores or port-faces. These cost £18 apiece, and were invaluable because they enabled a perfect new bore or seating to be obtained without removing the cylinder, in less time than would have been involved in removing and replacing it.

Robeys and Fodens had developed tractors from their steam wagon designs – in fact, Fodens had built them for many years. Robeys also used their wagon engine and boiler to power a tandem steam roller, with chain drive to the rear roll, which was full width, in line with and behind the other.

The boiler had a circular firebox which required no stays: it can be

Fig. 164. Robey 'high-speed' tractor No. 43165 built in 1927.
D. H. Yarnell, Esq.

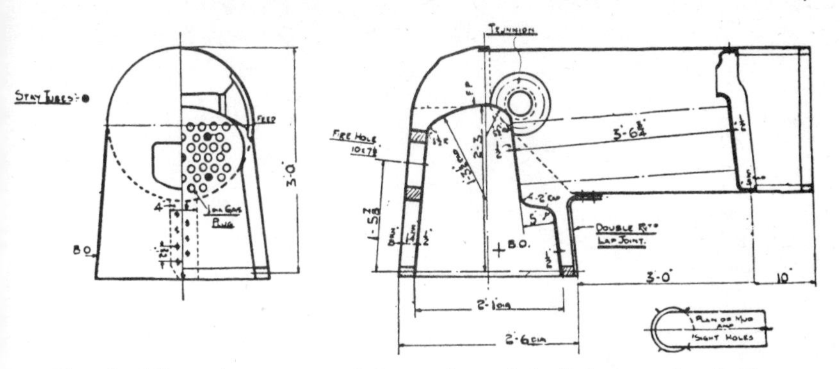

Fig. 165. The arrangement and dimensions of the Robey stayless boiler.
A. C. Lawrence, Esq.

seen in Fig. 165, which Mr. A. C. Lawrence prepared from a Robey wagon boiler which he regularly inspected in the course of his professional duties. The photograph (Fig. 164) is of Robey tractor No. 43165 produced in 1927. Drive to the hind axle was by chain, and the water and fuel were carried behind the driver. The Foden arrangement was rather similar, but with conventional firebox.

In 1927 the latter firm introduced a new tractor, based on the boiler and engine of their 6-ton steam wagon, with cylinder 4¼ in. and 7-in. bore by 7-in. stroke. The big ends were of the marine type, and the eccentrics and the crankshaft were mounted in Hoffman roller bearings. There were three speeds to give 3, 6 and 9 m.p.h. at normal revs. Ackerman steering was fitted as standard, but chain type could be fitted to order.

The tractor was also available with creeper tracks, made by the Roadless Traction Company, instead of the normal hind wheels, and this was a real cross-country vehicle, capable of travelling through bog or sand, or over rough ground. Even with its front wheels off the ground, as when climbing a steep hummock or bank, it could still be steered by braking one track or the other.

A very successful 5-ton steam tractor was produced, too, by the Sentinel Waggon Works, based largely on steam waggon design, and one of these, built in 1923, was at work until well into the sixties, fully occupied in shunting and hauling railway wagons at Teignmouth Harbour, and to and from the main-line railway. It replaced a petrol-driven tractor, and was found to do more work in two hours than the latter could do in a day! Moreover, the comparative saving in fuel and oil more than covered its cost within 18 months. The Sentinel is now preserved.

An agricultural version of this tractor was also being developed, but was

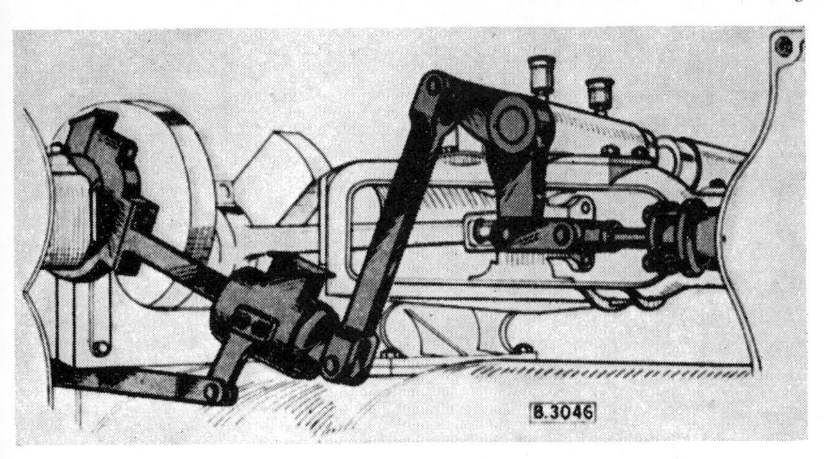

Fig. 167. Arrangement of the Marshall valve-gear.
Official catalogue.

dropped in favour of a half-tracked tractor. On test near Shrewsbury this hauled with ease two four-furrow ploughs in heavy clay, by direct traction. However, it was not received favourably by the agricultural world and, like the Foden half-track, was not proceeded with.

In 1933 came the culminating design from Marshalls of Gainsborough, the Class 'S' Series, of which there are still quite a number of rollers in existence, though I have not seen an 'S'-type traction engine personally since the last war. The compound traction is shown in Fig. 166, and what a lovely engine she is.

One of the first points of note is the patent Marshall valve gear, shown in more detail in Fig. 167. It is a radial gear, with only one eccentric per cylinder, allowing not only wider crankpins and thicker webs, but with a reduction in the number of working parts as compared with Stephenson link motion. There was a much greater area of bearing surface in the cylindrical slide, as compared with the link motion die-block, and the gear gave an improved steam distribution. Wick-feed lubricators were fitted to both the eccentric and the reversing slide.

It will be seen that the motion of the eccentric will cause the forward end of the eccentric rod to move in an oval path, working a bell-crank lever which in turn works the valve rod. The steam cut-off may be altered by varying the angular position of the reversing slide, and the engine is reversed by tilting the slide still further. An ordinary reversing lever and notched quadrant are used to work the cut-off and reverse. Piston valves are standard.

The hind wheels now have spokes riveted to the centres as well as to the rims, so that a broken spoke could be replaced easily. All gears, including the steerage worm and wheel, are enclosed in oil baths. The water pump is driven at only half the speed of the crankshaft (which Marshalls and other makers had done for many years). Ring-oiled bearings are used to carry the crankshaft, which has disc-cranks, fully balanced.

In 1930 there appeared the last Burrell showman's engine ever, and it was built by Garretts at Leiston (Fig. 172), though the name plates on the valve chests still said 'Charles Burrell and Sons Limited, Engineers, Thetford, England', as did the oval hubs of the hind wheels. The reason was that Burrells, along with other firms including Howards, had gone smash in the Agricultural and General Engineers' combine. The Burrell rights were taken over by Garretts, and thus it was that the last Burrell engines were built by a 'rival' firm.

The showman's engine was No. 4092 *Simplicity*, built for Mrs. Deakin of Brynmawr; it was a three-speed, 8-horse locomotive, spring mounted, and very lovely to look at. In due course she was taken over by Road Engines and Kerr of Glasgow, her dynamo and bracket were removed, and her canopy was cut down at the front. Thus she became a hard working and still handsome unit in a fine fleet of heavy haulage vehicles.

When road transport was nationalised after the war, she became or was said to be redundant, and was eventually purchased by a group of enthu-

Fig. 168. The last Burrell showman's engine, No. 4092 'Simplicity'.
R. G. Pratt, Esq.

Fig. 169. 'Simplicity' and 'Supreme', 'deglamorised', work in harness. *The North British Locomotive Co., Ltd.*

siasts for preservation. However, owing to a reason I prefer not to dwell on, she was scrapped and so a veritable Queen of the Road disappeared.

But her stable-companion, *Supreme*, the last Fowler showman's engine (No. 20223), and the last showman's engine ever to be built by any firm, has been more fortunate. She left the works in February, 1934, also for Mrs. Deakin, and she, too, became the property of Road Engines and Kerr, with her dynamo removed and canopy cut down. In their new guise they can be seen in Fig. 169, as they haul a railway locomotive for Egypt through the streets of Glasgow to the docks. All in a day's work – but what a magnificent picture!

In time, though, *Supreme* too became 'redundant', but after many vicissitudes including several years' stagnation in a Surrey scrapyard, she was acquired by a very keen enthusiast who has spent a great deal of time, effort and money on restoring her to original condition.

Meantime, however, another enthusiast, Mr. Sidney Harris, has spent nine years in building from works drawings a model of *Supreme*, one-eighth of full size, which is literally a perfect replica of her big sister, and I *mean* perfect. Should any reader doubt this statement, let him go along to the Science Museum in South Kensington, and let him try to find any imperfection, however slight. He'll be looking for a long, long time – for, after all, the model is literally *Supreme!*

17

HANDLING THE LOADS

Interdependence absolute, foreseen, ordained, decreed,
To work, Ye'll note, at ony tilt an' every rate o' speed.
KIPLING

IN EARLIER CHAPTERS, WE have noted a number of tasks, ordinary and extraordinary, carried out by traction engines and road locomotives, but it will not be out of place to give some more examples of these, starting with the showmen.

It was legal to haul up to nine vehicles until the passing of the new Locomotives Act in 1896, which cut the number down to a maximum of three, plus a water cart, unless the local Council agreed to a larger number. In the event, a few areas did allow four plus the water wagon, but over most of Britain the maximum remained at three, with a £10 penalty for not obeying the law. Needless to say, some wily showmen acquired indecently large 'water wagons', which could carry quite a lot of other tackle, besides a small amount of water to ensure that the majesty of the Law should not be affronted.

At the same time, when the man in blue was *not* visible, it is to be feared that the showmen's drivers did not always keep below the legal speed limit. It is recorded for example that one of Alfred Holland's engines took a bioscope show, weighing probably 40 to 45 tons, from Lincoln to Louth, a distance of 26 miles, in 1 hr. 40 min. True, this was in flat country, but 15 m.p.h. was moving, especially as this engine was on steel-straked wheels.

On long journeys across country, up hill and down dale, speeds were of course much slower, but an 11-hour day would usually average about 90 miles, with loads of anything from 30 to 45 tons. But of course, to quote the Fowler 8 n.h.p. *Big Lion*, at a quite ordinary 300 r.p.m. and with gear ratios of 11½, 18½ and 28 to 1, approximately, the respective road speeds were 6½, 4 and 2¾ m.p.h. A 7 or 8 h.p. loco was well on top of its load, and once clear of the towns it would keep on happily in third speed all day, except on a steep incline. So that when a showman was in a hurry (as he invariably was), to go from Liverpool via Leeds to Newcastle, a distance of 165 miles, or from Barnstaple to Birmingham (181 miles), he expected to, and did, make the journey in two 11-hour days, as a rule.

Fig. 170. Two Fowlers with an ingot mould at the Brightside Foundry, Sheffield.

Figs. 171 and 172.
Five road locos hauling a large anvil block in Sheffield.
The Brightside Foundry and Engineering Co., Ltd.

But what of the less glamorous but harder working locomotives of the heavy haulage contractors, such as Kerrs of Glasgow, Edward Box of Liverpool, Norman E. Box of Manchester, or Coupe Bros. of Sheffield? Here quite often the transporting of the load was only part of the work, which might involve demolishing a part of a building, or digging a large pit, to get the load in or out of place.

During the journey it might be necessary to cut down hedges or remove banks at the roadside; the late Norman Box told me that one particular load from Manchester to Sheffield involved taking out and replacing all the gaslamps through a large village *en route*. And on a photo in my possession, two of Kerr's McLarens are hauling two marine boilers at night, whilst linesmen are removing the overhead tramway wires to allow the boilers to pass beneath.

The Commercial Motor, discussing the subject as late as 1928, said: 'For very heavy work the ideal outfit appears to be a steam tractor (i.e., road locomotive – W. J. H.) hauling a multi-wheeled trailer or one or more special bogie trailers. The chief benefit with the steam tractor is the enormous power which it can develop and the use which can be made of its winding drum as an aid to loading and unloading; it is also a simple matter to equip tractors with powerful cranes.' Those are words which could be equally true today!

But in the early days of heavy haulage by steam, the only alternative was horse transport, and it is interesting to note that Pickfords, who in the 'thirties bought out Norman Box, Coupe Bros., and numerous other firms, still used horses for all really heavy transport until 1902, when they gradually changed over to steam.

These early days were pretty tough, but then so were the men who did the job. The trailers which carried the loads were shod with steel, and on plain bearings, weighing in the region of 10 tons to carry 20. Frequently they had no turntable, and it was necessary to skid them sideways round corners, with steel plates under the wheels, and a second engine pulling sideways with its wire rope. In confined spaces, jacks might have to be used to skid the bogie sideways, whilst on long hills the wooden brake blocks would catch fire at the most inconvenient times. Yet despite these conditions, loads of up to 100 tons were being handled in the early years of this century.

A smaller load than this – appreciably smaller – is seen in Fig. 170, though the weight of the ingot mould is not actually known. The photo was taken in Sheffield in the late 'nineties or early 1900's, and the engines are probably Coupes'. They are both Fowlers, with 8-ft. hind wheels, the compound with Boulton wheels. One of the engines could have managed the load quite easily, but for the fact that there was a steep incline leading out of the works yard of the foundry to the road.

With more massive loads, this same incline sometimes led to the use of as many as five locos being used together, and Figs. 171–2 show just such an occasion, probably in the 1920's. It must have been a real feat of co-ordination to start those five engines off together, and to keep them rolling together, especially starting on a slope.

Cornwall is famous for many things, of which not the least is its granite. In Winchester a handsome bronze statue of King Alfred is supported on a 40-ton granite pedestal which in turn stands on a 25-ton granite plinth. Both these blocks were hauled from the Cornish quarry of John Freeman and McLeod Ltd. to Penryn near Falmouth, in the manner seen in Fig. 173, where the load is suspended from stout wooden baulks carried on two bogies. In this particular photograph, the block is for the 40-ton pedestal.

These two engines are 8 n.h.p. Fowlers of about 1889, and the picture was taken in 1903. The engine nearest the camera was called *Zeta*, and the leading engine was probably *Absalom*. Incidentally, this is an illustration of using two engines, one for hauling and the other for braking, as will be mentioned shortly. Canopies were fitted to these locos in 1910, and they were scrapped in 1923, having spent a very hard and rough life indeed – but a most useful one.

Fig. 173. A 40-ton granite block for the King Alfred statue in Winchester.
John Freeman and McLeod Ltd., Penryn, Cornwall.

Fig. 174. Quite a light load for 'Titan'. Fowler No.

Norman Box started business in Manchester in 1906, but his father had been in heavy haulage in Liverpool for many years before that. The son built up a fleet of engines, and started to equip them with rubber tyres in 1913, commencing with his light tractors, but by 1922 all his heavies were on rubbers, too – some with cross-pads, rather like rubber strakes, but mostly on continuous treads. The heavies were mostly Fowler Big Lions (8 n.h.p.) or Super Lions (10 n.h.p.), but there were one or two other makes as well.

An early job of his is shown in Fig. 174, where *Titan* (No. 10325) – all the engines were named – mounted on Boulton wheels is on a task well within her capacity, hauling a Lancashire boiler on a local journey. The boiler itself sits on two four-wheel wagons, the front one being steerable, but on the rear one the turntable is made fast so that it cannot swivel. This *Titan* later was sold to a Sheffield steel firm, and a new Big Lion, No. 14843, received the same name.

On a good many jobs double heading was used where strictly speaking the haulage power of the lead engine was more or less superfluous, for a single engine could have managed the load on its own. In such cases the second engine was often there chiefly for its braking power downhill, where it would be attached at the *rear* of the load, to hold it back and prevent over-running or 'forcing' the front engine. And, of course, the second engine did come in useful going uphill, whilst even on the flat it enabled the other to take it easier.

Such a load is seen in Fig. 175, where McLaren locomotive *Rover* is double-heading the second *Titan*. The load is a large stator on an eight-

Fig. 175. McLaren and Fowler prepare to work in harmony.
Norman E. Box, Esq.

Fig. 176. Two Fowlers use their winding ropes to elevate a large storage tank.

wheeled bogie, of which the front four wheels are steerable. Note the spring in the drawbar between the two locomotives, to help to take up starting stress, and the steel plates under the bogie wheels, to prevent 'sinking in' of the load on relatively soft ground.

The next illustration (Fig. 176) shows two of the Fowlers using their winding drums to good effect in raising a storage tank from the bogies to its final position. This was at the Shell depot at Trafford Park: the engine nearer the camera is *Vulcan*, No. 14844, new with *Titan* just mentioned, in 1919 or 1920. The ropes were passed round snatch blocks attached to the upper girders, and slid the tanks up the baulks of timber with ease. I have another photo showing a single Fowler using its rope to haul a Lancashire boiler (which appears to be the same as that in Fig. 174). The boiler has been slid bodily sideways across a canal, on baulks, and is being pulled up the bank at a slope of about 1 in 3.

William Kerr of Glasgow had a good 'stable' of road locos, too, and Fig. 177 shows two of his 10 h.p. Burrells with a Lancashire boiler, which would be a light load for them. The engine nearest the load is No. 3419 *Clyde*, the last 10 h.p. road loco built by Burrell, and a 'special order' for Kerrs in 1912. She had cylinders $7\frac{1}{4}$ in. and $11\frac{3}{4}$ in. by 12 in., and weighed 17 tons 3 cwt. empty. Her hind wheels were 7 ft. by $20\frac{1}{4}$ in., before the cross-straked rubbers were fitted later in her career. She had a flywheel smaller than standard, the hub, rim and disc being in three separate parts riveted together. She was a three speed engine.

The leading engine is No. 1997 *Lord Roberts*, a two-speed loco which began life as a showman's engine in 1897. However, she quickly passed

Fig. 177. 'Lord Roberts' and 'Clyde' deliver a Lancashire boiler to the quayside.
Stuart P. Johnstone, Esq.

Fig. 178. Ready to off-load a huge steam accumulator at its destination.
Stuart P. Johnstone, Esq.

through the hands of several owners, and eventually came to Kerrs in 1902. Being a two-speed she did not work well with *Clyde* on a long journey, and Kerrs preferred to use her with one of their two-speed McLarens. They had several of these, all of 65 b.h.p. and built for the War Office during the 1914–18 war. When new they had two round tub-shaped fuel bunkers, but were rebuilt with normal type by Kerrs.

In the next photo (Fig. 178) one of the McLarens and *Clyde* are coupled together in front of that colossal steam accumulator, whilst *Lord Roberts* has been backed up at the rear. It seems likely that the first pair have hauled the accumulator to the factory where it is to be off-loaded, and that *Lord Roberts* is about to do some roping or pulling back of the load. She may well have been used as the 'braking' engine.

Many readers will have seen the stern half of the steam yacht *Turbinia*, the first vessel to be driven by turbines, in the Science Museum, but how many know that it was taken there from the Surrey Commercial Dock by a road locomotive? The load, some 40 tons, was carried on two four-wheeled bogies, pulled by a Fowler crane engine belonging to the London Traction Haulage Co. Ltd., a Pickford's subsidiary. This was in June 1927.

Fig. 179 shows an unusual combination of flying-boat and traction engine, with a 6 n.h.p. Marshall, built in 1886, used to launch the Blackburn 'Iris' flying-boat from the firm's slipway at Brough in Yorkshire, in 1928. This engine was hired from a Mr. Watson of Brantingham, a local village, and was exported to Belgium from Hull in 1950 in going order still. The same owner had two more Marshalls – a 7 and an 8 h.p. – and a Ransomes and a McLaren.

One big trouble in using steel-shod bogies with heavy loads was that frequently damage was caused to roads, which of course had to be made good by the haulier. The partial solution was to use more and wider wheels to distribute the weight more satisfactorily, but it was late in 1927 that Fowlers came up with the perfect solution – a trailer carried on 16 wheels, each with twin rubber tyres. It was actually designed to carry the exceptionally large pieces of electrical machinery which were becoming common, but it was the ancestor of most future heavy-load carriers.

The vehicle was designed to carry 85 tons, and in order to provide maximum clearance for bridges and under tram wires, the height of the loading platform was restricted to 2 ft. The trailer somewhat resembled a

Fig. 179. Veteran Marshall used to launch a 29,000-lb. flying-boat in 1928.
Blackburn and General Aircraft Ltd.

railway well-wagon, with raised ends resting on bogies. In this case, however, there were four bogies, each with four wheels: two side by side on the front steering bolster, and two attached at the rear.

Each bogie was independently mounted, and could tilt in a fore-and-aft direction, whilst each pair of wheels could tilt independently sideways as well, thus giving perfect flexibility. All wheels on the rear bogies had brakes, a hand wheel on each side working, through compensating levers, a pair of brake-shoes bearing on an internally machined surface on the inside of each wheel rim.

The platform itself actually consisted of seven girders side by side, built from plate and angle, with more than 4,000 rivets. All were single web except the broad central one, which had a double web wide enough to accommodate the kingpin of the fore-carriage. The overall length of the trailer was 37 ft., width 7 ft. 9 in., loading space in well 16 ft. 1 in., and ground clearance 11 in. The weight was 30 tons, and the cost £3,000 approximately.

It was in July 1928 that Edward Box's took delivery of Fowler Super Lion No. 17106, which was fitted with a crane designed to lift 12 tons at 8 ft. 6 in. radius, down to 4 tons at 12 ft. 6 in. radius. In actual practice, she once lifted a 17-ton boring mill on one job! Other feats of this engine include pulling a 100-ton Scammell loaded with an 80-ton girder bodily sideways to clear a corner in an awkward street in London, and double heading a 100-ton Scammell to move an ingot weighing 167 tons *net* in Sheffield.

Another of her jobs was in January 1939 when, now owned by Pickfords, she hauled the rudder of aircraft-carrier *Ark Royal* from Darlington to Birkenhead. It was 26 ft. long, 21 ft. wide, and 14 ft. high, being tilted up at an angle to reduce overall width. Including the trailer, the gross load was over 80 tons. But it is a fact that No. 17106 would take 120 tons gross on her own, in slow speed, as would her sister Super Lions. At the time of writing, this fine engine is still in use at Kingswinford in Staffordshire.

Other epic Fowler journeys include what was in 1937 the world's largest indivisible load, a steam accumulator 70 ft. long by 12 ft. diameter, from Annan in Scotland to the Beckton Gas Works, a journey of 321 miles. The engines concerned were 16263 *Talisman* and 17105 *Atlas:* the latter engine on her own had previously moved a 75-ton cylinder for paper production from Avonmouth to Bristol, and a 90-ton steam accumulator from Annan to Glasgow.

However, besides the ordinary jobs tackled by road locomotives and their smaller sisters, there were less conventional occasions when steam literally saved the day. For example, in November 1890, there was an explosion in the Middlesbrough Gas Works which rendered idle the gas engine driving the presses of a local newspaper. Undeterred, the proprietors borrowed a 15-ton steam roller, knocked a hole in the printing shop wall, and belted the flywheel to the presses. On another occasion, the *Lincolnshire Chronicle* was also printed by traction engine power.

During the last war, Holmans of Camborne developed a 'steam gun' which was demonstrated with the use of the local council's steam roller. Subsequently, this cheap and quickly made weapon, which hurled a Mills bomb, was fitted to trawlers and used to good effect against low flying Nazi aircraft.

Steam rollers also assisted mightily in the defence of Malta, and so in the African Victory, as testified by Air Marshal Sir Hugh Lloyd in his *Briefed to Attack*. They were used in repairing aerodromes after the tremendous bombing attacks, in building roads, and in making pens for the aircraft, for the bowsers, and for themselves. The Air Marshal says: 'If we lost a petrol bowser we felt like taking out our handkerchiefs and having a good cry, while the loss of a steam roller was about the equivalent of losing another Singapore.' And, during raids, 'it was a solemn duty to drive a roller into its pen, irrespective of the danger. Not one could be lost . . . The rollers . . . had to be guarded with our lives'.

Another use for steam in the second war was during the London 'Blitz', when road locomotives were brought in to help to demolish unsafe buildings. This was a very easy task, with the winding rope hitched to the walls – a touch of steam and down they came.

Again, Fowler ploughing engines were used in the laying of PLUTO, the petrol pipe-line run between England and France in 1943-4.

Of course, many hundreds of traction-engines, road locos, and their brethren were used in the 'first' war.

To return to a happier theme, traction engines were often used in early days to take Sunday school parties and the like on outings in wagonettes, and they came in useful on other occasions, too. For example, on every Royal celebration since Queen Victoria's Jubilee in 1887, traction engines belonging to the Morgan family, of Barlow in Derbyshire, have been used to brew tea for the village jollification.

The 6 h.p. Fowler No. 4267, new in 1882, performed this office for the Jubilees of 1887 and 1897, and for the Coronations of King Edward VII in 1902 and of King George V in 1911. Marshall No. 12218, new in 1884, was used at the Silver Jubilee in 1935, (not bad, when she'd celebrated her own *Golden* Jubilee the year before!), and at the Coronation of King George VI in 1937, whilst for the Coronation of Queen Elizabeth II, the engine used was 6 h.p. Burrell No. 3984, new in 1924. I had the privilege

Fig. 180. Fowler No. 15376 uses her 18-ton crane to lift a 15-ton Aveling roller.
Thomas Bridson, Esq.

of being present on the last occasion, and can confirm that 'traction-engine tea' is a very satisfactory beverage!

The production of traction engines ran down during the 1930's, and it is believed that the last general-purpose engine of all, a Foster, appeared in 1938. In 1946, Aveling-Barford produced a batch of steam rollers, and Marshalls received an order for 1,000 steam rollers of various capacities for India. Of these, the boilers and some components were produced at Gainsborough, and the other parts were made, and the rollers assembled, in India. An impressive ceremony was held when, in April 1948, the first batch of these rollers took the road. Flower bedecked, the first roller, *City of Delhi*, was decorated with the Indian good-luck sign, the swastika, and a coconut was broken on the front roll by the Minister for Industries and Supplies, accompanied by other government officials, and by Marshall directors and staff. 'The first Roller moved off amidst tremendous cheers, blowing its whistle, and followed by the other Rollers in excellent formation.'

Besides the engines kept by enthusiasts, there were still a few in more or less regular work up to the late sixties. Among these was the big Fowler No. 15376 owned by Robert Bridson and Son of Neston in the Wirral, which in Fig. 180 is shown with a post-war development, a crane capable of lifting 18 tons using her winding drum. In the picture she is lifting a 15-ton Aveling roller. This was the property of the local Council, but in her own 'stable' she had as companions Burrell road loco No. 3098, Fowler roller No. 17500, Marshall 'convertible' No. 68754, and two Sentinels, Nos. 8122 and 8942.

My last illustration shows *Excelsior*, Fowler No. 14862, then owned by Douglas Miller of Brighouse, as she rocks gently to and fro outside a model engineering exhibition in Halifax, generating electricity to draw the crowds. She is one of a batch of engines turned out

She was built in 1917 for the Ministry of Munitions, and subsequently converted to a showman's engine for Jacob Studt, Junior. At the present time the engine is known as *Evening Star*, and belongs to Monty Thackray of Old Malton. She too was one of the shining lights (literally) of the White Waltham Steam Fair of 1964.

Many readers will wonder why, with its many good points, the road steamer has become virtually extinguished. The answer is quite simple – it is partly because of prejudice, but largely because of vested interests. As early as 1831 we read how 'country gentlemen, *trustees of roads* (my italics – W. J. H.), farmers, coach proprietors, coachmen, post-boys, &c., opposed Gurney's steam carriages, and on the 22nd June, 1831, large heaps of stones were laid across the road . . . about 18 in. deep; whilst struggling

Fig. 181. To revive memories! 'Excelsior' rocks gently as she 'generates'.
Author's photo.

over the obstruction the axle was broken. Prohibitory turnpike rates ultimately turned these carriages off the road.' Nor should we forget the infamous Act of 1831 which required the man with the Red Flag to walk in front of any mechanically propelled vehicle, so that legally no such vehicle could exceed walking speed, though capable of much more.

Shortly after this, a line of steam coaches run by John Scott Russell (later of steamship *Great Eastern* fame) in Scotland was obstructed *by the road trustees* in a similar manner to Gurney's; a wheel broke, the whole weight of the coach rested on the boiler, causing it to burst, and five passengers were killed. But the Court of Session did not indict the road trustees – they ordered the coaches to stop running! Prejudice indeed!

The road tolls were tremendously against the steamer: we read of the charge for coal drawn by steam to be 4s. a ton, as against 3½d. per ton by horse. Then there were many bye-laws deliberately framed to the detriment of steam power, whereby, for example, one county authority forbade the use of a traction engine between the hours of 8 a.m. and 8 p.m., and the neighbouring authority forbade its use between 8 p.m. and 8 a.m. Even as late as the Locomotives Act of 1878, authorities were still given power to restrict the use for 8 hours out of the 24. In some cases this regulation meant that all working had to be done at night, and Fletcher says that many accidents, some fatal, could be charged against such local bye-laws.

Another anomaly was, said Thomas Aveling himself, 'if I send a boiler weighing 15 tons drawn by 15 horses over a country bridge and that boiler breaks the bridge I have nothing to pay, but if I send the same boiler over the bridge drawn by an engine weighing 8 tons, and that boiler breaks through the bridge, I have the whole expenses to pay'. And, of course, such work as timber carting and brick loading by horses was very bad for cutting up country roads, but no matter how deep the ruts caused by these carts, the haulier had nothing to pay. Yet 'let a traction engine . . . leave its footprints on the road's soft surface, the owner is at once arrested by the surveyor of the district, and the highway authorities . . . claim extraordinary expenses for damage incurred'.

The lesson has not been learned even today, of course, that highways and bridges should be suited to the traffic they have to bear, and not vice versa!

Another ridiculous regulation was that the safety valves must not be blown off. Picture a driver who has built up pressure knowing a steep hill lies ahead, when, by law, the man walking in front signals him to stop because of an approaching horse-carriage. How can he avoid the safety valves discharging? Especially if, as was usually the case, the horses were prancing and plunging instead of going past the engine. Then a locomotive must 'consume its own smoke' – consider a driver who has just replenished his fire, and who has to stop for a horsed vehicle. With no exhaust blast, the fire burns sluggishly, and how can he prevent smoke pouring from the chimney? The penalty for the former offence was up to £10, and for the latter up to £5 a day.

The Locomotives Act of 1878 gave one 'privilege' which nearly everyone mistakenly attributes to that of 1896 – it did away with the Red Flag, but a man still had to walk 20 yards in front of the engine – the previous distance being 60 yards – and now a legal speed limit of 4 m.p.h. in the country and 2 m.p.h. in cities, towns, and villages was imposed, with a £10 fine for offenders. County authorities were newly permitted to levy a licence fee of up to £10, with a penalty of £2 per day for non-observance. This was very hard on hauliers whose engines might work in several counties on their journeys, a separate licence being needed for each engine in each county.

Needless to say, when steam hauliers were haled to court by the Law, the magistrates nearly always were just the people most prejudiced against the use of steam haulage, and it is to be feared that the fines imposed frequently did nothing to enhance the supposed impartiality of British justice.

In 1896, *more than 60 years too late* for the proper development of the steam carriage, the Act was revised to permit lighter mechanically-propelled vehicles to travel up to a maximum of 20 m.p.h.; in 1903 steam tractors not exceeding 5 tons in weight were permitted to travel at 5 m.p.h., which as we have seen led to most makers introducing a tractor within that limit.

The development of the internal combustion engined vehicle was greatly encouraged by the 1914–18 war, but even so there was plenty of room for both – and for power, sheer strength, and durability the steamer was still paramount over the fast revving competitor which flogged itself to death in a comparatively short time. But the oil boom was on, and that oil had to find a market. So there was lobbying, intrigue, and advertising, besides vast research programmes on the i.c. engine which turned it and its vehicle into an even more complicated box of tricks than ever, without, however, giving it the inherent flexibility of the steam engine.

Then in 1930 and 1934 came the worst blows of all – new restrictions on axle loads, and other regulations, which were designed to drive the steamer off the roads altogether, and which virtually did so. Literally thousands of steam wagons, tractors, and road locos were taken off the roads because the punitive new regulations made it uneconomic to run them – one owner told me he received only scrap prices for two nearly new steam wagons, and the loss nearly broke him.

But what a different picture it *could* have been! Hancock, Gurney, Church, Dance, Maceroni – all these in the 1830's were able to run steam coaches, with regular and reliable services for months on end, at speeds of from 12 to 20 m.p.h. Trevithick before could have done the same. Rickett's steam carriages in 1858 could travel at like speeds, and Carrett's steam carriage of 1861 – a truly magnificently designed vehicle – earned its owner, Mr. F. Hodges, six summonses in six weeks, one for travelling at 30 m.p.h. Tangyes of Birmingham made an excellent steam carriage, and prepared to go into the business in an extensive way, 'but', as Richard Tangye says, 'the "wisdom" of Parliament made it impossible'.

Had Alfred Yarrow been encouraged there is evidence that he would have devoted his energies and vast intelligence to steam road locomotion instead of to marine work, with who knows what results? The Thomson road steamers, Lieut. Crompton's epic Edinburgh journey, the Burrell high-speed road locos for Turkey and Greece, the McLarens for France and India: all these show that had not prejudice, ignorance, and vested interests ruled the day in the nineteenth century, then by the end of that century steam road locomotion would have been in an unassailable position. We can imagine the private steam carriages, the regular bus and coach services in country areas, the tractors and steam lorries delivering goods, the heavies at their appointed tasks – and all at such a high state of development that the infant internal combustion could *never* have competed. By that time, the up-and-coming oil interests would have been happy enough to encourage development of oil firing for the smooth-running steamers, instead of the racketty i.c. engine.

But facts must be faced, and oil is paramount today. The steam locomotive is on its way out; power stations, factories and forges are being converted to oil firing: even the domestic scene is invaded by oil. Floods of oil are being imported whilst collieries are closed down and millions of tons of coal are stacked unused in worked-out quarries. More and more we depend on an imported fuel, whilst we know that it would not take even a major war to cut it off from us – the Suez crisis showed us that!

There are many of us to whom this doesn't make sense, but then we are told how old-fashioned and biased we are. Let us hope most earnestly that the situation never arises when this country *is* deprived of the bulk of its oil supplies: if it does, the devotees of oil will find out, too late for *all* of us, that old-fashioned ideas are sometimes best!

BIBLIOGRAPHY

If you borrow from one author, it's plagiarism: if you borrow from many, it's research. WILSON MIZNER

I HAVE INDEED 'BORROWED from many' in doing what I hope may be called quite fairly the research for this book, which, incidentally, has occupied much spare time over some twenty years, and I give below a list of works which have proved valuable to me.

Many of the journals named are now published no longer, of course, and most of the books listed are out of print, so that they are available only in libraries or in private collections. Some of the works named I am fortunate enough to own personally; others have been lent to me by friends; yet others have been studied at the local reference library, or at home through the library services.

Many people do not seem aware how extensive the latter really are: even the smallest public library should be able to obtain almost *any* book requested by the reader, through the Regional Loan Scheme or the National Loan Scheme. The staff of my own local library have always been most helpful, and I think that this is typical of almost any such staff in the country.

Journals and Newspapers

Allen's Activities
Brightside News
The Commercial Motor
The Civil Engineer and Architects' Journal
The Daily Graphic
Engineering
The English Mechanic and Mirror of Science
Feilden's Magazine
The Graphic
Industries
Meccano Magazine
Mechanics' Journal
Mettle
Model Engineer
Practical Mechanic's Journal
The Artizan
British Machine Tool Engineering
Cassier's Magazine
The Engineer
The Engineering Times
The Folkestone Chronicle
The Illustrated London News
Journal of the Road Locomotive Society
The Mechanical World
Mechanics Magazine
Pacific Rural Press
Steaming

Other Publications

Automobile Engineers, Proceedings of the Institute of
The Book of the Farm: H. Stephens, F.R.S.E., 1891
A Chapter in the History of the Traction Engine: W. Fletcher, 189?

Catalogues, Handbooks and other Official Publications of Numerous Firms
The Chronicles of Boulton's Siding: A. R. Bennett, 1924
A Century of Engineering: R. H. Clark, 1950
Chronicles of a Country Works: R. H. Clark, 1952
Civil Engineers, Proceedings of the Institute of
Engineering Facts and Figures, 1863
English and American Steam Carriages and Traction Engines: W. Fletcher, 1904
Farm Engineering, A Textbook of: John Scott, 1885
The Great Exhibition of 1851: Official Catalogue
The Great Exhibition of 1862: Official Catalogue
The Great Exhibition of 1862: *Practical Mechanics' Journal* Record of
The Highway Locomotives and Turnpikes Acts: A. Glen, 1879
Machinery of the 1862 *Exhibition:* D. K. Clark, 1864
Mechanical Traction in War: Lt.-Col. Otfried Layrix (undated)
Mechanical Engineers, Proceedings of the Institute of
Merveilles de la Science: Charles Figuier, 1867
Newcomen Society, Transactions of the
One and All: Autobiography of Richard Tangye, 1879
Patent Specifications – Numerous
The Practical Dictionary of Mechanics: E. H. Knight, 1884
Ransomes' Royal Records, 1789–1939
Road Traffic Act 1930, *A Memo on:* National Traction Engine Owners' Association
Royal Agricultural Society of England, 1839–1939, *A History of the*
Royal Agricultural Society of England, Journals of the
Steam and the Steam Engine: D. K. Clark, 188?
Steam Carriages: Alfred Yarrow, 1863
Steam Engine Builders of Lincolnshire: R. H. Clark, 1955
Steam Engine Builders of Norfolk: R. H. Clark, 1948
Steam Engine Builders of Suffolk, Essex and Cambridgeshire: R. H. Clark, 1950
Steam Locomotion on Common Roads: W. Young, 1861
Steam Locomotion on Common Roads: W. Fletcher, 1891
The Steam Portable Engine: W. D. Wansbrough, 1912
Steam Road Vehicles: H.M.S.O. (undated)
The Times *History of the War in South Africa*
The Traction Engine, 1842–1936: Gillford and Mullett, 1952
Traction Engines Worth Modelling: W. J. Hughes, 1950 (new revised edition, 1969)
Vienna Exhibition of 1873, *Official Catalogue of the*

INDEX

(**Bold figures denote illustrations**)